T0098592

The Other Talmud
The *Yerushalmi*

The Other Talmud
The *Yerushalmi*

Unlocking the Secrets of
The Talmud of Israel
for Judaism Today

Rabbi Judith Z. Abrams, PhD

For People of All Faiths, All Backgrounds

JEWISH LIGHTS Publishing
Nashville, Tennessee

www.jewishlights.com

The Other Talmud—The Yerushalmi:
Unlocking the Secrets of The Talmud of Israel *for Judaism Today*
© 2012 by Judith Z. Abrams

All rights reserved. No part of this publication may be reproduced, stored in a retrieval system, or transmitted in any form or by any means, electronic, mechanical, photocopying, recording, scanning, or otherwise, except as permitted under Sections 107 or 108 of the 1976 United States Copyright Act, without either the prior written permission of the Publisher, or authorization through payment of the appropriate per-copy fee to the Copyright Clearance Center, 222 Rosewood Drive, Danvers, MA 01923, (978) 750-8400, fax (978) 750-4744.

Requests to the Publisher for permission should be addressed to Turner Publishing Company, 4507 Charlotte Avenue, Suite 100, Nashville, Tennessee, (615) 255-2665, fax (615) 255-5081, E-mail: submissions@turnerpublishing.com.

Library of Congress Cataloging-in-Publication Data
Abrams, Judith Z.
The other Talmud—the Yerushalmi : unlocking the secrets of the Talmud of Israel for Judaism today / Judith Z. Abrams.
p. cm.
Includes bibliographical references.
ISBN 978-1-58023-463-4 (hc)
ISBN 978-1-68336-409-2 (pbk)
1. Talmud Yerushalmi—Criticism, interpretation, etc. 2. Judaism—21st century. I. Title.
BM498.9.A27 2012
296.1'2406—dc23

201200634510

9 8 7 6 5 4 3 2

Manufactured in the United States of America
Cover design: Tim Holtz
Cover photo: © Mary Lane/Fotolia.com

Published by Jewish Lights Publishing
An imprint of Turner Publishing Company
4507 Charlotte Avenue, Suite 100
Nashville, TN 37209
Tel: (615) 255-2665
www.jewishlights.com

Contents

Acknowledgments

No one writes a book alone, and in the case of this book, my debts of gratitude are tendered with great thanks.

Thanks go to those with whom I learn: Micky Rosen, Cathy Schechter, Rabbi Gordon Fuller, Rabbi David Lyon, Rabbi Mark Miller, Rabbi Adrienne Scott, and Cantor Robert Gerber (emeritus) of Congregation Beth Israel in Houston; and Barbara Sussman, Howard Stern, Bernice Kaufman, Beverley Sufian, Sondra Shapiro, Ellen Glass, and my students in the ALEPH rabbinical program, all of whom willingly stepped away from the Talmud they knew to explore the Talmud they didn't. God bless you for your wisdom, insights, and courage!

To Larry Dachslager, theater director of the Emery/Weiner School, for his help with the movie metaphors.

To Wendy Good, my friend in NOLA, for supplying parallels between a ravaged Jerusalem and a Katrina-ravaged New Orleans.

To Stuart M. Matlins, publisher of Jewish Lights, and Emily Wichland, vice president of Editorial & Production, for being open to a book on this topic. Thank you and God bless you!

And, of course, to my long-suffering family, who saw our home's already-limited shelf space burdened with more sets of Talmud than any one house should hold. To my husband, Steven, and my children, Michael, Ruth, and Hannah, this book is dedicated with much love and deep thanks.

Timeline

70 CE	Temple destroyed.
132–135	Bar Kokhba Revolt.
136	Jerusalem rebuilt as Aelia Capitolina.
164–180	Roman Empire weakened by smallpox and bubonic plague.
early 200s	Rome attacked by barbarians and weakened by civil war: twenty-nine emperors in forty-nine years.
212	By this time, there are Jewish communities in Spain, France, southern Germany, Italy, Greece, and Asia Minor.
259	Nehardea academy closes due to fire; Pumbedita becomes preeminent academy.
293	Tetrarchs, or collegiate emperors, realize Roman Empire is too big to be ruled by one emperor and Diocletian divides it into two.
315	Code of Constantine limits rights of non-Christians; Jews forbidden to enter Jerusalem except on one day of the year to mourn the Temple's destruction.
320	Council of Nicaea.
351	Revolt against the Romans in Israel is suppressed.
c. 429	Roman authorities abolish the office of *nasi*; Jewish community in Israel becomes poorer, and the center of rabbinical authority shifts to Babylonia.

Introduction

Moviemaking will serve as a guiding metaphor for our examination of the Yerushalmi, the Talmud of the Land of Israel. The art of filmmaking has more to do with Talmud than you might imagine. Both tell stories and convey information. Both depend heavily on editing to shape that information and make it intelligible. Both use "stock themes" and "stock scenes" to guide perception (e.g., wedding scenes, villains getting their due). Both cover important scenes in different ways. ("Coverage" in a film refers to the director's shooting the same scene ten times or more so that when the film is edited, the director has many options from which to choose. For example, a scene can be shot from a distance or close up.) To help you get a handle on a topic, we'll liken topics in the Yerushalmi to recognizable building blocks you find in movies.

So, imagine, if you will, that you're a Hollywood filmmaker. Together, we're going to make a movie that retells the history of the Jewish people in the years 200–425 CE. There have been many books and movies about this period, most of them conveying the following story:

> Once upon a time, we left Mesopotamia and settled in the Land of Israel, and then we went to Egypt. There, we were slaves but were freed by God through Moses and returned to Israel. There, we had good times and bad, but finally, in the year 70 CE, the Romans destroyed the Second Temple. And out of the ashes rose, phoenix-like, the great authorities of the Talmud, who set forth

Jewish law that would survive up until this very day. The center of Jewish learning moved first to Babylonia, where sages edited the Babylonian Talmud, and then to Europe, until pogroms forced the Jews to move to America and Israel. The end. (Tepid applause as the audience files out during the credits.)

The movie *we're* going to make, the story this book is going to tell you, is the far more compelling story you *don't* know. The bit about the Land of Israel is true, but imagine that as the soundstage of the movie you're directing.

The Script: Development Problems

The movie you see on the screen almost certainly didn't develop cleanly from a script to a green-lit project, to a shoot, and then to postproduction. Most scripts go through "development problems" in which funding appears and disappears, directors and stars sign up and then back out, and distribution deals are made and broken. The Yerushalmi experienced a *lot* of these development problems.

Almost certainly, when you hear the word "Talmud," you are hearing about the Talmud of the land of Babylonia, or the Bavli. Just as certainly, you've never been presented with its alternative, the Talmud of the Land of Israel, the Yerushalmi. That, in itself, should seem odd to you now that you think about it. Shouldn't the Talmud based in the land of the Bible be the one you know? Why did the Yerushalmi drop into "development limbo"?

How *did* the Bavli become the Talmud of choice? Like so much of Jewish history, it came down to chance. Put simply, the Romans subjugated the communities that would have been the natural constituencies for the Yerushalmi: the Jewish communities of northern Africa, the Mediterranean, and Israel. But the Romans never truly conquered the Jewish community of Babylonia. So it was "the last man standing," so to speak. Jewish life continued there, as it had for centuries, in relative stability, allowing the study of its Talmud to continue many centuries after the teachers of the Yerushalmi were silenced. The Bavli didn't win because it was better. It won through an accident of chance.

And so one generation handed down their learning to the next generation. But the Yerushalmi's star never fully waned. No less an authority than the Vilna Gaon, one of our greatest rabbinic teachers and authorities (1720–1797) and a huge fan of the Yerushalmi, advocated that it be studied more. This was a man who knew the Bavli back to front, but he was still enormously enthusiastic about the Yerushalmi.

The script for our movie comes from the Yerushalmi and is not that much different from the Bavli, the script used to tell the story above. They both talk about prayer, business ethics, Shabbat, holidays, and life-cycle moments. They both want you to say the *Shema* and *Amidah*. But the Yerushalmi gives us a different point of view on these topics. If the Bavli's script is *The Wizard of Oz*, then the Yerushalmi's is *Wicked*. Or you might think of it as the difference between *The Sound of Music* and a documentary on the Von Trapp Family Singers. These would be two movies about one group of people, doing one thing, but told in different ways and with different information.

The basis of the Yerushalmi is Mishnah, the philosophical document promulgated by Rabbi Yehudah Hanasi in 200 CE. The Mishnah describes an ideal Jewish world in which the Jews still live in the Land, tending to their agriculture and practicing animal husbandry. In the Mishnah, the Temple still stands, and the sacrifices are still the paramount form of Jewish worship. In addition, the rules of ritual purity and impurity still function as organizing principles in daily Jewish life. By the year 200 CE, this world exists only in the mind. In reality, the Romans rule the land, the Temple is wrecked, the economy is shattered, and almost nothing except endless taxes and wars organize Jewish life in the Land of Israel.

But the Jews of Israel weren't ready to give up the ghost. They maintained the hope of a full Jewish life in the Land. So they tried to negotiate the territory between dream and reality. The record of that negotiation is the commentary on Mishnah called Gemara. Mishnah, together with Gemara, equals Talmud.

Mishnah + Gemara = Talmud = Yerushalmi or Bavli

Gemara is as gritty as Mishnah is diaphanous. Mishnah is the theory. Gemara is the reality. Put it this way: if Mishnah is the pitch you, as a director, sketch out to your producers, Gemara is the working script from which you shoot. Both the Yerushalmi and the Bavli comment on the Mishnah in this way, and both are written in a combination of Hebrew and Aramaic.

Using our moviemaking metaphor, the difference between the Bavli and the Yerushalmi is something like the difference between making a movie for a regular theater versus making one for a 3-D theater and/or an IMAX theater. It's still the story of Judaism and the Jewish people. But the colors are richer, the action is bigger, the effects are more powerful in the 3-D/IMAX world of the Yerushalmi. Your actors have totally immersed themselves in the world they're creating. They live on the soundstage, that is, in Israel, and that informs their performance. If you've been to Israel, you know how effortless and rich Judaism is there. In Jerusalem, on Friday afternoons, the streets gradually empty out, the last bus for twenty-four hours rumbles by, almost empty, and then, forty minutes before Shabbat begins, the siren sounds over the whole city and you know that everyone's lighting their candles at the same time as you are. That's the 3-D, IMAX Judaism of the Yerushalmi. You could imagine the Yerushalmi is a pop-up book: you open it and Jewish living materializes.

Casting Is 99 Percent of Directing

Casting the right people is crucial to the success of our movie. Tell those grand sages of the Bavli to exit stage left and take their law book with them. Replace them with some very human, small-time teachers and thinkers. These guys are on the run from the Romans. They're trying to live their kind of Judaism in competition with other Jews who don't think they're doing it correctly. They're not creating law. No one takes them that seriously. They're outlining options. If you transported them to an Orthodox yeshivah today, they'd be tossed out on their ears for their relaxed, cooperative way of doing things.

The women, too, tend to be kind of glamorous. Again, if Central Casting sends you some yentas, send them packing. Many of the

Yerushalmi's women are rich, and they look it. They aren't Hollywood vixens. They're more like Meryl Streep. They're rich, smart, tough, and not about to be cowed by some guy no matter how smart or good-looking he is, even if he is their husband.

Behind the Scenes of Our Yerushalmi Script

At the Oscars, some truly obscure people win for art direction (which means the sets), "sound editing," and technical things of that sort. Without these "behind the scenes" people, we'd be back in the black-and-white, back-lot era of film, but it's not an aspect of filmmaking that gets a lot of publicity. Think of this section as a description of this "technical" part of our movie.

Versions

Some movies are released in different versions. There are original, digitally remastered, and anniversary editions of *Dumbo*, for example, and each edition has different extras. The Yerushalmi is something like this. There are two main versions: (1) the Venice edition, which contains the entire Yerushalmi in one volume, and (2) the P'nei Moshe edition, which comes in seven volumes. The former has almost no commentary, while the latter has lots. The Venice edition is laid out in columns, two columns on each side of the page, so a page is listed, for example, Y. Berakhot 3a, 3b, 3c, or 3d.

Venice edition of the Yerushalmi

The P'nei Moshe is laid out like a page of the Bavli: text in the middle, with commentaries around the edges of the text. Page citations are as they are in the Bavli: e.g., 3a, 3b, 4a, 4b.

This is a page of the P'nei Moshe edition of the Yerushalmi. The Mishnah and Gemara are in the middle, and the commentaries are laid out around them, much as they are on a page of the Bavli.

Compare the P'nei Moshe to this page of the Bavli:

A page of the Bavli in the standard Vilna Shas edition. The Mishnah and Gemara are in the center. Rashi is always the commentary closest to the spine of the book. The other major commentaries are arranged around the page.

Most scholarly works cite the Venice edition. Electronic versions tend to cite the P'nei Moshe version. ArtScroll is now producing a translation of the Yerushalmi that's more like the P'nei Moshe, but the pagination doesn't always line up one with the other. In this book, passages are cited according to the chapter and mishnah number and according to the P'nei Moshe and ArtScroll paginations, and sometimes with the Venice page numbers.

In the Yerushalmi, unlike in most of the Bavli, there can be great variety in the citations of the Mishnah. So in the Venice edition a passage could be chapter 4, mishnah 3 (4:3), and in the P'nei Moshe the same passage could be 4:5. There are also many manuscript variants. To add to the confusion, in the Yerushalmi a mishnah is sometimes called a *halakhah*; Gemara can also be called *halakhah*. So to clarify: *halakhah* can mean mishnah, or it can mean Gemara. In addition, in a discussion within the text, *halakhah* can mean "reliable tradition."

In *The Return of the King*, as Gandalf and Pippin prepare to meet the Steward, Gandalf tells Pippin not to mention A ... or B ... or C ..., and then he tells Pip not to talk at all. When it comes to the word *halakhah* in the Yerushalmi, it could be a mishnah, it could be Gemara, it could be a reliable tradition, and it also has a few other meanings. We're probably best served, as was Pippin, by not really translating the word at all in this book and looking at it more at a later time.

Some people use the abbreviations "J." (for "Jerusalem") or "P." (for "Palestinian") to refer to the Yerushalmi. We'll use the abbreviation "Y." When we are citing Mishnah only, we'll use the abbreviation "M." When we are citing Tosefta (a very early commentary on Mishnah), we'll use the abbreviation "T." The abbreviation "B." will signify a quotation from the Bavli. A page number preceded by a "V" indicates the Venice edition, "PM" is P'nei Moshe, and ArtScroll citations come with a number, a letter, and another number.

Translations

Have you ever noticed that when you watch a movie with subtitles, you soon get into a rhythm and it stops bothering you? There are three translations of the Yerushalmi into English.

Right now, the only complete English translation of the Yerushalmi is the one edited by Jacob Neusner, published by the University of Chicago, titled *The Talmud of the Land of Israel*, in thirty-one volumes. It's a useful place to start your learning. The text contains only English, whereas the other two translations offer the Hebrew/Aramaic as well as the English.

ArtScroll is now producing *An Annotated, Interpretive Elucidation as an Aid to Talmud Study* on the Yerushalmi. It gives you Hebrew and English, has good notes, and is the least expensive of the three. The texts on the pages facing the translations are well laid out, with useful indices that are well done indeed.

Yet another translation is now being produced, edited by Heinrich W. Guggenheimer and published by DeGruyter. It is an excellent translation, and is two-thirds finished, but it is very expensive (e.g., $200 per volume) when compared with the Neusner ($60 per volume) and the ArtScroll ($40 per volume).

The translations in this book are my own. I have consulted all three translations and used Jastrow's *Dictionary of Hebrew and Aramaic*. These translations have been made as "friendly" as possible, with brackets removed so that they read more fluidly.

Editing: What Makes *Hot Fuzz* Go from Stupid Cop Comedy to a Truly, Hysterically Funny Cop Comedy?

Editing is one of the things that makes a film great or terrible. Without good editing, a movie drags. With good editing, the movie rolls along at a pace that keeps you engaged. You might not even be conscious of the way a scene is cut. For example, if two people are sitting and talking, you might get an external shot of the restaurant, then one in which they are both in the frame, then close-ups of the individuals. The same is true when it comes to editing a Talmud. The editing of the British comedy *Hot Fuzz* takes it from a ludicrous story to a fast-moving, side-splitting comedy. It moves along in scenes that are often five-second (or less) bits of film strung together.

If the only kind of Talmud you've learned is the Bavli, there are some things you'll have to get used to when working with the Yerushalmi and the way it is composed and edited.

Aramaic

The Aramaic in the Yerushalmi is different from the Bavli's. But it's not that different and it's actually far easier than the Bavli's.

Seder Zeraim

The Yerushalmi covers *Seder Zeraim*, the Order of Seeds, which is all about food and agriculture and is not covered in the Bavli except for tractate Berakhot. This means a whole world of material that you may never have encountered before is now available to you.

Navigation

The Yerushalmi is easier to navigate. It sticks to commenting on the Mishnah much more than the Bavli does.

Stamma, **or the Editorial Layer**

Perhaps the most important difference between the Yerushalmi and the Bavli is that while there is stammaitic material in the Yerushalmi, it is different from the *stamma* in the Bavli. (The *stamma* is the late, anonymous, editorial layer of the Bavli.) First of all, it is there, even though there is much less of it than in the Bavli. The *stamma*'s voice in the Bavli gives rise to *pilpul,* that is, trying to reconcile every single statement within the entire Bavli, attempting to make it all agree consistently. The Yerushalmi does not lend itself to this futile effort. That means you can take it page by page and discussion by discussion without worrying about everything else the Yerushalmi has said at the same time.

An example from the Bavli may be in order here. In a discussion of whether a man should take his wife's advice or not, the Bavli offers two opinions. Rav says a man should *never* take his wife's advice, while Rav Pappa says he should *always* consult with his wife. The Yerushalmi would leave this alone. After all, some wives might give bad advice, and others might give good advice. In the Bavli, the *stamma* chimes in to settle the matter:

> It's not a problem! Don't consult your wife when it comes to worldly matters, but do consult her on domestic matters. Or there's another way to solve it. Don't consult her on religious matters, but do consult her on worldly matters. (B. Bava Metzia 59a)

This is classic Babylonian *stamma.* It barges in and fixes a "problem" that wasn't a problem in the first place. This happens all the time in the Bavli but rarely happens in the Yerushalmi.

Rhythm

The Yerushalmi's rhythm is different from the Bavli's, and for those used to studying the Bavli, it may take some getting used to. The Yerushalmi emphasizes a teaching's "pedigree" far more than the Bavli does. In fact, rarely do you find a teaching without learning who said it originally. In addition, the pace is far more clipped. It tends to be "Teaching A, Teaching B," with proof texts occasionally thrown in. Then the text moves on to the next topic, rarely exhibiting any attempt to decide between the two teachings or find a difference between them. This may catch you flat-footed the first several times you encounter it. Eventually, once you accept this rhythm, you'll find it enjoyable and refreshing.

Different Opinions, Not Halakhic Outcomes

This rhythm means that the Yerushalmi does not, in general, provide halakhic outcomes. Rather, it offers different opinions, then lets them exist, unharmonized, on the page. That means that *the Yerushalmi is affirming that there are multiple viable options from which to make one's choices when observing Judaism.*

Midrash

Rabbinic literature of the Land of Israel actually comes in two forms. There is the Talmud Yerushalmi, and then there is midrash, that is, commentaries on Scripture. Almost all the midrash collections we have today come from the Land of Israel. Some were produced at the same time as the Yerushalmi, while others were created after the Yerushalmi was closed.

All these differences may take a while to get used to. But what you'll find in the Yerushalmi is worth the effort, because, simply put, studying the Yerushalmi is just more fun than studying the Bavli.

How We'll Make Our Movie

So how do we make our movie? We'll do it scene by scene, bit by bit. We'll start by investigating daily life, then prayer, followed by Shabbat and holidays, and we'll finish with the major life-cycle moments. Remember, this is the sort of movie that you're going to want to see more than once. (The movie that comes immediately to mind for me is *Inception*. My daughter made me go see it, and I must say, it was one of the few times I sat through an entire movie without [a] falling asleep or

[b] figuring it out. As soon as it was over, I said, "I have to see it again.") The Yerushalmi is like that. You're going to want to come back and read it some more.

One Last Thing to Bear in Mind

We're focusing on Talmud, that is, on rabbinic Judaism. That would be like focusing only on Conservative Judaism. But there has always been a range of Judaisms from which one might choose. In other words, we're looking at two slices cut from the same pie when we compare the Yerushalmi and the Bavli. Just remember, there's an entire dessert cart that we're not sampling here, such as Karaite Judaism, the Judaism of Philo, and the Dead Sea Scrolls.

Part 1

Daily Life

Whether you credit Daniel Defoe, Benjamin Franklin, or Margaret Mitchell with the saying that the only two things you can truly count on in this life are death and taxes, it's a verity that would have rung true for Jews in the Land of Israel during the Yerushalmi's era. On the one hand, being part of the Roman Empire and straddling the strategically situated land bridge connecting Africa and Asia would have helped the Jews of Israel make a living in trade. On the other hand, the heavy hand of Roman taxes was a constant background drum beat in the Yerushalmi's world.

But those weren't the only taxes Jews were paying during this era. Above and beyond those tributes were the religious "taxes" they had to pay to support the Jewish community. And even beyond that was the almost-radical level of honesty in business that the sages demanded. If there is an orthodoxy of any kind in the Yerushalmi, it is in this area of honesty in business.

1

What Would Your Livelihood and Levies Be?

Location Scouting

Location scouting is one of the most crucial parts of making a film. Sadly, the sages of the Yerushalmi were stuck with some subpar locations. They did not live in Jerusalem. That city had been overtaken by the Romans. Instead, they lived in the north of Israel—in Tiberias, Sepphoris, Beit She'an, Beit Alpha, Lod, and Caesarea.

To be honest, they probably wished they lived in Jerusalem ... the Jerusalem where the Temple stood, the Jerusalem that was the center of Jewish life for a thousand years. They may have felt like New Yorkers transported to North Dakota. Their predecessors lived in Jerusalem, while they lived in Tiberias. The Yerushalmi attempts to ease the sting of this demotion:

> Said Rav Avin, "If the Holy One, blessed be He, had not made each place charming to those who live there, the Land of Israel would never have been divided up."
>
> And so it has been taught: There are three kinds of unique charm: a woman in the eye of her husband; a place in the eye of its inhabitants; a purchase in the eye of the purchaser.
>
> (Y. Yoma 4:1, 26a3, PM 20a; B. Sotah 47a)

It is almost as if the sages are reassuring themselves, and their fellow townsfolk, that it is possible to find happiness in northern Israel. True, it's not Jerusalem and the sacrifices are not offered there, but each of these towns has its own merits.

More important, the sages seem to be suggesting that happiness is a choice over which we have control. Where we live can come to seem as wonderful to us as Jerusalem was in its heyday.

What Would You Do for a Living?

There are so many people involved in making a movie: directors and caterers, actors and costumers, location scouts and secretaries, the list goes on and on. The ancient world had a range of professions, as well. The sages are mostly interested in Torah study, so what we find about people's professions has to be gleaned from various places. For example, we find a description of the enormous synagogue in Alexandria, Egypt. It was so big that a man had to stand on the bimah with semaphore-type flags to signal the congregation when to say, "Amen." Another reason they might have had to use the flags was that people were talking during services because of the seating arrangements:

> In the synagogue in Alexandria they did not sit mixed together. Rather, each group of workers sat by themselves. The gold-smiths sat by themselves, the silversmiths sat by themselves, the weavers by themselves, the bronze workers by themselves, and the blacksmiths by themselves. So that when a stranger came, he could join his fellow workers and be able to feed himself. And who destroyed it all? It was the evil Trajan.
> (T. Sukkah 4:6; Y. Sukkah 5:1, 28в1; B. Sukkah 51в)

Seating at services was organized along guild lines. And it makes sense that so large and rich a city would support so many artisans of luxury goods. The gold workers may have worked on the synagogue itself, which was said to have seventy-one golden thrones, each worth twenty-five talents of gold (Y. Sukkah 5:1). And people come to the synagogue to talk with each other just as much as they come to talk with God. The Trajan to whom the Yerushalmi refers was the Roman emperor from 98 to 117 CE, who was no friend of the Jews. There was scarcely a place where Jews lived that he did not control. His reach extended to Alexandria and the Land of Israel itself.

From other passages in the Yerushalmi we can deduce that these other trades were practiced in the days of the Yerushalmi:

Shepherding
Agriculture (terraced)
Glassblowing
Cutting glass, making mirrors
Olive farming and processing
Vineyards and wine production
Commerce
Charcoal burning
Making cosmetics
Weaving

Of course, the easiest path to wealth was probably the classic standby today: inherit it.

"Creative Accounting" v. Honesty in Business

It takes money to produce a film, and producers raise money by promising investors that they will have a share of the profits. It all sounds good until the Hollywood bookkeepers do some "creative accounting" that makes it appear that there are *never* any profits. (This was actually a joke in *Shakespeare in Love*, in which, instead of a salary, the actors were to receive a share of the profits ... which the producers knew would never materialize.) This is the exact opposite of the Yerushalmi's total, even radical, principle of honesty in business.

> Rabbi Shimon bar Kahana was supporting Rabbi Eliezer. They passed by a fence. Rabbi Eliezer said to Rabbi Shimon, "Bring me a chip so I can pick my teeth." Rabbi Eliezer reversed himself

and said, "Don't bring me anything, for if you do, everyone will do the same and ruin the man's fence."

Rabbi Chaggai was supporting Rabbi Zeira. They passed someone carrying a load of wood. Rabbi Zeira said to Rabbi Chaggai, "Bring me a chip so I can pick my teeth." He reversed himself and said, "Don't bring me a thing, for if you do, everyone will do the same, and the man's load of wood will be lost."

It's not that Rabbi Zeira was so punctilious a person, but rather, he wanted to show us how our Creator wants us to act.

(Y. HALLAH 4:5, 48B1)

What the sages are demonstrating here is not so much a legal position as a mind-set. Is it likely that taking a toothpick from one person would really hurt someone? Not very likely at all. But the sages understood that one small deed can be part of a sequence of deeds that *does* cause someone harm.

The last comment here has the feeling of a later addition. Rabbi Zeira was known to be an exceptionally pious person, so his behavior isn't really surprising. Yet someone must have objected. So we have this apologetic explanation. Rabbi Zeira was not trying to show off his piety. Rather, he was teaching a mind-set: everything belongs to God, and as such, everything has a degree of holiness to it.

Y. v. B.

Both Talmuds hold with the importance of absolute honesty in business. In fact, according to the Bavli (B. Shabbat 31a), the first question you will be asked after you die is, "Were you honest in business?"

What Kind of Taxes Would You Be Paying?

Before we even look at the Jewish taxes, Roman taxes need to be acknowledged:

Rabbi Abba said, "If you give charity from your purse, the Holy One, blessed be He, will guard you from tributes, from fines, from head taxes, and from crop taxes."

(Y. PEAH 1:1, 5A3)

One of life's eternal verities is that you can't throw a good war without a lot of tax revenue. And the Romans certainly liked to engage in war at every available opportunity. That means they levied lots of kinds of taxes. And the person who collected those taxes was, generally speaking, not a popular guy. But with the Yerushalmi, you always get both sides of the story ...

The Stock Villain = The Tax Collector

The sages uniformly hated tax collectors. They were "Snidely Whiplash" or the cowboy in the black hat. They were stock villains, rarely portrayed with any nuances. That's what makes the following story so interesting: the tax collector turns out to be the good guy.

In the waning years of the Second Temple, the Jewish people were ruled by pairs of leaders (zugot). You could think of them as the Speaker of the House and the Minority Leader of the House. The pair you probably know best is the last one, Hillel and Shammai. Hillel sort of represents the poor, and Shammai represents the rich.

A story contrasts the funerals of Yehudah ben Tabbai (one-half of a first-century-BCE zug) and the village tax collector, Bar Maayan. The former did not have a large crowd at his funeral, while the whole town turned out for the tax collector's funeral. The sages wonder about this, as they regarded tax collectors as scum and Yehudah ben Tabbai was considered an utterly righteous man.

What meritorious deed did Bar Maayan, the village tax collector, do? Heaven forfend! He never did a meritorious deed in his life. But one time he made a dinner for the senators, but they did not come. He said, "Let the poor come and eat the food, so that it not go to waste."

> There are those who say that he was crossing the market
> and he dropped a cake and it fell. He saw a poor man take it,
> and he didn't say anything, so as not to embarrass him.
>
> (Y. Hagigah 2:2, PM 11a, V 77d)

Reading between the lines, Yehudah ben Tabbai's heirs wondered how such a story could have (a) happened, (b) been recorded, and (c) been so hardy that it could survive all the way to the Yerushalmi. Maybe the tax collector wasn't such a bad guy. Maybe Yehudah ben Tabbai wasn't as beloved as we might have thought. What's important for us, here, is that the tax collector is the foil for the story, that is, a stock villain—the very one you'd least expect people to mourn.

Jewish "Taxes" and Their Enforcers

If you've ever stayed in a hotel in New York City, you know that there are federal and state taxes, and then there are taxes for just sharing the rarified air of that city. The Land of Israel had something like that. Produce and livestock in the Land of Israel were subject to all sorts of taxes/charity: leaving the corners of the field unharvested so that the poor can harvest this produce, first tithe, second tithe, terumah (a gift of one-sixtieth of the crop given to the priests), shekhichah (forgotten sheaves left in the field that the poor may collect), and challah. (This does not even touch on the incredibly complicated tariffs put on glass, building materials, people, and so on, through the application of ritual purity regulations.)

Collecting these "taxes" was a big problem in ancient Israel. A person who wasn't terribly punctilious about paying them was called an am ha'aretz, "a person of the land." The opposite of such a person was a chaveir (which today means "friend"). This gave rise to questions about "doubtfully tithed produce," that is, produce from which the agricultural taxes might or might not have been taken out. This caused a rift between the amei ha'aretz and the chaveirim, something like the rift some may experience today between those who keep kosher and their ultra-Orthodox relatives who think they don't keep kosher enough to eat in their houses.

Rabbi Pinchas ben Yair: The Enforcer

In a gangster movie, one of the stock characters is the enforcer. This is a big guy who's nice to you until you don't pay, in which case he breaks your arm. The fact that people didn't pay their Jewish "taxes" gave rise to a special, superhero-type enforcer, Rabbi Pinchas ben Yair. He led by example. He was so committed, even his animals paid these "taxes":

> Thieves stole Rabbi Pinchas ben Yair's donkey at night. They hid with it for three days, during which it ate nothing. After three days, they said, "Let us send it back to its master lest it die while it is with us and our cave will start to stink so much that we will be discovered." They sent it out. It went and stood outside its master's gate and began to bray.
>
> He said to his servants, "Open the gate, for the poor animal hasn't eaten anything in three days." They opened the gate for it, and it came in. He said to them, "Give it something to eat." They gave it barley but it refused to eat. They said to him, "Master, it doesn't want to eat." ... He said to them, "Have you removed from it the requisite tithes on account of doubt?" ... They hadn't, because animal feed is not liable to it.
>
> He said to them, "What can we do with this poor creature, since it is so stringent with itself?" So they removed the tithes due on account of doubt from the barley, and the ass ate.
>
> (Y. DEMAI 1:3, 7B1–7B2)

Rabbi Pinchas ben Yair was Rabbi Shimon bar Yochai's son-in-law. That, alone, would probably have qualified him for the "spiritually powerful but strange" category. (Rabbi Shimon bar Yochai was the one who stayed in a cave for thirteen years. Fire came out of his eyes when he was angry.) Rabbi Pinchas ben Yair was known for his incredible righteousness, and this dovetailed with, and may have been the source of, his ability to perform miracles.

The following stories in the Yerushalmi portray Pinchas ben Yair as a sage and magician, especially with mice:

> Two paupers deposited two bushels of barley for safekeeping
> with Rabbi Pinchas ben Yair. While the bushels were in his
> keeping, he sowed them and reaped them and gathered them
> in. When they came to take back their barley, he said to them:
> Bring camels and asses to carry all your barley.
>
> (Y. DEMAI 1:3, 7B2, PM 22A; DEUTERONOMY RABBAH 3:3)

So far, so good. Rabbi Pinchas ben Yair is acting most righteously, but
you'd expect nothing less from so great a sage. Then things get a little
stranger:

> Rabbi Pinchas ben Yair once went to a certain place. The villag-
> ers came to him. They said, "Mice are eating all our grain." He
> gathered the mice together. They began to chirp. He said to the
> villagers, "Do you know what they are saying?" They said, "No."
> He said to the villagers, "They are saying that the grain has not
> been tithed." The villagers said to him: "Pledge to us that if we
> tithe our grain properly the mice will not eat it all." He pledged
> to them, they tithed, and the mice stopped eating the grain.
>
> (Y. DEMAI 1:3, 7B3, PM 22A; DEUTERONOMY RABBAH 3:3)

Rabbi Pinchas ben Yair is giving the villagers courage. They're afraid to
tithe their grain because, between the tithes and the mice, they figure
they won't have anything left. He brokers a deal with the mice, and the
problem is solved.

Rabbi Pinchas's miracle working evidently became well known,
for even non-Jews requested his help:

> Once a pearl belonging to the king of Saracens fell, and a
> mouse swallowed it. The king came before Rabbi Pinchas ben
> Yair. Rabbi Pinchas said to the king, "Who am I, a conjurer?"
> The king said to Rabbi Pinchas, "I have come to you because
> of your reputation." Rabbi Pinchas gathered the mice together.
> He saw one of them walking like a hunchback. He said, "That
> one has it." He compelled it, and it disgorged the pearl.
>
> (Y. DEMAI 1:3, 8A1)

Word had apparently gotten around that Rabbi Pinchas ben Yair could negotiate with mice. The word for "conjurer," *chabar*, is spelled *chet-bet-reish*, the same letters that are used to spell *chaveir*, the one who is careful about tithes. Therefore, this is a lovely pun. These stories are just a few of many about Rabbi Pinchas ben Yair.

Sabbatical Year Produce

The sages had to balance the hard and fast lines the Torah drew with the ever-changing boundaries of real life. The rule for leaving the fields fallow once every seven years is sound agricultural theory. But putting it into practice was an administrative nightmare. The Torah states:

> Every seventh year, the land was to lie fallow. But the seventh year you shall let it rest and lie still; that the poor of your people may eat; and what they leave, the beasts of the field shall eat. In like manner you shall deal with your vineyard, and with your olive trees.
>
> (EXODUS 23:11; LEVITICUS 25:4–7)

Any plants that grew, uncultivated, in the seventh year were considered ownerless property. While anyone could eat them, no one was allowed to *sell* them. But what was to be done at the end of the seventh year? Could people buy and sell vegetables as soon as the new year began? Here, we find poor Rabbi Yehudah Hanasi outmaneuvered … by the leek lobby.

> They ordained that it would be permitted to import vegetables from outside of the Land of Israel to the Land of Israel.
>
> Even so, it remained forbidden to buy vegetables immediately at the end of the Sabbatical year.
>
> In the year following the Sabbatical year, Rabbi permitted the purchase of all vegetables from Israel immediately, except for leeks, which have a long growing season and require a great deal of care. Accordingly, we can assume that leeks for sale immediately after the Sabbatical year were tended during the seventh year itself.

What did the people of Sepphoris do with the leek? They covered it with sackcloth and ashes and brought it before Rabbi. They said to him, "How has this leek sinned more than all the other vegetables, such that it, alone, may not be purchased immediately at the end of the Sabbatical year?" As a result, Rabbi permitted the purchase of leeks immediately at the end of the Sabbatical year.

(Y. Shevi'it 6:4, 50b1–2, PM 37a)

Think how cute a leek would look if you put the roots up, making them "hair," and dressed it up as a "mourner." The larger discussion here in the Yerushalmi is a three-way tug-of-war among those who want to import vegetables, the sages who want to stop them, and the public that just wants some vegetables. In the end, the public wins.

Y. v. B.

These agricultural taxes weren't collected in Babylonia, so the tractates concerning these issues weren't even studied there.

2

Who Would Your Celebrities Be?

If Jerusalem was the Hollywood of the Jewish world, then who were the celebrities? Who would have been on the cover of *People* magazine? Well, the first thing to note is that it *wouldn't* have been the sages. When you read the Bavli, it seems as if the sages are the stars of the show. Reading the Yerushalmi, you get a more balanced view.

Priestly Watches

Priests were the A-listers of the age. They officiated at the Temple and made the sacrifices possible. They were physically absolutely blemishless. God's presence was as lethal as a runaway nuclear reactor, and the priests' perfect bodies constituted their safety suits.

When the Temple stood, and for centuries after that, the priestly watches continued to hold a certain kind of glamour. The watches supplemented the priests who worked in the Temple full time. Twice a year, for one week at a time, priests from different regions of Israel served in the Temple. While they were there, the folks at home would hold worship services.

Now, the sages weren't particularly fond of the priests. The priests were Israel's natural leaders, and the sages wished to supplant them. We can understand this with the following analogy. Imagine that we have only one hospital in all of America. If you want to have a heart bypass operation or chemotherapy, you have to go to this hospital.

It is the place of hope and last chances. Now imagine that Canada invades the United States and destroys that hospital. Afterward, you would nostalgically tell your children and grandchildren about what had been possible when that hospital stood and how much you wish you could have it again. In time, you would turn to acupuncture and homeopathic remedies as a substitute. But these would always be less than the gold standard that you had back in the day. The hospital in this analogy is the Temple. The doctors are the priests. And the homeopathic substitutes are the sages. You can see how they might resent the people's natural affection for the priests. Yet they were powerless to stop it.

Even the sages still honored the priestly watches in a small, symbolic way. There was a certain kind of sandal that was studded with nails. It sounded like Roman shoes. And this sound alone frightened the locals into a panic. Yet the sages permitted Jews to wear them. What is interesting is *why* they permitted them:

> How many nails may a sandal have for a person to be permitted to go about in it on the Sabbath without violating the rule about the sound of them frightening other Jews?
>
> Rabbi Yochanan said, "Five, for the five books of the Torah."
>
> Rabbi Chanina said, "Seven, for the days of the week...."
>
> Rav Acha said in the name of R. Chanina, "Nine, for the months of pregnancy."
>
> Rabbi [Yehudah Hanasi] would put eleven nails on one sandal and thirteen on the other (twenty-four total), for the twenty-four priestly watches.
>
> (Y. Shabbat 6:2, PM 35a)

Rabbi, who knew people who actually remembered the Temple's destruction, used this small act of defiance to remember the Temple and the priestly watches, while later sages began moving away from such nostalgia. This is the sort of quiet subversiveness that may have been some consolation to the sages. The shoes looked and sounded Roman, but the sages used them as symbols of Torah, holiness, and the priestly watches.

Of course, the priests were only part of the Temple's mystique. The following biblical verse is interpreted to show that the Temple was a cooperative enterprise:

> All the congregation prostrated themselves, the song was sung, and the trumpets blown all the way to the end of the burnt offering.
>
> (2 CHRONICLES 29:28)

The Yerushalmi makes each phrase indicate an essential part of the service in the Temple:

> "All the congregation prostrated themselves"—these are Israelites.
> "The song was sung"—these are the Levites.
> "And the trumpets were blown"—these are the priests.
> "All of this until the end of the burnt offering." Therefore, all are necessary for the sacrifice.
>
> (Y. PESACHIM 4:1, 28A4–28B1, PM 25A)

The proof text from Chronicles uses the word "all" twice. The sages parse this sentence to mean that you can't have the sacrifices without Israelites bringing offerings, Levites singing, and priests officiating. The priests might have been celebrities, but the sages, with their thoroughgoing democratizing bent, state that they were only one part of the picture. You need Kate Winslet and Leonardo DeCaprio to make *Titanic*, but you also need extras, grips, lights, musicians, and so on, too.

Scandal and the Priestly Watches

Celebrity scandal has a long shelf life ... extending all the way back to two-thousand-year-old shockers. Some of the priestly watches were not only famous, but they also were infamous. Take this shocking story about the priestly watch of Bilgah:

> The priestly watch of Bilgah is somewhat disgraced because of Miriam, a daughter of Bilgah. She became an apostate and

went and married an officer from a Greek royal family. When the Greeks conquered the Temple, she went and banged on the altar. She said to it, "Wolf! Wolf! You have destroyed the property of the Jews and not stood by them in their hour of need."

(T. SUKKAH 4:28 IN Y. SUKKAH 5:8, 33A1)

... And why didn't they remove the priestly watch of Bilgah from its place in the rotation entirely? You cannot do so, for Rabbi Shimon said in the name of Rabbi Yehoshua ben Levi, "It is difficult for God to uproot a genealogical chain from its rightful place."

(Y. SUKKAH 5:8, 33A1)

This passage reminds us that what happened in the Temple was local news for those who composed the Yerushalmi, something like celebrity news in Los Angeles. This woman's behavior might have been forgotten in the diaspora, but it was still a scandal in Israel.

Disabled Priests

The Yerushalmi offers an extremely rare view of priests with disabilities participating in a Temple rite:

As to walking around the altar seven times on Sukkot, it was taught: Priests who have physical defects participate in the procession. Reish Lakish asked before Rabbi Yochanan, "Now will maimed priests enter the area between the porch and the altar?" He said, "They were fit to do so."

(Y. SUKKAH 4:3, 24A1)

It's not hard to imagine how priests would be wounded in the line of duty. Priestly work involved knives and a great deal of backbreaking labor. And anyone can go into the courtyard near the altar as long as they are in a state of ritual purity. So wounded/older priests are allowed to take part on this happiest of holidays.

Other Celebrities: Helen and Munbaz

Every movie needs one or more producers who will put up the money to green-light the project. So who were the Yerushalmi's producers? Two of the most prominent patrons were Queen Helen and her son Munbaz.

Widowhood was a time of prosperity and independence for women then, just as it is for many women today. Widows wielded great power in synagogues and churches of this era, often contributing large sums of money for their construction. How do we know? You have only to look around any modern synagogue to find the answer: plaques as far as the eye can see, right? Plaques and inscriptions found in archeological remains testify to the antiquity of the relationship between plaques and fund-raising.

Helen lived in the first century CE and was the mother of King Munbaz of the Adiabene (Syria). Helen converted to Judaism in about 30 CE through the influence of Ananias, a Jewish merchant. Helen spent the latter part of her life in Jerusalem, where she built a palace. She died in 56 CE in Adiabene, but her remains were buried in Jerusalem on the Mount of Olives, where her tomb still stands today.

Helen was very generous. For example, she is remembered for making lavish donations to the Temple.

> Helen, Munbaz the king's mother, made a candelabra of gold
> over the entrance of the Sanctuary, and she also made a tablet
> of gold with the *sotah* portion (Numbers 5:11–31) on it.
>
> (M. YOMA 3:10)

The candelabra that Helen gave the Sanctuary was placed at the very top of the building so that, at sunrise, the light would hit it. It would glitter, reminding the inhabitants of Jerusalem that it was time to recite the morning *Shema* (T. Yoma 2:3).

The scroll with the *sotah* portion refers to that passage in the Torah concerning a woman who is suspected of adultery. This passage from the Torah is written down and combined with earth and water. The suspected adulteress drinks it in order to determine whether she has actually been unfaithful.

Just imagine a couple in marital distress who comes to the Temple for this ritual. The priest would have to find a scroll, roll it to the right place, get some parchment, ink, and so forth. The couple might be waiting an interminable amount of time. With Helen's gift, it was almost like going to a drive-through at a fast-food joint. They'd be done within an hour.

This mishnah is one of three *mishnayot* (M. Yoma 3:9–11) that contrasts those who are remembered favorably and those who are remembered unfavorably for their contributions to the Temple or their lack thereof. Those who contributed lavish or simply practical improvements to the Temple are remembered with praise. Those who had special skills in preparing materials for the Temple or in singing or writing and who refused to teach those skills to others were remembered for shame. Helen is the only woman in either group.

Rabbi as Celebrity

Some stars are so well known that they are referred to only by their first name, for example, Cher, Madonna, Bono. Rabbi Yehudah Hanasi was so well known that he was referred to simply as "Rabbi." Rabbi Yehudah Hanasi, the promulgator of our Mishnah, was a celebrity in his own right for several reasons. He was a famous sage of distinguished lineage and fabulous wealth that allowed him to represent the Jews to foreign potentates (think: a Rothschild). Here's one story about him that actually has a connection with America:

> Artaban sent our holy teacher [Rabbi] a single priceless pearl. Artaban said to him, "Send me something that is of comparable worth." Rabbi sent him a mezuzah. Artaban said, "What? I sent you something priceless, and you sent me something that is worth two nickels." Said Rabbi to him, "Both your treasures and my treasures cannot compare to what I sent you. Not only that, you have sent me something that I must safeguard, while I have sent you something that safeguards you, as it is written, 'When you walk it will lead you, when you lie down it will

watch over you, and when you are awake it will talk with you'
(Proverbs 6:22)."

(Y. PEAH 1:1, 7B2; GENESIS RABBAH 35:3)

Artaban was a legendary Persian ruler who, according to Christian
tradition, set out to meet the Three Wise Men with three great gems: a
sapphire, a ruby, and a pearl. He never achieved his goal and, Christian
legend has it, gave his gems to the needy instead. The Smithsonian
National Museum of Natural History has a 287-carat cabochon star
sapphire called the Star of Artaban.

If he had wished to do so, Rabbi could have reciprocated with as
lavish a gift as he had been given. But in this case, he chose to take the
"teachable moment" and educate the king about values, and valuations.

Rabbi Yochanan and Reish Lakish

While it is highly doubtful that Rabbi Yochanan and Reish Lakish
were celebrities in their day, they earn a place among celebrities of
the Yerushalmi because, without them, there would be no Yerushalmi.
Rabbi Yochanan is literally on every single page, often paired with his
study partner and student Reish Lakish. Before a disagreement ended
their relationship (and Reish Lakish's life), he was, almost literally,
Rabbi Yochanan's right-hand man.

Once, Rabbi Yudan Hanasi heard a teaching of Reish Lakish's
and was outraged. He sent guards to arrest Reish Lakish,
and they roughed him up. Reish Lakish ran for it and fled
to Magdala [near the Kinneret], and some say, to the village
Hittayya [a town in the hills near Tiberias].

The next day, Rabbi Yochanan and Rabbi Yudan Hanasi
went up to the meetinghouse. Rabbi Yudan asked Rabbi
Yochanan, "Why does my master not give us a teaching of
Torah?"

Rabbi Yochanan began to clap with one hand.

Rabbi Yudan said to him, "Do people clap with only one
hand?"

He said to him, "No. For Reish Lakish is not here. Just as one hand cannot clap, I cannot teach Torah without Reish Lakish here."

(Y. SANHEDRIN 2:1)

Rabbi Yochanan depended on Reish Lakish to sharpen his wits and challenge his arguments.

Given this, it may seem odd that an intellectual argument turns into a dispute so acrimonious that it results in Reish Lakish's death. In the Bavli (Bava Metzia 84a), we find a very detailed story about the relationship between these two sages. Briefly told, Rabbi Yochanan "converts" Reish Lakish from a gladiator to a sage. The two are study partners and sharpen each other's learning through arguing. But one day, Rabbi Yochanan steps over the line. Harsh words fly; Rabbi Yochanan is narcissistically wounded and casts an evil eye on Reish Lakish, who then dies. Rabbi Yochanan is then inconsolable. Eventually, to end his misery, the sages pray that Rabbi Yochanan dies, and he does.

This well-developed story is not found in the Yerushalmi. The only reference we have to this fight between Rabbi Yochanan and Reish Lakish is this passage:

Rabbi Yochanan went three years without going to the meetinghouse because of his sorrow over Reish Lakish's death. At the end of this time, Rabbi Elazar saw in his dream: Tomorrow Sinai [Rabbi Yochanan's nickname] will come down and teach you something new.

(Y. MEGILLAH 1:11, PM 14B, V 72B)

Compared with the story's Shakespearean tone in the Bavli, the account of the break between Reish Lakish and Rabbi Yochanan in the Yerushalmi is guarded, veiled. All we know is that Reish Lakish is gone and Rabbi Yochanan is so sad about it that he stops teaching for three years. The different spins the two Talmuds put on this story are intriguing. Surely those in the Land of Israel would have a better institutional memory of what happened than those in Babylonia. But why, then, is there so much more detail in the Bavli? One has the impression of hearing about a scandal in the British monarchy in two different ways: (1) from a tabloid, looking to spill the maximum amount of dirt (the Bavli) and (2) from a loyalist paper that only wants to report that the problem is solved (the Yerushalmi). Perhaps it was Rabbi Yochanan's role as creator and editor of the Yerushalmi that suppressed the lurid details that the Bavli recounts. (Or the Bavli makes them up!)

Y. v. B.

The Yerushalmi emphasizes the priesthood more than does the Bavli. The Bavli portrays the sages as central stars far more than the Yerushalmi does. If we were to refer to this using our movie metaphor, in the Bavli, the sages' names would be above the movie title on the poster. In the Yerushalmi, the priests would be the ones with the top billing.

For Us ...

Well, when we (the Jewish people) lived without a country of our own, under oppressive regimes, our rock stars were the great rabbis of every age. But in Israel (and in America, today), we have all sorts of celebrities: Hollywood directors, Bar Rafaeli and her ilk, Nobel laureates, famous physicians, secular scholars, titans of business, and philanthropists. Today's Jewish world is much more like the world of the Yerushalmi than the Bavli and the Lithuanian yeshivahs that were its heirs. The Yerushalmi's celebrity system is *our* celebrity system.

3

The Obnoxious Rich Kid
How Would You Feel about
Those Jews in Babylonia?

The movies love to lampoon the rich and entitled, while still making their lives seem glamorous. In the *Harry Potter* world, this character is Draco Malfoy. He has tons of money and even lots of magical talent. The Weasleys, the impoverished but loving family, feel one-down to the Malfoys, even though they eventually win it all.

Those Jews in Babylonia had a well-established community. They'd been there since the First Temple was destroyed in 586 BCE. They lived in a rich land with lots of water (i.e., the Tigris and Euphrates Rivers). The Romans hadn't subdued them. They were on easy street compared with the Jews in the Land of Israel.

And yet, if you lived in Israel, you had a history that was even longer than the one that the Babylonians Jews had. And you lived in the place where almost all your foundational stories happened and where the First and Second Temples stood. You *lived* your history through the streets you walked, the food you ate, and the cultural artifacts you created. Part of you might have felt jealous of the Babylonian Jews: they were richer and lived in greater safety than you did. But even with all its challenges, part of you felt proud to live in Israel.

There was a great deal of communication between these two communities. Indeed, some prominent sages acted as "traveling salesmen." They brought the latest Jewish knowledge from Israel to the Jews in Babylonia. In addition, it seems that many Jews from Israel visited Babylonia as tourists. How do we know? Because the Yerushalmi gives us the itinerary the Israeli tourists would take. Here were the top five tourist sites that Israeli tourists saw in Babylonia:

> One who sees Babylonia must recite five blessings:
> 1. When he sees the Euphrates River, he says: Blessed … who makes the works of creation.
> 2. When he sees the statue of Mercury [Hermes], he says: Blessed … who is patient.
> 3. When he sees Nebuchadnezzar's house, he says: Blessed … who destroyed this wicked one's house.
> 4. When he sees the place of the fiery furnace and the lion's den, he says: Blessed … who performed miracles for our forefathers in this place.
> 5. When he sees the place from which they quarry gravel for idolatrous purposes, he says: Blessed … who speaks and acts. Blessed … who decrees and upholds His word.
>
> (Y. BERAKHOT 9:1, 86A1–86A2)

The statue of Mercury/Hermes could have been a heap of stones to which passersby would add a stone to show their respect. The Israeli tourists would see such stones and say the blessing, marveling at God's patience: He does not destroy such idols right away. Nebuchadnezzar destroyed the First Temple. The tourists praise God for punishing him. When they see where Daniel was saved from the oven and/or the lion's den, they say a blessing that should sound quite familiar: "… *she'asah nisim la'avoteinu bamakom hazeh.*" This is almost exactly the prayer we say when we light the Hanukkah candles. The quarry may have been what played-out quarries are now: places of destruction and barrenness, a visible fulfillment of God's decree against Babylonia.

Hillel: The Archetypal Babylonian

The archetypal Babylonian who came to Israel to make his mark was Hillel. He wanted to make an impression as soon as he got to town.

Then he got smacked upside the head with a helping of Yerushalmi-style karma.

> When Hillel came to Israel from Babylonia, he offered all sorts of teachings, but the people did not accept his teachings until he said, "I have heard these traditions from Shemayah and Avtalyon." When they heard this from him, they stood and appointed him *nasi* over them.
>
> He then began to chide them, saying, "What caused you to need this Babylonian, i.e., me? It's because you failed to serve the two great men of the world, Shemayah and Avtalyon, who were sitting with you."
>
> As soon as he chided them, a teaching disappeared from him. They asked him, "What should we do for the people who did not bring their knives to slaughter their Passover lamb before the Sabbath?"
>
> He said to them, "This tradition I have heard but I have forgotten. Leave it to Israel to determine it. If they are not prophets, they are the children of prophets." It turned out that whoever's Passover offering was a lamb would stick the knife into the wool, and if it was a kid, he tied it between his horns. As soon as he saw this happening, he remembered the tradition, saying, "Thus I heard from Shemayah and Avtalyon."
>
> (Y. PESACHIM 6:1, PM 39A–B)

This is a classic tale of karma and comeuppance for Hillel. Imagine an American rabbi going to Israel today and hectoring people about their Jewish observance. He would have his hat handed to him in short order and made to work on a kibbutz to burn off his pride.

Tensions Between Sages in Israel and Babylonia

Rabbi Yochanan, the central figure of the Yerushalmi, certainly didn't think much of his Babylonian colleagues. For example, he told off one Babylonian sage:

O Babylonian! You have crossed three rivers and have been swamped.

(Y. Shabbat 7:2, PM 43b)

This is typical. He regularly berated the Babylonians with whom he came into contact (e.g., Y. Shabbat 6:2 and numerous other places).

Israeli Pride

Regardless of how much they might have envied the Babylonians, the sages of Israel were proud of their country's religious life and its products. One of the ways they expressed that pride was by legislating that the produce of the Land of Israel was preferred for religious duties. When it comes to lighting the Shabbat lights, one sage mandates that olive oil, a product of Israel, is the only acceptable oil:

Rabbi Tarfon says, "They kindle the Shabbat lamp only with olive oil."

(M. Shabbat 2:2)

The Jews of the diaspora have their representatives, too, in that very same mishnah:

The sages permit all kinds of oil on Shabbat: sesame oil, nut oil, radish-seed oil, fish oil, gourd oil, tar, and naphtha.

(M. Shabbat 2:2)

It would seem that there's still quite a fight over this mishnah, because Rabbi Yochanan ben Nuri, a contemporary of Rabbi Akiba, pleads the case of the diaspora communities:

Rabbi Yochanan ben Nuri got up on his feet and said, "What will the people in Babylonia [Iraq] do, who have only sesame oil? What will the people of Medea [Iran/Persia] do, who have only nut oil? What will the people of Alexandria [Egypt] do, who have only radish oil? What will the people of Cappadocia [Turkey] do, who have neither one nor the other?"

(T. SHABBAT 2:3; Y. SHABBAT 2:2, PM 16B)

In other words, the Yerushalmi recognizes that not everyone lives in "olive oil" country. The sages of the Yerushalmi want people to observe Shabbat, but they believe that the Israeli way is the best way. Even though the sages of Israel can't legislate that lamps be lit only with olive oil, they can certainly make it the preferable form of light.

Y. v. B.

Understandably, the Bavli paints quite a different picture of this relationship. While they do show respect for the Israeli colleagues, they see themselves as the stars of the show and the ones who hold all the power. And time and circumstance conspire to make this idea become reality.

For Us ...

This whole scenario should sound very, very familiar to you. Just look at how Israelis think of American Jews today, and the picture will come into clear focus. We are the second largest community of Jews, and we certainly live in greater abundance and safety than do Israelis. Yet they (and we) often hold the notion that Israelis know how to "do Jewish" better than we do. Their way is the most authentic, and their environment is more Jewishly saturated. How many Israeli scholars-in-residence have come to your community? How many American scholars go to Israel? It's probably a ratio of 9:1. Look in your synagogue gift shop. How many exports of Israel do you find there? Probably a great many.

Israelis today often look askance at Jewish life in America. We are "other" and, often, "less." There is undeniably something wonderful about Jewish life and learning in Israel, but vibrant Jewish life exists here, as well.

4

Right and Wrong, Crime and Punishment

Obviously, an ethical mandate for a society has to describe what is right and what is wrong and what happens as reward for the former and punishment for the latter. But these categorizations depend on time and place. For example, in America, openly carrying around an Uzi would seem hostile at best and illegal at worst. In Israel, however, lots and lots of people carry Uzis openly as they go to and from their military posts. Indeed, I once remember being on a crowded bus in Jerusalem on Friday afternoon jammed next to a soldier who had an Uzi right in my back. That I didn't mind. It was the fact that he still had the clip in that I minded. Still, I didn't feel threatened, because it was normal for that time and place. Similarly, right and wrong in the Yerushalmi was, in some ways, unique to that time and place.

What Would Your Greatest Virtues Be?

The greatest good in Hollywood is money and/or Oscars. The Yerushalmi's greatest virtues are the ones they set out at the very beginning of tractate Peah:

> These are the things without measure: leaving corners of a field unharvested, first fruits offering, appearing at the Temple on the festivals with sacrifices, acts of loving-kindness, and Torah study.

> These are the things whose fruit a person eats in this world and whose principal remains in the World to Come: honoring father and mother, acts of loving-kindness, bringing peace between a man and his fellow, and Torah study is equal to them all.
>
> (M. PEAH 1:1)

I would suggest that the sages thought Peah would be the first tractate of the whole six orders of the Mishnah. Why? Because the entire rest of Mishnah is pretty much nothing *but* measuring things: time, animals, even the size of the human soul (which turns out to be the size of a breadbox). But here, in this mishnah, the sages are saying, "Yes, we'll be laying out measurement after measurement. But we acknowledge, from the start, that there are some things that go beyond measurements." It's a global statement on the nature of goodness and the limits of the "argument" that the sages will set forth in the entire Mishnah.

So what happened? Why was this changed? After some period of time, offerings in the Temple and agricultural "taxes" were replaced by praying as a central pillar of Jewish "being." It was likely *after* this shift took place that tractate Berakhot was moved to the very front of the Mishnah as a whole. If you think about it, tractate Berakhot has very little to do with agriculture, which is the order of the Mishnah in which it is contained. So the sages' original starting point for Judaism, as expressed in M. Peah 1:1, was caring for the poor, supporting the Temple, kindliness, and Torah study.

As the Gemara comments on this mishnah, what we see is one long, glorious introduction to Jewish life based on generosity, kindness, and study. Since this mishnah is not covered in the Bavli, this material is dismantled and dispersed widely in various tractates in that document.

This mishnah is significant in that it also explicitly relates actions to rewards, not just in this life, but also in the next. As a rule, the Mishnah doesn't talk about the World to Come, with a few notable exceptions (e.g., M. Sanhedrin 10:1–5). So for the Mishnah to mention it here is unusual and, we could theorize, meant to drive home the message that there are some good things of which we can't have too much. Note that deeds of loving-kindness and Torah study are the two mitzvot that make both lists.

It's good, too, to think of what is *not* on this list. Keeping kosher and the Sabbath, procreating, and having a deep mystical relationship with God are not mentioned here. The Yerushalmi finds these things to be important but understands that not everyone can have these experiences. M. Peah 1:1 is a list for both men and women.

What Would Your Worst Sins Be?

In so very many movies, the hero or heroine needs to fight against "the Dark Side." So what is the Yerushalmi's "Dark Side"? Our passage at the beginning of Peah not only tells us what the sages considered to be the greatest virtues, but it also tells us what they considered to be the worst sins:

> And corresponding to these four good things (in M. Peah 1:1), there are four things for which punishment is exacted from a person in this world while the principal remains intact for him in the World to Come. And these are they: idolatry, illicit sexual relations, murder; and gossip is equal to them all.
>
> (Y. Peah 1:1 8A1; T. Peah 1:2)

The first three sins require no explanation. But the fourth bears some discussion. Gossip is worse than idolatry, sexual sins, and murder rolled *together*. And it is the sin in which almost all of us indulge every single day. It poisons all three parties involved: the one who says it, the one who hears it, and the one about whom it is spoken. Gossip is Torah study's evil twin: it is the worst use of language, while the other is the best possible use of language.

While these four are the worst sins, there are certainly other sins that could be included in a list of "ten worst sins" in the Yerushalmi. We have this story about a fellow named "Mr. Five Sins," who prays for rain and his prayer is answered (usually a sign of great righteousness):

> Rabbi Abbahu summoned "Mr. Five Sins" and asked him, "What is your trade?" He said to him, "I do five sins every day: hiring prostitutes, cleaning up the theater, bringing home their garments for washing, dancing, and playing the flute before them." Rabbi Abbahu asked, "What good deed have you done?" He said, "One day I was cleaning the theater, and a woman came and stood behind a pillar and cried. I said to her, 'What's the matter?' She said, 'My husband is in prison and I wanted to see what I can do to free him [i.e., work as a prostitute].' So I sold my bed and cover and gave the proceeds to her. I said, 'Here is your money: free your husband, but do not sin.'" Rabbi Abbahu said to him, "You are worthy of having your prayers answered."
>
> (Y. TA'ANIT 1:4, PM 5A–B, V 64B)

The sins Mr. Five Sins engages in are mostly working in the licentious aspects of Roman culture: promoting prostitution and working in the theater (think: Caesar's Palace in Las Vegas). The woman is desperate: her only prospect of freeing her husband is to become a prostitute. Mr. Five Sins worked with prostitutes every day and wanted to save this woman from such a fate. Because Mr. Five Sins saves this one woman from falling into prostitution, he is worthy of having all his prayers answered. In general, though, adopting Roman culture and/or cooperating with the Romans was considered a sin.

Sin Causes the Temple's Destruction

Movies and books are often focused on figuring out the characters' backstories. The *Bourne Identity* and *Harry Potter* movies and books are good examples. When something terrible happens to us, either as individuals or as a people, we want to know what we did to cause it so we can avoid that behavior in the future. Our ancestors were no different:

> The First Temple was destroyed only because they worshipped idols, practiced fornication, and committed murder. And so it was in the case of the Second Temple as well....

During the time of the Second Temple they devoted themselves to Torah and were meticulous about tithes, and every kind of good manners was found among them. On what account did they go into exile? Because they loved money and hated one another without cause. This teaches you that hatred of one another is evil before God, and Scripture deems it equivalent to idolatry, licentiousness, and bloodshed.

(T. MENACHOT 13:22).

Rabbi Zeira, Rabbi Yaakov bar Acha, and Rabbi Avunah were in session. They said, "Baseless hatred is worse, for the First Temple was rebuilt, while the Second Temple was not."

(Y. YOMA 1:1, 6A1–6A2, PM 4B, V 38C)

The First Temple was destroyed on account of the Jews doing the "three big sins." But it was the petty arguing and nursing of grudges that caused the Second Temple to be destroyed and *stay* destroyed. This is very much in line with our passage about the four great sins, above. In essence, gossip was to blame for the loss of the Temple.

Y. v. B.

This is one of the most striking points of divergence between the Yerushalmi and the Bavli. For the former, the greatest sin is to betray one's countrymen. For the latter, the greatest sin is to betray Judaism religiously. You could think of it as the difference between treachery for Israelis, which would mean being a traitor to the country and/or its military, while treachery to Judaism in America would be faithlessness to our faith.

For Us ...

The big take-home is how heinous a sin the Yerushalmi considers gossip to be. The big sin then is the big sin now: gossip. Just. Don't. Do. It.

Rogues Gallery: Sinning Sages

What would *Guys and Dolls* be without Nathan Detroit and his gang of gambling addicts? Or what would *Oliver* be without Fagin's pickpocketing boys? The Yerushalmi has its own rogues' gallery, peopled by some sages who, let us say, fall off the wagon.

Rabbi Eliezer

In many a movie, there is an intense, smart character who borders on dangerously strange (think: Nicholas Cage and Samuel Jackson in almost any role, or Heath Ledger as the Joker in *The Dark Knight*). Rabbi Eliezer ben Hyrcanus is this sort of personality in rabbinic literature. He was one of the greatest sages who ever taught. A contemporary of Rabban Gamliel (and his brother-in-law) and Rabbi Yehoshua, and teacher of Rabbi Akiba, he was known to have tremendous learning and knowledge. He also performed magic, sometimes to his detriment and to the detriment of others. His wife, Rabban Gamliel's sister, was called Imma Shalom, possibly an honorific title. (She certainly earned it; Rabbi Eliezer was not the easiest person with whom to live.) She is only mentioned once in the Yerushalmi:

> It happened that a student taught in front of his teacher, Rabbi Eliezer [thereby, effectively, upstaging him]. Rabbi Eliezer said to his wife, Imma Shalom, "He'll not live out this week." And before a week passed, he died. His students said to him, "Rabbi, you are a prophet." He said to them, "'I am neither a prophet nor the son of a prophet' (Amos 7:14). Rather, I have received a teaching that any student who says a reliable tradition in front of his teacher has earned the death penalty."
>
> (Y. SHEVI'IT 6:1, 44A1–44A2)

This is actually a pretty typical story for Rabbi Eliezer. What's interesting is that Imma Shalom is described in the Bavli as having the ability to control her husband and his temper to some degree. Here, she's portrayed as a passive bystander. Rabbi Eliezer was finally excommunicated (Y. Moed Katan 3:1, 81c–d; B. Bava Metzia 59a–b) for his high-handed ways. (Rabbi Eliezer was excommunicated for a number of reasons. First of all, he was tried for heresy, but he was found innocent on those charges (T. Hullin 2:24). Second, he was a sorcerer, not a fatal flaw in and of itself. But third, he refused to abide by the rules of engagement when scholars disagreed. And it was this, combined with these other factors, that finally tipped the scales in favor of his excommunication.)

Interestingly enough, this is why the students of the sages had to ask Imma Shalom about her sex life rather than asking Rabbi Eliezer. The sages accepted the Greek/Roman idea that the manner of sexual intercourse had an effect on the beauty of a couple's offspring. Judging by their children's appearance, it was clear to the students that Rabbi Eliezer and Imma Shalom had great sex, and the students were looking for some pointers. However, they were forbidden to speak with Rabbi Eliezer, since he'd been excommunicated. So, they asked Imma Shalom, who told them, in rather explicit terms, what it was that made Rabbi Eliezer so great in bed. (Look it up for yourselves; it's in the Bavli—that's all you're getting from me.) Clearly, Rabbi Eliezer was as expert at sex as he was on everything else. Even though the teachings of a named individual are not usually taken as a basis of practice in the Mishnah, Rabbi Eliezer's rulings about how often a husband must offer to have sex with his wife became the norm.

Rabbi Eliezer and the Oven of Achnai

Some of our sages, even our greatest sages, had serious issues with sin. Rabbi Eliezer, for example, had problems getting along with those who disagreed with him. In what is one of the most famous stories in rabbinic literature, his disagreements with his colleagues come to a head in what was the equivalent of a shoot-out at the OK Corral. But the way it's told in the Yerushalmi is different from the way it's told in the Bavli. First, in the Bavli, it's placed in the commentary to a mishnah about hurt feelings. In the Yerushalmi, it's placed in the commentary to a mishnah that talks about being released from a state of excommunication. Ordinarily, according to the Mishnah, people did not cut their hair during the intermediate days of a festival. However, the following people were allowed to do so:

> And these are they who may cut their hair during the intermediate days of a festival: the one who comes from a country located across the sea, and the one who comes out of captivity, and the one who leaves prison, and the one who was excommunicated who the sages just released from his state of separation.
>
> (M. MOED KATAN 3:1)

The Yerushalmi's version of the oven of Achnai story makes a great deal of sense in the context of this mishnah. It is discussing what happens at the *end* of a period of excommunication. One immediately resumes participation in normal life, signified here by the cutting of one's hair. The Bavli, too, could have put the oven of Achnai story in the commentary to this mishnah. However, it wanted to underscore a different point, the seriousness of hurt feelings, in its retelling of this tale. Here's the Yerushalmi's version:

> The sages wanted to excommunicate Rabbi Eliezer. They said, "Who will go and let him know that he has been excommunicated?" Said Rabbi Akiba, "I will go and let him know." Rabbi Akiba went to Rabbi Eliezer and said to him, "My teacher, my teacher, your colleagues are excommunicating you."
>
> Rabbi Eliezer resolved to test the correctness of the sages' decision and took Rabbi Akiba outside and said, "Carob tree, carob tree, if the tradition is according to their words, be uprooted!" And it was not uprooted. "If the tradition is according to my words, be uprooted." And it was uprooted. "If the tradition is according to their words, return." It did not return. "If the tradition is according to my words, return." It returned.
>
> *All these signs and the tradition is still not according to Rabbi Eliezer? Said Rabbi Chanina, "Ever since the Torah was given, it*

was not given except 'to follow a majority opinion' (Exodus 23:2).
But is it possible that Rabbi Eliezer does not know that we follow the
majority? So why would he make such a vigorous demonstration,
knowing that the majority must win?"

Rabbi Eliezer did not lose his temper until they burned all
the things cooked in an Achnai oven, which he had declared
insusceptible to ritual impurity, before his very eyes. For there
(M. Keilim 5:10) they taught, "If he cuts the oven into which
an impure animal fell into segments and puts sand between
the segments, Rabbi Eliezer says it is not susceptible to ritual
impurity, but the sages say it is susceptible to ritual impurity.
And such an oven is called an oven of Achnai."

Said Rabbi Yermiyah, "A great visitation happened on that
very day: every place upon which Rabbi Eliezer cast his eyes
was burned. And not only that but even one grain of wheat
would be half burnt and half unburnt depending upon which
half of the grain of wheat he had looked at with his glaring
gaze.

"And the pillars of the sages' meetinghouse vibrated.
Rabbi Yehoshua said to the walls, 'If colleagues are arguing
with each other, what does it matter to you?' And then a
Heavenly Voice came forth and said, 'The tradition is according
to Eliezer, my son.' Said Rabbi Yehoshua, 'The Torah is not in
heaven!' (Deuteronomy 30:12)...."

One time Rabbi Eliezer was passing through the
marketplace and he saw a woman cleaning her house. She
threw out the dirt from her house, and it fell on his head. He
said, "It appears to me that today my colleagues will bring me
close to them soon and lift the ban of excommunication so that
I might fulfill the following verse, as it is written, 'From the
ash heap He lifts up the needy. To sit him with princes, with
princes of His people. He sets the barren one of the house as a
happy mother of many children' (Psalm 113:7–9)."

(Y. MOED KATAN 3:1, PM 10B, V 81C–D)

Y. v. B.

The Yerushalmi's version of the oven of Achnai story ends with Rabbi Eliezer feeling that his excommunication is over, while the Bavli's story ends like a Shakespearean tragedy: dead bodies litter the stage. There are other significant differences between the two versions of this story.

In this telling of the oven of Achnai story, Rabbi Eliezer does not immediately perform magic in public. Instead, he goes out of town, where no one but he and his best student, Rabbi Akiba, can see what happens. He also gives his colleagues respect by "testing" their ideas to see if they are right. In addition, the carob tree doesn't remain uprooted. It returns to its spot, leaving no sign around which Rabbi Eliezer's supporters could rally.

Rabbi Yehoshua, Rabbi Eliezer's partner and temperamental opposite, provides the counterbalance to Rabbi Eliezer's demonstration. Unlike Rabbi Eliezer, Rabbi Yehoshua assiduously avoids confrontations and almost never demands his rights (e.g., B. Berakhot 27b). He is also very poor. Rabbi Eliezer, for all his flamboyance and spiritual power, his social standing and his wealth, is still on the outside. Poverty-stricken Rabbi Yehoshua remains the quintessential insider, protecting his institution from harm, even defying a voice from heaven to do so.

Rabbi Yehoshua stops the walls of the Academy from falling, thereby physically preserving the majority of sages who are ruling against Rabbi Eliezer. He refutes the Heavenly Voice as well, thereby spiritually preserving the sages' authority. (Note that, unlike the version in the Bavli, God doesn't laugh with delight during this fight.) It may have been that the "shock waves" that followed Rabbi Eliezer's excommunication were so great that they seemed to rock the foundations of the Academy. You need only think of times when you have been in an institution during a period of great emotional turmoil and turnover and think how little stability there was (and how little productivity) to understand this situation.

This story in the Yerushalmi is balanced. Actions bring equal reactions. Rabbi Eliezer is cast off and brought back. Rabbi Eliezer makes demonstrations that are countered by Rabbi Yehoshua. The sages burn Rabbi Eliezer's bread, and he burns theirs in return. This demonstrates a principle that underlies much of biblical and rabbinic literature: *middah k'neged middah*, "measure for measure." That is, the energy that one sends forth is the energy that one receives.

A note on editing is in order. If you look at the part of the passage that is in italics, above, you can tell that it's a later interpolation. Later sages wonder how Rabbi Eliezer can raise such a fuss. By the time this story "jells" everyone knows that a majority vote wins every contest. So this interpolation tries to address what is a problem for later readers. The foolproof way to ascertain whether something is an interpolation is to read the passage without it. Try it. You can see that the passage reads quite nicely without this paragraph.

Elisha ben Abuyah: Good Guys Gone Bad

As Darth Vader was the greatest Jedi to be seduced by the Dark Side in *Star Wars*, and as Tom Riddle was Hogwarts's most brilliant student to be ensnared by evil in *Harry Potter*, so the Yerushalmi has a great sage who became a terrible sinner: Elisha ben Abuya.

As we saw above, Rabbi Eliezer was a powerful magician who generated and controlled fire. At the circumcision celebration of Elisha ben Abuyah, Rabbi Eliezer and Rabbi Yehoshua left the party, went into a side room, and began to study. At that moment, as they tapped into Torah's essential energy, fire came down and surrounded them (Y. Hagigah 2:1, V 77b). This had a drastic effect on the eight-day-old's life.

> "The end of a thing is better than its beginning" (Ecclesiastes 7:8) so long as it is good *from* its beginning. And so it happened to me.
>
> My father, Abuyah, was one of the richest people in Jerusalem. When the day of my circumcision came, he invited

all the important people of Jerusalem.... When they had eaten and drunk, they began stamping their feet and dancing. Rabbi Eliezer said to Rabbi Yehoshua, "While they are occupying themselves in their way, we will occupy ourselves in our way." So they sat down and engaged in the study of the Torah, from the Pentateuch to the Prophets, and from the Prophets to the Writings. And fire fell from heaven and surrounded them.

Abuyah said to them, "My masters, have you come to burn my house down around me?"

They said, "God forbid! But we were sitting searching through the words of the Torah from the Pentateuch to the Prophets and from the Prophets to the Writings, and the words were as alive as when they were given from Mount Sinai. And the fire shone around us as it shone from Mount Sinai. And what was the essential attribute of their being handed over at Sinai? They were given only by fire."

Abuyah, my father, said to them, "My masters, if this is the power of the Torah, if this son of mine lives, I will dedicate his life to Torah."

Because his original intention was not pure, that is, not for the sake of heaven, therefore, it was not realized for me.

(Y. Hagigah 2:1, V 77b, PM 9a–b)

Because Elisha's father wanted his son to learn Torah to gain power, rather than out of love for the Torah and for God, his whole career as a sage was blighted from its very beginning. It's not hard to imagine Abuyah, a wealthy and powerful man, being impressed by this display of power. But worshipping God's power, instead of God's self, is a form of idolatry. And in this case, it had disastrous effects on Elisha.

Y. v. B.

Like the oven of Achnai story, the account of Elisha ben Abuyah's life differs between the Yerushalmi and the Bavli. In both versions, however, he is depicted as the ultimate traitor to the sages. He acquires the moniker "Acher," "the Other." This might indicate that he is outside the group. It might also allude to a religious spin-off of Judaism called *Zera Acher*, "A New Seed." In the Yerushalmi, his heresy is betraying the Jews to their enemies, while in the Bavli his heresy is dabbling in gnosticism, the belief in two deities, rather than monotheism.

Response to God's "Unfairness"

Other experiences turned him against the sages, as well:

> Why did all this happen to him? Once Elisha was sitting and studying in the plain of Gennesaret, and he saw a man climb to the top of a palm tree, take a mother bird with her young, and descend safely. The following day he saw another man climb to the top of the palm tree, take the young birds, and release the mother. When he descended, a snake bit him, and he died. Elisha thought, "It is written, 'If you chance to come upon a bird's nest, in any tree or on the ground, with young ones or eggs, you shall not take the mother with the young. You shall let the mother go, but the young you shall take to yourself; that it may go well with you, and that you may live long' (Deuteronomy 22:6–7). Where is the welfare of this man, and where his length of days?" He did not know that Rabbi Yaakov had explained it before him: "That it may go well with you," in the World to Come, which is wholly good. "And that you may live long," in the messianic era, the time that is eternal.
>
> (Y. HAGIGAH 2:1, PM 9B)

The Torah explicitly promises long life for the performance of only two mitzvot: honoring one's parents, and shooing a mother away from her nest and taking only the eggs. Yet the boy who followed the Torah did not live. A similar injustice might also have added to Acher's defection:

Some say he defected because he saw the tongue of Rabbi Yehudah the Baker, dripping blood, in the mouth of a dog. He said, "This is the Torah, and this is its reward! This is the tongue that brought the words of the Torah as befits them. This is the tongue that labored in the Torah all its days. This is Torah, and this its reward [*Zo Torah v'zo s'kharah*]? It seems as though there is no reward for righteousness and no resurrection of the dead."

A third theory as to why Elisha left the sages goes back to a prenatal influence:

Some say that when his mother was pregnant with him, she walked past some idolatrous temples and smelled their particular kind of incense, and the odor pierced her body like the poison of a snake.

(Y. Hagigah 2:1, V 77b, PM 9b)

Whether he "went rogue" because of prenatal, childhood, or adult experiences, Elisha became the enemy of the sages.

Elisha targeted the sages for elimination.

Who is Acher? Elisha ben Abuyah, who slew the young scholars of the Torah. They say, "He used to kill every disciple he saw mastering the Torah."

Moreover, he used to enter the schoolhouse, and when he saw the pupils in the presence of the teacher, he would say, "What are these doing here? This one should be a mason. This one should be a carpenter. This one should be a fisherman. This one should be a tailor." When they heard this, they would leave the teacher and go and become workmen. Of him Scripture says, "Let your mouth not lead you into sin" (Ecclesiastes 5:5). For he ruined his own good deeds.

Also, at the time of the persecution, the Romans made the Jews carry burdens on the Sabbath. But the Jews arranged it so that two people should share one load, because two people doing one piece of work are not liable in regard to Sabbath violation. Elisha said, "Make them carry the loads by themselves." They went and made them carry the loads by themselves, but they arranged to unload them in an area that could be classified neither as private ground nor as public area, so that they might not bring them out from private to public ground [which is forbidden]. Elisha said, "Make them carry bottles that will break if left lying around."

(Y. HAGIGAH 2:1, PM 9A, V 77B)

In a move that presaged the canton service of young Jewish boys in the Russian Army, he forced children who would have been sages to go into different careers. He also caused Jews to sin. Knowing all the rules made it possible for him to close all the loopholes the Jews wanted to use to keep themselves from violating Shabbat.

Y. v. B.

Whether Elisha actually killed some students, diverted students away from Torah study, or made all sorts of Jews violate the Sabbath, we have three forms of betrayal that the Yerushalmi finds most heinous. In the Yerushalmi, apostasy is political and communal betrayal of the Jewish people in general, and of the sages in particular. In the Bavli, apostasy is believing in a dualistic world order and is expressed through personal immorality and ritual transgressions.

For Us ...

What disgraces Judaism may vary according to one's location. Disloyalty to one's country might cast shame on a Jew in America, but it would be truly shocking for a Jew whose country was the State of Israel. Apostasy for a diaspora Jew is more likely to consist of theological, moral, or ritual betrayal of the Jewish tradition. It is like the difference between political sabotage and wearing a cross.

5

How Can Judaism Compete with Christianity?

Our movie isn't the only one playing at the multiplex. So how are we going to sell tickets for our movie when we're up against big, established franchises such as Roman paganism and Christianity? Well, in truth, it's a bit of a tough sell.

Intentions Count

The Jews of Israel lived under a ferocious Roman occupation that made it difficult (or outright dangerous) to perform any mitzvot. So the sages of the Yerushalmi give their readers a way to deal with this uncomfortable reality. In all likelihood, you have been taught that we are held accountable only for our deeds, not for our thoughts or intentions. The Yerushalmi offers a different perspective:

> God considers a good intention as a good deed, but a bad intention does not count as a bad deed....
>
> When does this apply? With regard to a Jew. But with non-Jews, it is the opposite: The Holy One, blessed be He, does not consider a good intention as a good deed. And God regards a non-Jew's bad intention as a bad deed....
>
> It was taught: Rabbi Shimon ben Yochai says, "If a person was totally righteous his whole life but at the end he rebelled, he has lost everything he accomplished in his entire life.

"If a person was utterly evil his whole life but in the end he repented, the Holy One, blessed be He, receives him."

Rabbi Yochanan said, "And not only that, but all the sins that he committed are counted as good deeds."

(Y. PEAH 1:1, 9B1–2)

Under the Romans, the Jews of Israel were dealing with some extreme conditions. They might have had all the good intentions in the world, but the price for acting on those intentions might have been too high. Since the price of loyalty to Judaism was great, the rewards had to be similarly great.

Defection rates must have been high. Think of the pressure to adopt (or appear to adopt) paganism or Christianity. The fact that *any* Jews remained faithful must have been remarkable in that time and place. So the sages of the Yerushalmi would want to reward even the *desire* to do the right thing, as that may have been the best some could do.

The Afterlife and Limbo in the Yerushalmi

In the movies, we expect that the villain will suffer and the righteous will prosper. Some "movies" of the Yerushalmi's day, such as Christianity, were selling just that—heaven and hell. So what was the Yerushalmi selling? That's a little bit problematic. The sages had very fluid ideas about the afterlife. There is a place of punishment called *Gehinnom*, that is, Hell, and a place of reward called *Olam Haba*, that is, the World to Come. Heaven itself has seven levels and many different kinds of angels. The Yerushalmi even describes a Jewish limbo. So who goes there?

Rabbis of Caesarea said, "The children of non-Jews and the soldiers of Nebuchadnezzar's army, who were forced into service, are neither alive in the World to Come nor are they judged and assigned to *Gehinnom*. Regarding these people, Scripture says, 'They will sleep an eternal sleep' (Jeremiah 51:57)."

(Y. BERAKHOT 9:1, 88A2)

The sages had mercy on soldiers who were conscripted against their will. Likewise, children who were raised as idol worshippers and did not reach the age when they could have chosen Judaism would not be held responsible for the sins they unknowingly committed.

Y. v. B.

Christianity was a challenge for the sages in both Israel and Babylonia, although Zoroastrianism was a strong threat with which the Jews in Israel did not have to struggle.

For Us ...

It appears that the fight over how to weigh intentions versus actions was not a done deal in the Yerushalmi. In other words, it didn't have to turn out the way it did. We could have a Judaism that resembles much more closely ... Christianity.

Within living memory, whole populations of Jews faced regimes every bit as toxic as the Romans (e.g., the Nazis and the Soviets). To "do Jewish" was tantamount to signing your death warrant in those environments. This passage seems tailor-made for such situations.

6

Tefillin and Tallit
Essential "Props"
and "Costumes"

Sometimes, costumes and props take a movie from mundane to classic. What would *The Wizard of Oz* be without the ruby slippers? What would *Gone With the Wind* be without the dress made out of velvet curtains? What would the *Lord of the Rings* trilogy be without that ring, which almost always gets its own "personal" close-up every time it's shown?

Jews have their costumes and props, too. And they inform the "performance" every bit as much as those items do in a movie.

Saying the *Shema* isn't just something we do with words. It includes a concrete set of actions and items, particularly tefillin. Nowadays, when we wear tefillin, we put them on for the morning recitation of the *Shema* and then take them off until the next morning. We say some prescribed blessings as we wrap them on our arms and put them on our heads. We all know what they look like: black, leather boxes. Everyone knows that, right?

Well ... according to the Yerushalmi, that isn't how it was at all. The Yerushalmi records that ideas about tefillin were still in flux and there was a great deal of variety in the way this mitzvah was done.

> If one makes his head-*tefillah* round, this is a dangerous practice that does not fulfill the commandment. To put them on the palm

of the hand is the manner of heresy. To overlay them with gold
or put that of the hand on one's sleeve is the manner of outsiders.

(M. MEGILLAH 4:9)

We can conjecture that the Mishnah forbids round tefillin, gold
tefillin, and tefillin worn on the palms or sleeves because people were
actually wearing such items in these ways. There used to be many
different sorts of tefillin, which may have identified Jews as being
members of different groups (think: knit *kippah* versus fedora). The
sages who wrote the Mishnah were likely members of the "black,
leather, square tefillin" group, and they were trying to outlaw every
other group's version of this mitzvah. This may be why the sages
designated so many details of their version of tefillin as having come
from Sinai and Moses. "A tradition to Moses from Sinai" (*halakhah
l'Moshe miSinai*) is a technical phrase that means, "We don't have a
scriptural leg to stand on, but we want it to be this way." In other
words, "Do it because I said so." The "black box" contingent could
reflect Judaism's democratizing principle at work. The plainest, and
perhaps least expensive, sort of tefillin were to become the norm.

There was also diversity in the way this mitzvah was performed.
For example, some sages wore their tefillin all day long.

After recovering from an illness, Rabbi Yannai used to wear his
tefillin all day long for three days. This teaches that illness cleanses
the body [they can't be worn in a state of ritual impurity]....

Rabban Yochanan ben Zakkai never took off his tefillin.
Not in the summer; not in the winter. And Rabbi Eliezer, his
disciple, also acted accordingly.

(Y. BERAKHOT 2:3, 20B3–21A1)

Do they *ever* take the tefillin off? Yes. They didn't wear them in the
Roman-style bathhouse, which was an important institution in the
world of northern Israel. The sages did not want the tefillin to come
into contact with any form of nakedness, so they had a "tefillin check
boy" at the bathhouse.

Rabban Yochanan ben Zakkai would wear tefillin until he reached Yaakov the Thermasarius [from the Greek word for warmth]. And when he returned from bathing, Yaakov would give the tefillin back to him.

And when he gave them to him, Rabban Yochanan ben Zakkai would say this to him: "Two arks went along with the Israelites in the desert—the ark of the covenant and the ark of Joseph's bones. The nations of the world said, 'What is the nature of these arks?' Israel said to them, 'This is Joseph's coffin, and this is the ark of the Life of the world [Chei ha'olamim].' And the nations of the world ridiculed Israel and said, 'Is it possible that a coffin [a death box] goes alongside the ark of the Eternal [a life box]?' And Israel said, 'It is because Joseph guarded what was kept in the ark.'"

And why did Rabban Yochanan tell this story to the bath attendant?... Joseph merited kingship because he kept the commandments of the Holy One, blessed be He. We merit all this honor only because we keep the commandments of the Holy One, blessed be He. And you, Yaakov, want to prevent us from keeping these commandments. So hurry up and give us back our tefillin!

(Y. BERAKHOT 2:3, 21A1–21B1)

Rabban Yochanan ben Zakkai's beautiful metaphor of the arks with which the whole people of Israel always traveled and the tefillin with which Jews traveled truly suggests that the tefillin should always be worn as long as one is awake.

There are options for how one says blessings regarding tefillin:

In what way does one recite the blessings over tefillin?

Rabbi Zerikan in the name of Rabbi Yaakov bar Idi: When one puts on the tefillin of the hand, what does he say? Blessed ... who sanctified us with His commandments and commanded us concerning the commandment of tefillin [l'haniach tefillin].

When he puts on the tefillin of the head what does he say? Blessed ... commanded us concerning the commandment of putting on tefillin [*al mitzvat tefillin*].

When he takes them off what does he say? Blessed ... and commanded us to keep His statutes....

Rabbi Abbahu sat and taught in the evening with his tefillin on sideways to keep track of them.

(Y. Berakhot 2:2, 2:4 21b1–21b2)

The bottom line is that there were many ways to wear and bless tefillin. They could be square or round. They could be covered with leather or gold. They could be worn all day long, save bringing them into contact with nakedness. You could say a blessing when putting them on and when taking them off. The tefillin were reminders of God's love and protection, which stretches all the way back to the Exodus from Egypt, when two precious boxes guarded the whole people in their desert wanderings.

But wait ... there's more!

Women, Tzitzit, and Tefillin

We've already seen, here, a far wider variety of ways of observing this mitzvah than we might have expected. But that's not the end of the surprises. There even seems to be enough leeway in the Yerushalmi to allow women to wear tefillin:

Whence do we learn the exemption for women from reciting the *Shema* and wearing tefillin? "And you shall teach them to your *sons*" (Deuteronomy 11:19) and not to your daughters. Whoever is obligated to study Torah is obligated to wear tefillin. A challenge to that teaching is raised: Saul's daughter Michal used to wear tefillin. And Jonah's wife used to go up to Jerusalem on the pilgrimages and the sages did not object.

(Y. Berakhot 2:2/2:3, 21b3–22a1)

First, we have a pretty standard derivation for excluding women from wearing tefillin. Sons, not daughters, are explicitly mentioned. (Of course, the Hebrew really means "children," not just "sons.") Then there seems to be a clarifying comment. If you're obligated to study Torah, you have to wear tefillin. *Everyone* is supposed to study Torah (M. Peah 1:1). It's a positive mitzvah with no time limit set on it. Only positive mitzvot with a time limit exclude women. So the two statements cancel each other out.

(The evidence for women wearing tzitzit is even more compelling. By 220 CE, the sages all agreed that women were commanded to wear tzitzit, with one lone sage dissenting. In *all* such cases, except this one, the anonymous majority wins against the named minority. It's actually amazing that women ended up *not* wearing them. The Bavli records that one sage, Rav Yehudah, made sure to put fringes on the aprons of the women in his household [B. Menachot 43a].)

At least one slave (whose status is often likened to that of women) was known to wear tefillin. Rabban Gamliel's slave Tavi wore them:

> It is taught: Rabban Gamliel's slave Tavi would wear tefillin, and the sages did not protest his actions [even though slaves are exempt from the mitzvah of tefillin].
>
> (Y. Sukkah 2:1, 11b1)

Tavi was more than just one of Rabban Gamliel's slaves. He was a member of the family. Rabban Gamliel sat shivah for Tavi when he died (M. Berakhot 2:7). Tavi's wife, Tavita (both slaves' names come from the word meaning "good," i.e., *tov*), was also exceptionally well versed in Jewish practice:

> It happened that Rabban Gamliel's serving girl, Tavita, was carrying wine for drinks. She inspected herself to see if her period had begun before lifting up each jug of wine.
>
> When her period started, she said to Rabban Gamliel, "My teacher, I have seen a dark red stain on my garment."
>
> Rabban Gamliel felt shaken up at the possibility that the wine had been rendered ritually unclean.

> She said to him, "I checked myself before lifting each jug, so only this one is rendered impure."
>
> (Y. NIDDAH 2:1, PM 6A)

In the parallel version of this text (Leviticus Rabbah, *Metzora* 19:4), Rabban Gamliel is so happy he exclaims, "May your life be given to you, even as you have restored mine to me!"

So we see that rules that we think of as hard and fast, such as that women don't wear tefillin or tzitzit, aren't so hard and fast at all in the world of the Yerushalmi.

Y. v. B.

The Bavli is considerably less open to variation in the observance of tefillin and tzitzit. For them, the square-black-box-and-no-women-allowed contingent has won.

For Us ...

We can reclaim the Yerushalmi's flexibility when it comes to tzitzit and tefillin. We can surround ourselves with the words of the *Shema* on our bodies, using art and technology that are available to us. We can unleash our creativity *and* be part of a long tradition that embraced a variety of ways to approach this mitzvah.

7

Who, Beside Rabbis, Was Running the Jewish Community?

There are all sorts of people who play supporting roles on and off camera to make a movie. Whole armies of costumers, electricians, assistant directors and second assistant directors, drivers, and stunt performers are needed to make a film, even if they are never in front of the camera.

So who was the "crew" of the Yerushalmi's world? This passage gives us some ideas:

> Ten cups of wine are drunk in a mourner's home: two before the meal, five during the meal, and three after the meal. After the meal, the first cup was for *Birkat Hamazon*, the second for those who did acts of kindness, and the third for those consoling the mourners. When Rabban Shimon ben Gamliel died, they added three additional cups: one for the *chazzan hak'nesset*, one for the *rosh hak'nesset*, and one for Rabban Gamliel. But once the *beit din* saw that they were becoming drunk, they ruled that these three additional cups stop, and they returned to the ten-cup standard.
>
> (Y. Berakhot 3:1, 34a1; B. Ketubot 8b; B. Pesachim 110a)

The wine of the sages' days had a very low alcohol content, something like light beer today. But even ten light beers would put most of us under the table, and apparently things had gotten out of hand at these post-burial meals. Those who helped bury the body and those who brought the food for the mourners were toasted. The first cup of wine after the meal was standard at every meal. We still have a vestige of that cup of wine today: the third cup of wine at the Passover seder.

At some point after Rabban Gamliel's death, three additional cups were added. It is likely that Rabban Gamliel's memory was honored at funerals because he saw what a ruinous effect exorbitant funeral expenses were having on people. He mandated that he be buried in the simplest shrouds possible, instead of linen and silk. Rabban Gamliel was leading by example. As a billionaire, he could have afforded shrouds of gold if he so desired. Instead, he made this ruling and showed there was a better way.

So we know about Rabban Gamliel, but who were the *chazzan hak'nesset* and the *rosh hak'nesset*? No one is really sure. They had something to do with running the service. Guggenheimer hypothesizes:

> The *hazan* [sic] was not only the reader in congregational prayers, but also the general organizer of religious affairs. In outlying communities he was the ritual slaughterer and the conduit through whom questions of religious practice were addressed to the Academies.... He had to recite the prayer at the end of a study session.
>
> (GUGGENHEIMER, Y. BERAKHOT, P. 360 NOTE 116)

T. Sukkah 4:6 says that the *chazzan hak'nesset* in the great synagogue of Alexandria would wave semaphore flags to signal the congregation when to say, "Amen." (If you think of some of our largest synagogues without sound systems, you can see why this might be necessary.) He's "the crew" who makes sure there's film in the camera and the extras all do what they're supposed to do. The *rosh hak'nesset* was the head of the community and was responsible for synagogue upkeep as well as maintenance of the cemetery (T. Sotah 7:7–8). In the end, there isn't much certainty about what these people did.

Our passage describes a community that is in a state of "becoming"; it's evolving and changing, going in one direction, then in another. People spend too much on funerals … until Rabban Gamliel convinces them to do otherwise. They drink some toasts, then augment that number, then prune that number back. Nothing is very tied down and there's lots of flexibility. In a sense, this is what directors call "coverage": they shoot a scene from many different angles and give the actors many different directions so that, when it comes time to edit the film, they have a great deal of footage from which to choose. The Yerushalmi gives us lots of "coverage" of services and synagogues from which to choose.

Rabbis Who Do It All

For some movies, directors like to have "triple threats"—actors who can act, sing, and dance. And then, as now, some communities want rabbis who can do everything. They should have twenty years of experience, be thirty-five years old, love working with teenagers and have a passion for visiting the elderly, have great family lives, and be in the office fifteen hours a day. This is nothing new. Then, as now, communities wanted a leader who could perform all the necessary rabbinic functions:

> Rabbi Shimon ben Lakish went to Botzra. They came to him and said, "Show us a person who sermonizes [darish], judges [dayyan], writes [sofer], sings/reads or takes care of the syna-gogue [chazzan], who can fulfill all our needs."
>
> (Y. SHEVI'IT 6:1, 46B1)

Reish Lakish is asked to find such a person to send to Botzra (in Moab). Moab is not in the Land of Israel, hence, no Jew from the Land of Israel should go there. Reish Lakish finds a Babylonian to do this job, which Rabbi Yochanan okays. Rabbi Yochanan is saying that there's Israel, and then there's everywhere else. Regardless, it's a good picture of what rabbis did to serve the Jewish community.

8

How Would You
Be Reading Torah?

The sages of the Yerushalmi didn't want services to run so long that they became a burden to the congregation. One of their greatest mechanisms for controlling the length of Shabbat services was reading the Torah on the triennial cycle (a practice that has been adopted by many Reform and Conservative congregations today). Instead of reading every word of the whole Torah portion each Shabbat, they would read a third of it, thereby covering all of it over the course of three years.

More Coverage: Translation Is a Must

Sometimes there is no one right way to play a scene but actually many right ways. The director shoots a variety of ways the scene can be played and chooses one later. And there were many right ways to read the Torah.

The sages were not interested in a speed-reading of the Torah text. They wanted the congregation to understand the words. And they were aware that few people might understand the Hebrew. So they insisted on having the text translated into the language the people would understand, be it Aramaic, Greek, and so on:

> Rabbi Zeira said in the name of Rav Hananel, "'And they read from the book, from God's scroll, explaining; and they made

meaning [v'som sechel] and the people understood the reading' (Nehemiah 8:8). This refers to Scripture."

"Explaining" refers to the translation.

"And they made meaning" refers to proper articulation [t'amim].

"So that the people understood the reading" refers to the tradition [masoret].

And there are those who say: This means the grammatical constructions.

And there are those who say: This means the first words of the successive verses.

Rabbi Zeira in the name of Rav Hananel: "Even one who is experienced in reading the Torah, as was Ezra, should not recite it from memory."

(Y. MEGILLAH 4:1, 34B1–34B2, PM 28B)

The verse from Nehemiah seems to have many apparently extraneous words. The sages therefore assign each word its own meaning. But there is no set version as to what those meanings might be. It could mean translating or a traditional interpretation (masoret) or grammar or a *Reader's Digest* summary. Perhaps different groups explained the verses different ways, some translating, some explaining grammar, and some giving summaries.

In this same passage, we find out that some congregations read from a book and some from a scroll, and some stood while reading, while others sat. Some people read and translated; others didn't think this was the right way to do the Torah reading. Some people read the Torah without a blessing or with different blessings than we know. The catalogue of variety goes on and on. In other words, there is no single right way to read Torah, according to the Yerushalmi. There is no standardization. There are *lots* of right ways.

Who Are the Yerushalmi's "Extras"?

Before the days of computer-generated imagery, if you wanted a crowded scene, you had to have a lot of extras (think: the crowd scenes in *Gandhi* or *Cleopatra*). Like communities of every age, sometimes the congregations in the Yerushalmi had trouble scratching together a minyan. In a discussion of how many *aliyot* to the Torah there are, we find this:

> "On Shabbat, seven people have *aliyot*" (M. Megillah 4:2). And if they want to call more, they do call more. And all figure in the number of seven, even a woman, even a minor. But they do not bring a woman to read Scripture in public.
>
> (T. MEGILLAH 3:11)

This leaves open the tantalizing possibility that there could be more than seven *aliyot* and that women and children could have *aliyot* to the Torah.

Y. v. B.

The biggest difference between the two Talmuds is the difference in the ways the two approach the Torah reading cycle. The Babylonian cycle completes the entire Torah every year.

9

Con Men and
Characters in Disguise

S tories featuring con men (e.g., *The Music Man, The Sting, Dirty Rotten Scoundrels*, and *The Freshman*) are standard fare in the movies. The Yerushalmi has its own con men, specifically people begging for charity who don't really need it.

> Rabbi Yochanan and Rabbi Shimon ben Lakish went to bathe in the public baths of Tiberias. A poor man met them and said, "Acquire merit by me and give me some charity." They said to him, "When we return we'll give you charity." When they returned, they found him dead. They said, "Since we did not acquire merit during his lifetime, let us care for him in his death." While they were occupied with burying him, they found a pouch of *dinars* hanging on him. They said, "That is what Rabbi Abbahu said in the name of Rabbi Elazar: 'We have to give thanks to the dishonest among them, because if there were no dishonest persons among them, if someone refused to give charity to a person who was requesting alms, he would be punished immediately.'"
>
> (Y. PEAH 8:8, 73A2)

Perhaps Rabbi Yochanan and Reish Lakish were in a hurry, or perhaps Shabbat evening was approaching. Regardless, they brushed off the beggar. When they saw the results, however, they resolved to bury him and show him kindness in that way. (Since the man had money, one wonders how he died. Surely if he'd been on death's door from hunger, the sages would have noticed. So his death likely came suddenly and, perhaps, violently.) They found a great mercy in the man's "posing": we really are bound to help those in need, so those who take without truly needing are actually a godsend, as they introduce a factor of uncertainty into the process.

The Straight Man: The Honest Townsfolk

In almost every con-man movie you need the mark, who is often the honest townsfolk. In *The Music Man*, the townsfolk are as upright and upstanding as one could possibly imagine: no flash, just solid Iowan values. Our honest townsfolk in the Yerushalmi are those folks who deserve charity but will neither ask for it nor take it easily. Some sages found a way around this impediment.

> Rabbi Yaakov bar Idi and Rabbi Yitzchak bar Nachman were in charge of giving out the charity money for the community. They would give Rabbi Oshaya's father-in-law, Rabbi Chama, a *dinar*, and he would give it to others.
>
> Everyone would gossip about Rabbi Zecharyah, Rabbi Levi's son-in-law. They said that he didn't need charity but was taking it. When he died, they checked and found out that he would give away this money to others who were in need.
>
> Rabbi Chinena bar Pappa would distribute charity at night. One time the chief of the spirits met him and said to him, "Did the rabbi not teach us, 'Do not move the boundary of your neighbor' (Deuteronomy 19:14) [meaning, 'You are infringing on my turf!']." Said Rabbi Chinena to him, "But it is also written, 'A gift in secret overturns anger' (Proverbs 21:14)." The spirit gave up and fled from him.
>
> (Y. PEAH 8:8, 73A2–73A3)

This seems to be the photonegative of the beggar in the story with Rabbi Yochanan and Reish Lakish. Here, we have sages who are eager to give charity and think up clever ways to do it.

The Underdog Catches a Break: Dealing with Financial Adversity and Giving Charity

Everyone loves a story in which an underdog comes out on top. We rejoice when Cinderella goes to the ball and marries Prince Charming, vanquishing her evil stepmother and stepsisters. The story of the underdog who finally catches a break is a standard theme in literature and movies. And the tougher the underdog has it, the more glorious the deliverance is.

One such underdog is Abba Yehudah, a formerly generous giver who fell on hard times.

Once it happened that Rabbi Eliezer, Rabbi Yehoshua, and Rabbi Akiba went up to the sands of Antioch to collect funds for the sages.

There was a certain man there, named Abba Yehudah. He would give charity generously. One time, he lost all his money, and he saw our rabbis and despaired of helping them. He went home and his face was filled with suffering.

His wife said to him, "Why are you so downcast?"

He said to her, "Our rabbis are here, and I do not know what I can do for them."

His wife, who was even more righteous than he, said to him, "You have a single field left. Go and sell half of it, and give the proceeds to the sages."

He went and did as she recommended. He came to our rabbis and he gave them the proceeds.

Our rabbis prayed on his behalf. They said to him, "Abba Yehudah, *May the Holy One, blessed be He, make up your loss.*"

When the sages went their way, Abba Yehudah went down to plough the half field that he had left. His cow fell and broke a leg. He bent down to lift up the cow, and the Holy One, blessed be He, opened his eyes and he found a treasure. He said, "It was for my own good that my cow broke its leg."

When our rabbis returned, they asked about him, saying, "How are things with Abba Yehudah?"

People said, "Who can gaze upon the face of Abba Yehudah, Abba Yehudah of the oxen! Abba Yehudah of the camels! Abba Yehudah of the asses!" So the sages realized that he had recovered his wealth.

Abba Yehudah went to the sages and asked how they were. They said to him, "How are you doing?"

He said to them, "Your prayer on my behalf has born fruit and fruits of fruits." They said to him, "Even though others gave more than you did, you were the one whom we wrote down at the top of the list."

The sages seated Abba Yehudah among them and said the following verse about him: "A man's gift makes room for him and brings him before great men" (Proverbs 18:16).

(Y. Horayot 3:4, PM 17b, V 48a; Leviticus Rabbah 5:4)

There's a lot to love in this story. First, this passage gives us a prayer (in italics) to say to one who is going through financial misfortune. Second, Abba Yehudah's wife is described as holier than him. Third, Abba Yehudah, following his wife's suggestion, gives charity even when he has so much less to give. And, fourth, God rewards this act of faith with plenty.

This is yet another example of the Yerushalmi's belief in their brand of karma, that is, the energy you receive is the energy you sent out. At the end of the story, we find out that Abba Yehudah was not merely generous, but he was also *happy* to give. Others gave more than he did, but because he did so with such *menschlichkeit*, the sages always put him first on their list. And by the story's end, he is at the top of their list, this time as their biggest donor.

Karma: Justice Prevails

It is almost axiomatic in storytelling and moviemaking that justice must prevail. I am reminded of a story about the movie *Fatal Attraction*. They were showing test audiences the film. Some audiences saw the villainess killing the couple. Other audiences saw the villainess being killed. People hated the former and loved the latter. They wanted to see justice prevail. They wanted everyone to get what's coming to them.

The Yerushalmi shares this desire for balance and justice. The Yerushalmi expresses the belief that everyone will get what's coming to them:

One who possesses fifty *zuz* and trades with these must not take *peah*. And anyone who does not need to take and does take will not pass from the world before he will become dependent on other people for charity. And anyone who needs to take and does not take will not die of old age before he will support others from his own wealth. Of such a person, Scripture says, "Blessed is the man who trusts in God, and God shall be his trust" (Jeremiah 17:7).

And it is also true of a judge who judges according to the true law.

And anyone who is not lame or blind or limping and makes himself appear to be one of these will not die of old age until he becomes like one of them, as it is said ("And he who seeks evil, it shall come to him" [Proverbs 11:27]; and it is further said), "Justice, justice shall you pursue" (Deuteronomy 16:20).

And any judge who takes bribes and perverts justice will not die of old age before his eyes have grown dim, as it is said, "And a bribe you shall not take, for the bribe blinds the sighted" (Deuteronomy 16:19).

(M. PEAH 8:9; MEKHILTA KASPA 3 ON EXODUS 23:8; SIFREI DEUTERONOMY 144; B. KETUBOT 105A–B)

There are a few technical concepts we need to know to understand this mishnah. This mishnah begins with the concept of "money that works." Someone who has fifty *zuz* and who uses that money to conduct business does not need charity. This is different from a person who has fifty *zuz* but has no opportunity or ability to use this money to support himself.

Just as tractate Peah begins with an exalted statement about charity and mitzvot, so it ends with this exalted statement of the larger consequences of righteous and sinful behaviors. As you sow, so shall you reap.

A note about variant texts of the Yerushalmi is in order here. The material in italics, above, is found in only one of the five main manuscript variants of the Yerushalmi. The portion in italics is omitted in all the other versions. Frankly, it's a much neater version of the mishnah without that addition. This sort of thing happens a great deal more often in the Yerushalmi than it does in the Bavli. With or without this addition, the message is clear: as you sow, so shall you reap.

Another mishnah expresses this idea of karma, as well:

> Samson went after his eyes, therefore the Philistines gouged out his eyes, as it is said, "And the Philistines took hold of him and put out his eyes" (Judges 16:21). Absalom was overly proud of his hair. As a result, he was suspended by his hair. And because he had intercourse with ten of his father's concubines, they put ten javelins into him, as it is said, "And ten young men that bore Joab's weapons surrounded Absalom and smote him and killed him" (2 Samuel 18:15). And since he deceived three parties—his father, the court, and Israel (as it is said, "And so Absalom stole the hearts of the men of Israel" [2 Samuel 15:6]")—so three darts were thrust into him, as it is said, "And he took three darts in his hand and thrust them through Absalom's heart" (2 Samuel 18:14).
>
> (M. SOTAH 1:8; MEKHILTA, TRACTATE SHIRATA 2, ON EXODUS 15:1)

Suffering comes as a consequence of, and in a similar fashion to, sin. Reward follows the same pattern:

> And this principle also applies to goodness. Miriam waited and watched over Moses one hour, as it is said, "And his sister stood afar off" (Exodus 2:4). Therefore Israel waited for her for seven days in the wilderness, as it is said, "And the people did not journey until Miriam was brought back" (Numbers 12:15).
>
> Joseph merited the privilege of burying his father, and none of his brothers was greater than he, as it is said, "And Joseph went up to bury his father, and there went up with him

both chariots and horsemen" (Genesis 50:7–9). Whom have we greater than Joseph, since none but Moses occupied himself with burying him? Moses merited burying the bones of Joseph, and there is no one in Israel greater than he, as it is said, "And Moses took Joseph's bones with him" (Exodus 13:19). Who is greater than Moses, seeing that none save the Almighty occupied Himself with burying him, as it is said, "And He buried him in the valley" (Deuteronomy 34:6). And this applies not only of Moses, but also of all righteous people, as it is said, "And your righteousness shall go before you; the glory of God shall gather you" (Isaiah 58:8).

(M. SOTAH 1:9–10)

Each of the biblical stories mentioned above is carefully crafted to highlight the symmetry pointed out in these *mishnayot*. The Bible is the source of the principle of *middah k'neged middah*, "measure for measure," or in other words, justice prevails.

Rewards come to those who practice righteousness. The case of Miriam is an illustrative one. Miriam and Aaron rebel against Moses's authority. Miriam is stricken with leprosy as a result and then healed by Moses's impassioned prayer (Numbers 12:1–13). She must be isolated from the camp for seven days because of her temporary state of ritual impurity. The Torah explicitly states that the entire camp waited for her during this seven-day period and did not resume their journey until she could rejoin the camp. Tosefta, commenting on this passage, points out that the ratio of reward to goodness is five hundred times greater than the measure of retribution for sin (T. Sotah 4:1). According to Tosefta, and the many examples it brings there (T. Sotah 3:1–4:19), punishments are distributed with an even hand, but rewards for good deeds are dispensed generously.

The idea of *middah k'neged middah*, measure for measure or, as we would say, karma, is found in numerous places in the Yerushalmi:

Rabbi Chaggai said in the name of Rabbi Shmuel bar Nachman: It once happened that a certain righteous man would dig pits, ditches, and caves for the benefit of passersby. Once, his daughter was crossing a river on her way to be married and the river washed her away.

Everyone came to her father, wishing to console him, but he refused to be consoled. Rabbi Pinchas ben Yair came and tried to console him, but he refused to be consoled. He said to the townspeople, "Is this what you call a pious man? He's rebelling against God's judgment [which isn't righteous]."

They said, "Rabbi, thus and so would he do, and thus and such befell him." He said, "Is it possible that he should honor his Creator with water and that God should strike him so terribly with water?"

Immediately, a report spread in the town that the man's daughter had come back. Some say that she was caught on a branch. And some say an angel came down in the shape of Rabbi Pinchas ben Yair and saved her.

(Y. Demai 1:3, 8b1; Y. Shekalim 5:2; Deuteronomy Rabbah 3:3; B. Hullin 7a; B. Bava Kamma 50a; B. Yevamot 121b)

Clearly, this is a popular story; it's quoted all over the place! It's part of a large collection of stories about the piety of Rabbi Pinchas ben Yair. If this were a Western, he'd ride into town wearing a white hat.

Reish Lakish, who was a Roman gladiator before he was a sage, recognized Rome's corruption:

Reish Lakish went up to pay his respects to Rabbi Yehudah Hanasi. Rabbi asked him, "Pray for me, for this Roman government is exceedingly evil." Reish Lakish told him, "Take nothing from anyone and then you will not have to give anything to anyone." While Reish Lakish was sitting with Rabbi, a woman came in, bringing Rabbi a dish with a knife in it. He took the knife and returned the dish to the woman. At that moment an imperial courier came in and saw the knife, took a fancy to it, and took it. Toward evening, Reish Lakish went to pay his respects to our Rabbi again and saw him laughing. Asked Reish

Lakish, "Why are you laughing?" Rabbi said, "An imperial courier came in, saw the knife I took from the woman, coveted it,
and took it away." Reish Lakish said, "Did I not tell you that
if you do not take anything from anyone, you will not have to
give anything to anyone?"

(GENESIS RABBAH 78:12; B. PESACHIM 118B)

Corruption could seep in and contaminate even the best community
leaders. This is another tale of Yerushalmi-style karma. Just as Rabbi
took the knife, the imperial courier took it from him. If Rabbi had
listened to Reish Lakish and forgone the knife in the first place, then he
would not have had to suffer its loss.

Even in a world riddled with irrational cruelty, the Yerushalmi
expects that there is some order, some balance, some justice that will
make sense of people's lives. The wicked *will* be punished, and the
righteous *will* be rewarded.

Perhaps this was even more important to the sages of the
Yerushalmi than it was to the sages of the Bavli. In an utterly chaotic
world, there had to be some glimmer of rationality or people would
simply sink into despair. And one of the few things the Jews in the
Land of Israel could control was the kind of energy they sent out into
the world. They could "prime the pump" with justice and kindness,
hoping to receive justice and kindness as a result.

Y. v. B.

Both Talmuds subscribe to this concept of biblical interpretation.
Since it is an idea that originates in midrash and Bavli quotes more
midrash than does Yerushalmi, we find it more frequently in Bavli.
Just remember that the Yerushalmi should be seen as a "frater-
nal twin" of the midrash collections. So just because it isn't in the
Yerushalmi doesn't mean the sages of Israel weren't thinking about
it. They simply slotted it into different documents.

10

Who Would
Your Enemy Be?

The movie equivalent of your enemy is the Nazi Party and the SS. They strike fear in your heart just by showing up on the screen in uniform. And they keep succeeding in killing the Jews. The good guys don't come to the rescue, and anyone who survives is the exception, not the rule.

The Yerushalmi's enemy is Rome. And he's not going away. And he's not getting weaker. This is not how the story is supposed to go. Enemies come and go. The superpowers of the biblical and Second Temple worlds were the river empires of the Tigris/Euphrates and the Nile. As one would expand, the other would contract, in a dynamic "push me–pull you" over the land bridge that was straddled by Israel. Usually, these great empires weren't terribly interested in Israel's highlands, where the Jews lived. The great powers would have hugged the coast as their most efficient route to the other great empire. However, they would vanquish the highland communities if they resisted.

Israel's fate is very much akin to the fate of the Baltic states over the last hundred years. Germans, Poles, and Russians would march through the Baltic states (Lithuania, Latvia, Estonia), claim them, and then move on to the rich interior of the enemy (e.g., the German invasion of the Ukraine and Russia in World War II), only to be forced out by the Soviets. And just as the Baltic states had small windows of freedom, so Israel and Judea occasionally tasted autonomy.

But such freedom was squashed by the Romans' continued domination of Israel. They remained dangerous. There seemed to be no détente. They were so frightening that just the sound of their shoes caused pregnant women to miscarry (Y. Shabbat 6:2). The Yerushalmi reflects how immediate the threat remained in the Land of Israel:

> How then does Rabbi Chiyya the Great interpret the verse, "You shall purchase food from them for money, that you may eat; and you shall also buy water from them for money, that you may drink" (Deuteronomy 2:6)?
>
> It means, "with food you shall purchase Esau," that is, Rome will like you for giving them food. Once you have fed him, break him. If he is hard on you, purchase his goodwill with food. And if you cannot subdue him, give him ample funds.
>
> (Y. Shabbat 1:4, PM 10a)

The Bavli reports that one of the wealthiest people in Israel, Nakdimon ben Gurion, did in fact buy water from the Romans so that the Jews could have enough during the Passover pilgrimage season (B. Ta'anit 19b–20a). (It's difficult to determine whether there's any factual basis for that story. It doesn't show up in any sources written in the Land of Israel, and it is told in a fanciful way.) Our passage, above, suggests a sort of triage of hostility, based on the story of Jacob (a stand-in for Israel) and Esau (a stand-in for Rome). Just as Jacob fed Esau some stew and then took his birthright (Genesis 25:30–34), the Jews should feed Rome and then break its hold on the land. If that doesn't work, at least make sure the food turns into a guarantee of friendship. If that doesn't work (sigh), then pay a lot of taxes.

A Smothering Sense of Danger

This smothering sense of danger shows itself time and again in the Yerushalmi:

> Said Rabbi Chiyya bar Ba: "When you go out as a troop against your enemies, guard yourself from every evil thing"

(Deuteronomy 23:10). Does this mean that if one does not go out, one does not have to guard? Rather, we learn from this that Satan only brings charges against a person in a time of danger.

Said Rabbi Acha bar Yaakov: "If harm should befall him on the journey" (Genesis 42:38). Lo, will harm not befall him at home? Rather, we learn from this that Satan only brings charges against a person in a time of danger.

Rabbi Bisna in the name of Rabbi Liyya: It is written, "They said to him, 'Thus says Hezekiah: This day is a day of distress, of rebuke and of disgrace; children have come to the birth and there is no strength to bring them forth'" (Isaiah 37:3). Lo, is that not the case on any other day? Rather, we learn from this that Satan only brings charges against a person in a time of danger.

Rabbi Aibu bar Negri: It is written, "When he is judged, let him be found guilty" (Psalm 109:7). "Let him come forth justified" is not written here, but rather, "Let him come forth guilty." We learn from this that Satan only brings charges against a person in a time of danger.

Said Rabbi Bar bar Kina: In the case of a board stretched from one roof to the next, even if it is ever so broad, it is forbidden to walk across it. Why? We learn from this that Satan only brings charges against a person in a time of danger.

Rav said: One who dwells in a shaky house turns the Angel of Death into his creditor....

Said Rabbi Levi: In three situations, Satan is waiting to prosecute: one who makes a trip all by himself, one who sleeps by himself in a closed-up house, and one who sets sail on the Mediterranean.

(Y. Shabbat 2:6, PM 19b)

The feeling we get from this passage is that danger is looming around every corner. Even more interesting, the phrase "Satan only brings charges against a person in a time of danger" is found only in sources from the Land of Israel.

Every day for the Jews of Israel is a time of danger in this era, so Satan is always able to prosecute. "A shaky house" is an idiom meaning that only a perfectly righteous person's merit will keep the house from falling down (e.g., Nachum Ish Gamzo, Y. Peah 8:9; B. Ta'anit 21a; B. Rosh Hashanah 16b). This is a society on a knife's edge of existence. The tiniest disturbance or carelessness can cause catastrophe. It sounds very much like the life of Jews in the Soviet Union. Being seen in the wrong place, associating with the wrong people, or learning Hebrew was enough to cause you to lose your job or go to prison.

In one other way, Jewish life during this period was like Jewish life in the Soviet Union. In both cases, a slip of the tongue could condemn a person to imprisonment, the Gulag, or death:

> Why does the snake bite one limb but all the limbs feel it? The snake replied, "Why do you ask me? Ask the talker who speaks here and kills in Rome; who speaks in Rome and kills in Syria."
> (Y. PEAH 1:1, 9A3)

The Roman occupation makes what might have been merely idle gossip an instrument of murder.

Craven, Incompetent Government Officials

From the Keystone Kops to the misguided Ministry of Magic in the *Harry Potter* franchise, incompetent government officials are a standard enemy against whom a hero must fight. Sadly, they were real for the sages of the Yerushalmi. And the sages are just as tough on Jewish leaders who are in any way corrupt as they are on the Romans. There is no love lost between the sages and those who won their high offices through bribes:

> Rav Mana used to ridicule those who were appointed to office through money. Rav Ammi applied to them the verse, "Don't make for yourself gods of silver or gods of gold" (Exodus 20:20).
> Said Rabbi Yoshiyah, "And the tallit that he wears is like a donkey's saddlecloth."

While Rabbi Zeira and one of the sages were sitting together, one of those who were appointed to office through money passed by. The sage said to Rabbi Zeira, "Let us appear to recite Mishnah, so that we will not have to stand up for him."

(Y. Bikkurim 3:3, 23b3–24a1, V 65d)

Usually, one stands before an elder, a judge, or one who has great Torah knowledge. Here we see a different picture: one of realpolitik, in which some officeholders have not truly earned their positions and the sages who don't want to show them any honor. (There is a rule that you should never interrupt Mishnah recitation, e.g., B. Shabbat 10a, B. Hagigah 12b.)

Y. v. B.

The Romans are seen as a malevolent force in Bavli, but in a muted way. They did, after all, destroy the Temple, but the pain and the anger are muffled by miles and centuries of distance from the event itself.

For Us ...

Politics is a tricky game, then as now. We always need to heed Reish Lakish's advice: deal with everyone with integrity and not avarice. Send out the energy you want to receive in return.

How Do You Carry Out Warfare?

The Jews of Israel carried out warfare in a manner similar to the way Butch Cassidy and the Sundance Kid conducted their affairs. They only succeeded using guerilla-style tactics, and they were only one step ahead of the law. And, of course, in the end, they lost.

The truth is that the Jews for whom and about whom the Yerushalmi is written hadn't often had great success when it came to waging war. We do have Megillat Ta'anit, which lists happy days in Israel's past when the Jews achieved great victories or had miraculous salvations. But by the time of the Yerushalmi, the only events from that scroll that were still celebrated were Purim and Hanukkah.

Making war is an exercise in history. Armed forces live on their communal memories of lessons learned from previous battles, both positive and negative. Once there was a definitive break in time when Jews no longer fought successfully or, even worse, fought and brought disaster upon the Jewish people, it seems that this body of knowledge was no longer passed down through the generations. This resulted in a people who did not know how to wage war effectively.

From this position of military inferiority, especially in contrast to the might of the Roman Empire, what could the sages of the Yerushalmi teach? They actually took a rather reasonable approach: hope and wait. One day, they maintained, Rome will fall and we'll be rid of them. In the meantime, they looked to Scripture for inspiration. In Genesis Rabbah, they turned Esau/Edom into a stand-in for Rome, while Jacob/Israel was Israel. Haven't you ever wondered why Esau is always painted as such an evil character by the midrash? If you read Scripture as it's written, he's actually an okay guy. He's certainly nicer than Jacob—the trickster, literally "the heel." It's because the sages of the Yerushalmi, casting Esau as Rome, imputed all of Rome's bad qualities to Esau. They were assuring their listeners that one day, Israel/Jacob will overcome Esau, just as he does in the Torah.

Civil Disobedience

While the Jews of Israel in the time of the Yerushalmi could not effectively wage war openly, they were encouraged to resist the Romans via civil disobedience:

Rabbi Shmuel bar Sosartai went to Rome. The queen lost her bracelet, and he found it. A public announcement went out through the city: One who returns it within thirty days will receive such and such a reward; but after thirty days, he will be beheaded. He returned it after thirty days. She asked him, "Haven't you been in the city and heard the public announcement?" He said, "Yes, I heard the announcement." She said, "And what did it say?" He said, "One who returns the bracelet within thirty days will be rewarded, but one who returns it after thirty days will be beheaded." She asked him, "So why didn't you return it within the thirty-day time limit?" He said, "So that no one should say that I acted out of fear of you. Rather, I wanted people to know that I acted out of fear of the Merciful One." She said to him, "Blessed is the God of the Jews."

(Y. Bava Metzia 2:5, PM 8a, V 8c)

This is just one of a number of similar stories that all end with the phrase "Blessed is the God of the Jews." The common theme in these stories is that the Jews behave with great piety, and this endears them to various rulers. Such stories may have been told to inspire Jews to resist Rome's might.

Martyrdom

When all else fails, the Yerushalmi tells us to consider martyrdom:

The son of Trojianus [Trajan, c. 117 CE], the evil one, was born on the ninth of Av, and the Jews were fasting. His daughter died on Hanukkah, and the Jews lit candles.

His wife sent him a message, saying, "Instead of going out to conquer the Barbarians, come and conquer the Jews who have rebelled against you."

He thought it would take ten days to reach Israel, but he got there in five. He came and found the Jews studying the following verse: "The Lord will bring a nation against you from afar, from the end of the earth, as swift as the eagle flies, a nation whose language you do not understand" (Deuteronomy 28:49).

He said to them, "What are you studying?"

They said to him, "We are studying this verse [Deuteronomy 28:49]."

He said, "This verse refers to me. I thought I'd arrive in ten days and arrived in five [i.e., I came here swiftly]."

His legions surrounded them and killed the men.

He said to the women, "Obey my legions and I shall not kill you." They said to him, "As you did to those on the ground, do to us who are still standing." He mingled the women's blood with the blood of their men, until blood flowed into the ocean as far as Cyprus. At that moment the horn of Israel was cut off, and it is not destined to return from its place until the son of David will come.

(Y. SUKKAH 5:1, 28B3–28B4; ESTHER RABBAH, PETICHTAH 1:3)

This passage describes the destruction of the Jewish community in Alexandria, Egypt. It is set against the background of the destruction of the Jewish communities in Alexandria and Cyprus in 117 CE. The story suggests that Jews preferred martyrdom to enslavement. It is also possible that this is told as an inspirational story to raise the morale of a people worn down by one Roman victory after another.

Y. v. B.

By the time the Bavli closes (c. 650 CE), memories of Jews' military might have long faded into legend. Martyrdom, on the other hand, remains a sadly relevant part of Jewish life. We have but to remember the thrilling novelty of the creation of the State of Israel and its mighty armed forces to realize what a radical paradigm shift it was. For the first time in some two thousand years, the Jews reclaimed their right and ability to effectively wage war. One event that the sages of the Yerushalmi did not live to see was that Rome, like so many tormentors of the Jews before it, finally did crumble, while the Jews survived. Perhaps perseverance was the Jews' most effective weapon.

For Us ...

There is really only one way to win, says the Yerushalmi. No matter how militarily powerful your opponent is, *your* power lies in scrupulous virtue. Even armed with the finest tools of war, virtue is always a good complement to violence.

Part 2

Building Blocks
of Prayer

Almost every Jewish prayer service has the same basic building blocks: some warm-ups, the *Shema* and Its Blessings, the *Amidah*, and some closing prayers. But that's only prayer in the synagogue. The sages of the Yerushalmi envisioned a life constantly filled with prayer. These are the building blocks with which you might be less familiar. The Yerushalmi wants you to pray all day long, to be constantly aware of God's gifts as God gives them to you. It's a highly disciplined faith of gratitude and awareness. But it has room for personal creativity. The Yerushalmi's prayer practice also has its own distinctive kind of mysticism, a mysticism that is embedded in the prayers we use to this very day. In addition, the sages of the Yerushalmi practiced meditational techniques while praying. There is a great deal they can teach us that can enhance our spiritual practice today.

11

The Toolbox of Prayers

Think of the moment in a film when the underdog triumphs. What does he do in his moment of glory? Is he content to simply triumph, or is he punching the air with his fist? He's probably doing the latter. He has to win by the rules, but he expresses it as a moment of triumph that is higher than just winning a game. Adding that extra "punctuation" is how the Yerushalmi approaches prayer. The building blocks of prayer are the same as they are in the Bavli: (1) the *Shema*, (2) the *Amidah*, and (3) blessings before and after enjoying things and before doing mitzvot. But the Yerushalmi takes these basic building blocks and uses them as stepping-stones to a higher spiritual plain.

Meditation and the *Shema*

The sages of the Yerushalmi didn't believe in rushing headlong through services. They augmented their prayers with meditative techniques. For example, when reciting the first verse of the *Shema*, they would stretch out the last word, *echad*, "one":

> Summachos bar Yosef said, "One who prolongs the word *echad* lengthens his days and years for good."
>
> Rabbi Yermiyah used to greatly lengthen his pronunciation of the word "one." Rabbi Zeira said to him, "You don't have to stretch it out so much. Rather, lengthen it just long enough to enthrone God in heaven and on earth in the four directions of the world."
>
> (Y. BERAKHOT 2:1, 18B3)

In classic Yerushalmi fashion, we have two options, both of which stand as valid. We should stretch out the last word, but how long to do so is up for discussion. This is almost certainly based on the story of Rabbi Akiba's martyrdom at the hand of the Romans. He understands that we should love God with all our souls, even as God takes that soul from us. He fulfills this precept by reciting the *Shema* as he dies, stretching out the word "one" until he dies (B. Berakhot 61b). In commemoration of this devotion, others elongated the word "one" as a way of helping them focus on this sentence in prayer, which must be said with deep intention.

Rabbi Yermiyah apparently holds out a bit too long for Rabbi Zeira's taste. If we didn't know Rabbi Zeira to be the modest and righteous character he is, we might hear a bit of sarcasm in his rebuke to Rabbi Yermiyah. After all, it would still take a person a good bit of time to envision God in heaven and the four corners of the world. Perhaps Rabbi Yermiyah is holding up services with his lengthy *echad*. The Yerushalmi doesn't like people who make services too long (see chapter 15). Or perhaps we're seeing a side of Rabbi Zeira that is rarely on display. Perhaps even the pious Rabbi Zeira wanted to get through services in some reasonable amount of time.

If this were the Bavli, the *stamma* would now come into the picture, finding ways to justify each statement so that there would be a way, no matter how strained, to split the differences and allow all these ideas to exist on the same page together. The Yerushalmi is obviously comfortable letting all these practices sit, unharmonized, on the page. Refreshing! You get to choose.

When the Prayer Book Needs a Ruthless Editor

Often, the "director's cut" of a movie is much better than the version that came out in theaters. It has extra scenes that help fill out the story. But sometimes the director's cut bogs down the narrative and makes the film worse. Scenes that the director wisely deleted find their way back into the film. Prayer in Judaism can become like this unwieldy director's cut: things get added, and the editor never shows up.

In standard Jewish practice, the *Amidah*, the prayer par excellence, is said three times a day. The Yerushalmi links this to the three states of consciousness a person experiences during the day:

> From whence do they derive the obligation to say three prayers a day? Rabbi Shmuel bar Nachmani said, "They correspond to the three changes people experience each day.
>
> "In the morning a person must say, 'I give thanks to You, Lord my God and God of my fathers, that You have brought me from darkness into light.'
>
> "In the afternoon a person must say, 'I give thanks to You, Lord my God and God of my fathers, that just as I merited seeing the sun in the east, so may I merit seeing it in the west.'
>
> "In the evening he must say, 'May it be Your will, Lord my God and God of my fathers, that as I was in darkness before and You have brought me to light, so may You once again bring me forth from darkness to light.'"
>
> (Y. Berakhot 4:1, 43a2)

Could these three simple prayers take the place of the *Amidah*? It would certainly be easier for the average Jew to remember this format as opposed to the entirety of the *Amidah*. As we shall see, this is just one of the many options the Yerushalmi provides for "doing Jewish" that are every bit as authentic and legitimate as the ones in our prayer book, which was taken, by and large, from the Bavli. The Yerushalmi also assumes that you are praying and thanking God all day long.

The *Amidah*

The *Amidah* has three basic "acts," just like a three-act movie. The meat of the movie, and of the *Amidah*, is the second act. In *Groundhog Day*, for example, the first act is setting up "the day." The second act is the protagonist's learning to live the same day over and over again. The third act is that last day, when he finally gets it right. (In my eyes, this is one of the most spiritually meaningful films, ever.) Or in a trilogy, this is the second movie, when everything seems scattered and the outcome is in doubt (think: *Lord of the Rings* or *Star Wars*).

When we pray the *Amidah*, the main prayer of the service, today it can sound like "blah, blah, blah." You could close your eyes, open the prayer at random, put your finger on the page, and the prayer on that page would sound pretty much like the prayers on every other page. When it is davened at high speed, it certainly sounds like one undifferentiated mass.

Nothing could be further from the way the sages of the Yerushalmi prayed the *Amidah*. To them, it was a step-by-step spiritual blueprint for individual and communal redemption. (As you go through this section, you might want to have a prayer book at hand, open to the weekday *Amidah*, so you can see how the Yerushalmi's description lines up with what is in the prayer book today.) The first three blessings of the *Amidah* are always present:

1. *Avot*: God of our ancestors.
2. *Gevurot*: God's might.
3. *Kedushat Hashem*: Praising God's name as holy. (This prayer's key line, "Holy, holy, holy ..." [Isaiah 6:3], is an important part of *Heichalot* mysticism. Every time you hear, "Holy, holy, holy," in a service, you should imagine making your way through seven celestial halls on your way to the highest heaven, where God dwells.)

The last three blessings are always present:

1. *R'tzei*: Asking God to accept our prayers.
2. *Modim*: Thanking God for accepting our prayers.
3. *Shalom*: Thanking God for the gift of peace.

With this framework in mind, we can now look at the intermediate blessings. The first three blessings and the last three blessings are praise of God. The middle blessings deal with the needs of all creatures:

Grant us knowledge.
Now that You have granted us knowledge, accept our repentance.
Now that You have accepted our repentance, forgive us.

Now that You have forgiven us, redeem us.
Now that You have redeemed us, heal our sickness.
Now that You have healed our sickness, bless our years with plenty.
Now that You have blessed our years, gather us together.
Now that You have gathered us together, judge us in righteousness.
Now that You have judged us in righteousness, humble our opponents.
Now that You have humbled our opponents, exonerate us in judgment.
Now that You have exonerated us in judgment, build Your house for
us, and hear our entreaties and accept us into it.

(Y. Berakhot 2:4, 25a1–25a2)

The daily *Amidah* is not a jumbled list of requests for God's help. It is a logical, step-by-step program for ultimate redemption. You can't repent without understanding what you've done, and you can't be forgiven without repentance. Nor can you be redeemed until you've been forgiven, the redemption taking the form of healing. We then come to the communal requests of the *Amidah*. These blessings are a step-by-step program of what the Messiah will do. In the messianic era, we will each right our own ship morally, then be gathered together and be found innocent in God's eyes, and as a consequence, God will defeat those who've harmed us and punish them. We will then have the Temple rebuilt for us, and our prayers thence will be heard and accepted.

In this version of the *Amidah*, we find two very interesting things. First, this version of the *Amidah* would give us a total of seventeen blessings, not the eighteen as it is traditionally known, nor the nineteen blessings you'll find in most prayer books today. Second, there is no mention of restoring the Davidic kingship or even the rebuilding of Jerusalem.

We can only theorize about this, but it's not hard to imagine that Jews in the Land of Israel, who were thrashed by the Romans under the leadership of descendants of David, wouldn't be so anxious to have another such king back in power. Alternatively, it might have been dangerous to request such a thing out loud in Israel at that time. And a prayer for Jerusalem might cut too close to the bone, as well. At this point, it was still a Roman city, and Jews couldn't get anywhere near the place. It might also be that the Roman rulers would take offense at prayers that essentially called for their ouster.

The *Amidah* developed gradually over time. Everyone knew the basic outline of the prayers, but whoever was leading services could riff on these basic themes, within reason. In this sense, the *Amidah* would almost always have some new element to it, that is, they had daily creative services.

There may have been another way in which services had a great deal more variety than they have now. A *piyyut*, a liturgical poem based on the weekly Torah portion, was woven through the Shabbat service. So every Shabbat, the prayers were slightly different. There were three kinds of individuals who ran services in this system: the *chazzan*, a person who ran services, who in those days functioned as both a prayer leader and a *gabbai*; a *payytan*, a poet, who added the week's poetry to the framework of prayers laid down by the *chazzan*; and the *darshan*, who translated and explained the Torah portion.

Short Services, Please

You might think that with three prayer leaders, services would be interminably long. However, the one thing the sages of the Yerushalmi didn't want was a long service.

> How do we know short prayers are better? From what was taught: Lengthening prayer is shameful.... One who shortens his prayer is praiseworthy.
>
> (Y. Berakhot 1:5, 14a2)

In other words, the congregation has only so much concentration to devote to the service. The sages of the Yerushalmi understood the natural creative tension between adding something new to services each week (a *piyyut*) and needing to prune services to keep them from running too long. The idea that it is good to be creative *and* keep services to a reasonable running time sounds a great deal like liberal Jewish movements' ideas about prayer today.

Giving Thanks

The Yerushalmi documents that the congregants and the sages made up their own individualized versions of one the *Amidah*'s blessings in particular: the blessing for thanksgiving.

> When Rabbi Yasa came from Babylonia to Israel, he saw them bowing and whispering during the prayer of thanksgiving in the *Amidah*. He said to us, "What are they whispering?..."
>
> While the leader recites the blessing, the congregation says in an undertone:

> "We thank You,
> Master of all creatures,
> God of praise,
> Rock of the worlds,
> Eternal life,
> Maker of creation,
> Resurrector of the dead,
> who kept us alive and sustained us,
> who gave us merit and helped us,
> and brought us near to give thanks to Your name.
> Blessed are You, O Lord, God of thanksgiving."

> Rabbi Ba bar Zavda in the name of Rav said: "We thank
> You, for we are obligated to thank Your name.
> 'My lips will shout for joy when I sing praise to You; my
> soul also, which You have rescued' (Psalm 71:23).
> Blessed are You, O Lord, God of thanks."

> Rabbi Shmuel bar Mina in the name of Rabbi Acha said:
> "Thanksgiving and praise to Your name.
> Greatness is Yours.
> Power is Yours.
> Glory is Yours.
> May it be Your will, Lord, our God, and God of our
> fathers, that You support us when we fall,

and straighten those who are bent.
For You are full of mercy,
and there is none besides You.
Blessed are You, O Lord, God of thanksgiving."

Bar Kappara said:
"We kneel to You,
we bend to You,
we bow deeply to You,
we kneel to You.
For to You every knee must bend,
every tongue must swear.
'Yours, O Lord,
is the greatness
and the power
and the glory
and the victory
and the majesty.
For all that is within the heavens and in the earth is
        Yours.
Yours is the kingdom, O Lord,
and You are exalted high above all.
But riches and honor come from You, and You rule over all.
In Your hand are power and might;
and Your hand makes great
and gives strength to all.
And now we thank You, our God, and praise Your glori-
        ous name' (1 Chronicles 29:11–13).
So now, our God, we thank You
And praise Your glorious name
With a whole heart and
With a whole soul we bow.
'All my bones shall say:
Who is like You,
Saving the poor from the one stronger than he

and the poor and the destitute from one who robs him?'
With all our heart, and with all our soul, we prostrate
    ourselves.
'All my bones shall say: O Lord, who is like You? You
    who delivers the weak from him who is too strong
    for him; saving the weak and the needy from him
    who despoils him' (Psalm 35:10).
Blessed are You, the God of thanks."
(Y. Berakhot 1:5, 14B3–15A1)

From a practical standpoint, the Yerushalmi is validating people's license to say their own blessing of thanks, to themselves, during the repetition of the *Amidah*. In other words, the bare bones of the *Amidah* are not enough to express one's gratitude. The sages of the Yerushalmi understood that part of prayer must be unscripted and personal. If it's all by rote, then it lacks something essential. In terms of practical use today, each one of these versions of the thanksgiving prayer is a beautiful, authentic composition, and we are free to adopt them and adapt them for our own prayer services. Bar Kappara's prayer ought to sound very familiar. It's almost a word-for-word section of the *Aleinu*.

An Attitude of Gratitude: Ben Zoma's Prayers

Sometimes, the big picture is made manifest through tiny details. In *Schindler's List*, which is in black and white, the only color used is to show just one little girl, in a red coat. Yet, by focusing on just one person in a sea of people, the enormity of the Holocaust is brought out dramatically.

One of our sages, Ben Zoma, had the ability to look at the tiniest of details and learn great things from them. Ben Zoma was one of the four sages who engaged in mystical speculation (T. Hagigah 2:3). After his spiritual journey, Ben Zoma could not relate to reality. However, we have this teaching of his, perhaps from before his adventure, which expresses a sense of gratitude and fosters an elevated state of awareness of all the gifts one has while one has them, almost as if he sees everything through a microscope:

When Ben Zoma saw a Jewish crowd in Jerusalem, he would say, "Blessed be He who created all these people to serve me. How hard did the first person have to struggle to toil before he could eat a piece of bread: he seeded, plowed, reaped, sheaved, threshed, winnowed, separated, ground, sifted, kneaded, formed loaves, and baked them, and only then could he eat. But I arise in the morning and find all these foods ready before me.

"How hard did Adam toil before he could put on a garment: he sheared, bleached, separated, dyed, spun, wove, washed, and sewed, and only then did he find one shirt to wear. But I arise in the morning and find all these pieces of clothing ready before me.

"How many skilled craftsmen are industrious and rise early to their work. And I arise in the morning and all these things are ready before me."

And so Ben Zoma would say, "But what does a bad guest say? 'What have I eaten of this homeowner? And what did I drink from this homeowner? I ate only one piece of food. I drank only one cup of his wine. He went to all this trouble to provide for his wife and children, but not for me.'

"What does a good guest say? 'Blessed be this homeowner! May he be remembered for good! How many kinds of wine did he bring before me! How many dishes did he bring before me! How much effort did he expend for me! All this effort he took for my sake.' And so Scripture says, 'Remember, so that you will aggrandize His work that men see' (Job 36:24)."

(Y. BERAKHOT 9:2, 88A4–88B1; T. BERAKHOT 6:5)

Ben Zoma realizes the transience of human existence (i.e., we are guests on this earth—here today, gone tomorrow). He also fosters the awareness of our interconnectedness and that everything we enjoy is a gift. So we should approach life with a sense of gratitude, while understanding our place in the cosmos.

Responses to the Priestly Benediction

The Priestly Benediction is one of the high points of a worship service. In Orthodox or Conservative synagogues, the priests (*Kohanim*) go up to the bimah, cover themselves fully in their *tallitot*, and recite the blessing (Numbers 6:24–26), echoing the words of the prayer leader, who sings it to them.

They are covered up because, as they stretch out their hands in the shape that Mr. Spock of *Star Trek* made famous, God's lethal presence rests upon them. (Leonard Nimoy grew up watching Orthodox *duchening*, as it is called, and when they asked him to come up with a hand greeting for Vulcans, he immediately thought of this gesture and the accompanying prayer for peace.)

The Priestly Benediction is a finely crafted prayer of fifteen words and sixty letters. The following layout shows how the words are constructed:

God bless-you and-keep-you.
(*Y'varekh'kha Adonai v'yishm'rekha.*)
God will-shine His-countenance upon-you and-grace-you.
(*Ya'eir Adonai panav eleikha vi'chuneka.*)
God will-raise His-countenance upon-you and-give you peace.
(*Yisa Adonai panav eilekha v'yaseim l'kha shalom.*)
(NUMBERS 6:24–26)

Today, we respond to each line of the blessing by saying, *Kein y'hi ratzon*, "Be this God's will." The Yerushalmi offers us two different options:

One who see the priests in the meetinghouse [*beit k'neset*], Rav Huna says: He says, "Bless the Lord, O you His angels [*Barakhu Adonai malakhav*]" (Psalm 103:20).

For the second (Numbers 6:25), he says, "Bless the Lord, all His hosts [*Barakhu Adonai kol tzeva'av*]" (Psalm 103:21).

For the third (Numbers 6:26), he says, "Bless the Lord, all His works [*Barakhu Adonai kol ma'asav*]" (Psalm 103:22).

In the *Musaf* service he responds to the Priestly Benediction in this way:

For the first line of the blessing, he says, "A Song of Ascents. Come bless the Lord, all you servants of the Lord, who stand by night in the house of the Lord" (Psalm 134:1).

For the second, he says, "Lift up your hands to the holy place and bless you the Lord" (Psalm 134:2).

For the third, he says, "May the Lord bless you from Zion" (Psalm 134:3).

(Y. Berakhot 1:1, 5a1–5a2)

Psalm 103 is a song of praise to God and ends in the three verses cited, which rhyme. The responses invite ever-wider circles to bless God: angels, stars, and then all of creation. We could also interpret the verses from Psalm 134 as referring to ever-widening geographical locations: the Temple, the Temple Mount, and the city of Jerusalem (i.e., Zion).

The Yerushalmi assumes that the congregation knows the psalms and can recite them back to the priests. In this way, the Yerushalmi democratizes the Priestly Benediction. Yes, only priests can offer it. But there must be a congregation to whom it is offered. And the congregation responds with Scripture verses of their own. These verses bless the priests, so everyone participating gets his or her own blessing, priests and congregants alike.

For the New Moon

The Jewish calendar is a solar-lunar one, in which the sighting of the new moon is very important. The Yerushalmi says that there is a blessing to say upon seeing the new moon:

Blessed ... who renews the months [*m'chadeish chodashim*].

(Y. Berakhot 9:2, 89b6)

This is close to the blessing we say on this occasion today, but it's actually more lyrical. In the prayer book it says, "Blessed ... who sanctifies the new moons" (*Barukh atah Adonai, m'kadeish roshei chodashim*). The words "new" and "month" come from the same Hebrew root, *chet-dalet-shin*, and the Yerushalmi's blessing underscores that connection: *m'chadeish chodashim*. The emphasis is on renewal, a message the Jews of the Land of Israel would have embraced.

Prayers from the Cutting Room Floor

Directors shoot hours and hours of film, but a movie is only two hours long. What happens to the footage that isn't chosen to be in the film? It ends up on the cutting room floor. Or, if the director is very attached to this footage, it becomes part of the director's cut or extras on a DVD.

This phenomenon also occurred with our prayer book. The sages composed many prayers, only a fraction of which we know today. The Yerushalmi shows us all sorts of prayers "from the cutting room floor" that you've never seen and are really good.

Prayers for Healing

People needed healing in the sages' day every bit as much as we need it now. In a discussion on whether one can put amulets on a wound on Shabbat, the Yerushalmi allows for some wiggle room:

> They do not recite a verse of Scripture over a wound on Shabbat. And to read a Bible verse over a mandrake is forbidden and lo, it has been taught: They would recite the psalm for the afflicted in Jerusalem.... And what is the psalm for the afflicted? "O Lord, how many are my foes! Many are rising against me; many are saying of me, 'There is no help for him in God'" (Psalm 3:2–3) and the whole psalm (and in addition, or in its place, Psalm 91:1–9).
>
> (Y. SHABBAT 6:2, PM 36A, V 8B)

This is an example of the Yerushalmi tacking back and forth, displaying remarkable flexibility. First it says that they don't recite a formula against the demon, but then it turns out that some people do recite a Scripture verse for healing on Shabbat. So we have lots of variety and no hard-and-fast rules. This is also an example of the Yerushalmi using Scripture as one of the basic building blocks of prayer. Not surprisingly, psalms are often used, because they express pleas and thanksgiving to God.

Another blessing that one doesn't hear often is one that might be quite heartfelt:

> Said Rav Avun, "What blessing does one who drinks purgative waters say? 'Blessed ... who created healing waters [*Barukh ... shebara mei r'fu'ot*].'"
>
> (Y. Berakhot 6:8, 70b2)

Here is a blessing that deserves to be adopted, adapted, and placed in our "spiritual toolbox," especially at the rate new medicines are being created these days.

A Blessing for Dessert

The system of blessings that we have now mandates a set format for all blessings. They all begin with *Barukh atah Adonai, Eloheinu Melekh ha'olam*. But this was not an accomplished fact in the days of the Yerushalmi.

> It was taught (T. Berakhot 4:5): Rabbi Yose says, "Anyone who changes the formula that the sages fixed has not fulfilled his obligation." Rabbi Yudah says, "Anyone who changes a food from its original form and didn't change its blessing has not fulfilled his obligation." Rabbi Meir says, "Even if he said, 'Blessed be the One who created this nice thing [*Barukh shebara hacheifetz hazeh*],' over any kind of food, he has fulfilled his obligation...." A precedent-setting story happened with Rav when one Persian man came to him and said, "I eat my bread, but I don't know how to bless it, and I say, 'Blessed is the Master of this bread [*Barukh divra hadein pita*].' Have I discharged my obligation?" Rav said, "Yes."
>
> (Y. Berakhot 6:2, 64b1–64b2)

In the Yerushalmi, blessings are not set. Any expression of thanks to God is legitimate. This is as it should be. Often, these days, people are afraid to say a blessing because they don't know the "right one" to say, resulting in no blessing at all. According to this Yerushalmi, personal thanks in any form is good spiritual practice. It's worth noting that Rabbi Meir (a great authority from the Land of Israel) and Rav (a great authority from Babylonia) both agree that "Johnny-Six-Pack-Jew" doesn't have to master a whole set of complicated blessings. Thanking God, no matter the form, is good enough for them.

12

Ad-Libbing

While the crew holds the script sacrosanct, actors are rarely troubled with the script's holiness. They often improvise the dialogue. And sometimes what they say actually shows up in the film. Unsurprisingly, Jews put in their two cents when it comes to making up prayers along the way.

A Blessing for Honesty in Business

The sages created a system in which every mitzvah is preceded by a blessing. Yet some of these blessings can be found only in the Yerushalmi. For example, we find the following case of Rabbi Chaggai and Rabbi Yermiyah going into a grocery store to inspect its scales for accuracy. Rabbi Chaggai eagerly recites a blessing over the mitzvah of examining the scales, and Rabbi Yermiyah approves:

> Rabbi Chaggai and Rabbi Yermiyah went to the stores to inspect the scales for accuracy, and Rabbi Chaggai jumped in and said a blessing [... *asher kid'shanu b'mitzvotav v'tzivanu l'takein hami-dot v'hamoznaiyim ul'takein hash'arim*, "... who sanctified us with His commandments and commanded us to check measures and scales and to check the prices"]. Rabbi Yermiyah said to him, "You have acted rightly, because all mitzvot require a blessing."
>
> (Y. BERAKHOT 6:1, 60A1–60A2)

Ad-libbing *berakhot* (blessings) is clearly supported by the Yerushalmi. You don't know a blessing that fits your immediate circumstances? You can make one up that fits your situation. And it's not as if these two sages are mere extras in our film. Rabbi Yermiyah, originally from Babylonia and a student of Rabbi Zeira's, became the leader of the Jewish community after Rabbi Zeira's death. Rabbi Chaggai was also a student of Rabbi Zeira and was a respected leader in Tiberias, as well. They were both active around 320–350. Given today's conditions of lax economic morality, it might be a good time to revive this blessing's usage. This is a blessing that you won't find in our prayer books. It is only in the Yerushalmi.

Making the Best of a Bad Situation

At this point in history, the Jews of the Land of Israel had to have been hardy souls to make it through their trials. And so, they developed blessings for making the best of a bad situation:

> If one's wine turned to vinegar, he says, "Blessed be the true Judge." If he goes to drink it, he says, "For all came into being by His word." If one saw edible locusts, he says, "Blessed be the true Judge." If he goes to eat them, he says, "For all comes into being by His word." If one saw fruit that did not ripen, he says, "Blessed be the true Judge." If he eats them, he says, "For all comes into being by His word."
>
> (Y. BERAKHOT 6:3, 65B1)

We say blessings over bad things as well as over good things. God is the author of the totality of our fate and gives us both the bitter and the sweet. This passage is a template for how we express this through blessings. If one's wine turns to vinegar or swarms of locusts arrive or a drought causes the fruit not to ripen, one says the blessing associated with all unhappy events: "Blessed be the true Judge." However, if one makes the best of a bad situation and consumes the vinegar, locusts, or unripe fruit, then one says the general blessing over food: "Blessed is

God, for all comes into being by His word." (I often call this the little black dress of *berakhot*, because it works for every kind of food.)

When Someone Else Experiences Financial Loss

In 2008, many people experienced grave financial loss. This is a situation that the sages of the Yerushalmi understood. When the Romans destroyed the Temple, they also destroyed the thriving economy that went with it. The Yerushalmi demonstrates how to respond to such situations with prayer:

> To one whose slave or animal died you say to him, "May God restore your loss" [*Hamakom yimalei chesronkha*].
>
> (Y. BERAKHOT 2:8. 29B2)

The owner himself would say, "Blessed is the true Judge," while those around him would say this prayer *to* him and on his behalf.

Passing Through a Cemetery

That desire for renewal finds voice in another blessing. Walking among Jewish graves that the Romans would have filled, the Jews expressed their hope that these Jews would rise again and live in the land in which they'd died.

> One who passes through a graveyard says, "Blessed is the One who resurrects the dead."
>
> Rabbi Chiyya in the name of Rabbi Yochanan says, "One says, 'Blessed is the One who is faithful to His word and resurrects the dead.'"
>
> Rabbi Chiyya in the name of Rabbi Yochanan says, "One says, 'You are the One who knows your numbers, and He will awaken you and will remove the dust from your eyes. Blessed are You, God, who resurrects the dead.'"
>
> Rabbi Elazar in the name of Rabbi Chanina says:
> "The One who created you with justice

and sustained you with justice
and took you out of life with justice
and who will, in the future, revive you with justice,
is the One who knows your numbers,
and He will remove the dust from your eyes.
Blessed is the One who resurrects the dead."

(Y. BERAKHOT 9:2, 90A2)

Resurrection of the dead was an important feature of the sages' faith. (As today, not all Jewish groups in those days believed in resurrection of the dead.) After the Bar Kokhba Revolt, the Jewish population of Israel was decimated. Redemption and vindication must have seemed like far-off dreams. These four blessings are a whisper of hope and defiance. The Romans may have appeared to have won, but this blessing says, "It ain't over 'til it's over." Note how the Yerushalmi gives options without picking one as "the proper one." You can say any one of the four, or you can make one up along similar lines.

On Seeing a Rainbow

The heavens were a source of inspiration, especially for the sages of the Yerushalmi, who were *Heichalot* mystics. They conceived of their spiritual journeys as trips through vast swaths of space and time. So when they would see something as rare as a rainbow, they saw it as a special sign of God's presence—a reminder of the rainbow that God bestowed on Noah after the flood.

> One who sees a rainbow in the clouds says, "Blessed are You, God, who remembers the covenant." Rabbi Chiyya in the name of Rabbi Yochanan: "Who is faithful in His covenant and remembers the covenant. Blessed ... who is true in His covenant and who remembers His covenant."
>
> (Y. BERAKHOT 9:2, 90A3)

God made a covenant with Noah, agreeing not to destroy the world ever again. The sign of this covenant is the rainbow (Genesis 9:12–13). So, to the sages of the Yerushalmi, a rainbow was an echo of that biblical promise. During this era, Jews in Israel might have doubted whether God would remain faithful to the covenant. These blessings are either a reminder or a hope that God will remain faithful to that promise. Again, the Yerushalmi offers options without indicating a preference for any one of them.

Options for *Havdalah*

In the Yerushalmi, the form and substance of *Havdalah* was still being hammered out:

> Rabbi Elazar ben Rabbi Hoshaya: "As long as one mentions no fewer than three kinds of 'divisions.'"
>
> Rabbi Yochanan said, "They should say no less than three, and those who say more should not add more than seven 'differences.'" ...
>
> Levi said, "They should mention only the 'separations' that are in the Torah."
>
> Nachum ben Rabbi Simai said in the name of his father, "Even if one says a single 'separation' it is enough."
>
> (Y. Berakhot 5:2, 57a1)

The Yerushalmi entertains the notion that *Havdalah* may mention anywhere from one to seven "differences" (*havdalot*). It also seems that each sage had his own ideas about how to determine the differences to be mentioned. (Not surprisingly, the Yerushalmi turns to Scripture, as it often does.) Here are some of the *havdalot* in Scripture:

Genesis 1:4: the separation between light and darkness
Genesis 1:7: the separation between the upper and lower waters
Leviticus 10:10: the separation between holy and regular
Leviticus 10:10: the separation between the pure and impure
Leviticus 20:26: the separation of Israel from the nations
Deuteronomy 10:8: God's separation of the tribe of Levi from the
  other tribes

1 Chronicles 23:13: Aaron and his sons' separation from the rest
    of the priests

There are many other "differences" in Scripture the sages could have
selected.

The Yerushalmi also provides a prayer for *Havdalah*:

> May the impending six days of creation that are coming to
> us begin in peace. Rabbi Abba adds, "And cause us to hear in
> those days joy and gladness." Rabbi Chizkiyah says in Rabbi's
> name, "Make us understand, and teach us."
>
> (Y. BERAKHOT 5:2, 57A3)

The key thing here, aside from the possible variants for our own
observance, is the obvious flexibility in the liturgical system. We can
use this template to recapture much of the flexibility that our prayers
may now lack.

These are just a few of the blessings and prayers you can find only
in the Yerushalmi. These prayers are every bit as legitimate as those
we find in our prayer book, which is based on the Bavli. Great sages
created them and used them. In other words, we needn't be limited
by what we find in the prayer book. The Yerushalmi offers all kinds of
different ways to bless God.

13

What Would Your Mysticism Be?

Angelina Jolie appeared in a mystery/adventure film, *Lara Croft*. She went farther and farther into the mystery, eventually escaping the bonds of time and talking to her deceased father. She faced danger at every turn.

Believe it or not, the mysticism of the Yerushalmi is something like the *Lara Croft* movie. The mysticism of this era is known as *Heichalot* mysticism: the mysticism of the seven heavenly halls. The seeker/worshipper would journey through vast swaths of time-space and brave dangers of fire, ice, and killer angels. At the end of each hall, the prayer would recite the *Kedushah*: "Holy, holy, holy is the Lord of hosts, the whole earth is filled with God's glory" (Isaiah 6:3). The journey was dangerous, filled with traps to ensnare those not pure of heart.

> From the earth until the first heaven is a 500-year journey. And from one heaven to another is a 500-year journey. And the thickness of a heaven is a 500-year journey. And the same is true of each and every heaven.... Even to traverse the hooves of the *Chayyot* [heavenly beings] is a 515-year journey ... equal to the numerical value of the word *yesharah* ["shall dwell," "covering," "straight," or "unified"; see Ezekiel 1:7]. See how high God is above His world, yet when a person enters into a meetinghouse (*beit k'neset*) and stands behind the pillar and prays in a whisper, the Holy One, blessed be He, listens to his prayer.
>
> (Y. BERAKHOT 9:1, 87A1)

The journey through the seven heavens is a long and arduous one. The Bavli gives us more details (B. Hagigah 12b–13a) about what, precisely, is in those heavens. For the sages of the Yerushalmi, those spaces are almost unimaginable and unimaginably vast. God is glorious, but far away. Living as they did in the difficult political and economic conditions of Roman-ruled Israel, it seems understandable that God might seem so far away. But the Yerushalmi offers hope: that distant God hears our quietest prayers.

Nishmat as Mysticism

Nishmat is a prayer said on Shabbat and festivals as we finish up the introductory psalms of praise. *Nishmat*'s aim is to give us perspective: it is as impossible to fully recount God's glory as it is to count all the raindrops. Indeed, *Nishmat* originates as a prayer of thanksgiving for rain:

> Rabbi Yehudah bar Yechezekel said: "Father would say a blessing when rain fell:
>> May your name
>> be magnified,
>> and sanctified,
>> and blessed,
>> and glorified, our king [*Yitgadel v'yitkadash v'yitbarakh v'yitromeim shimkha Malkeinu*],
>> for each and every drop of rain that You cause to fall for our sake. For You separate each and every drop from the others, as it is said, 'For He forms drops of water, into separate drops of rain' (Job 36:27)." ...
>
> Rabbi Yose bar Yaakov went to visit Rabbi Yudan of Migd'lya. When he got there, rain began to fall. And he heard a voice saying, "A thousand and a thousand thousands, a myriad and a myriad of myriads times must we give thanks to Your name, our king, for each and every drop of rain that You cause to fall for us. For You repay with goodness those who are guilty."
>
> (Y. BERAKHOT 9:2, 90B2; GENESIS RABBAH 13:15; DEUTERONOMY RABBAH 7:6)

Rabbi Yehudah's prayer begins with words you know: *Yitgadal v'yitkadash v'yitbarakh, v'yitromam shimkha Malkeinu.* Why are there so many synonyms? Why are there so many reflexive verbs, which, in Hebrew, begin either with *yit, tit, mit,* or *hit?* The answer: mysticism.

Aleinu and *Kaddish*:
Not Just Cleanup but Mystical Ascents

The high point of *Lara Croft* is her meeting with her father. The part of the service that corresponds to this climax is *Aleinu* and *Kaddish.* But what is the emotion most people, clergy or laity, feel upon hearing the call to rise for *Aleinu?* Relief. The service is almost over. This is definitely the ninth inning. What a pity that two of our most powerful prayers of ascent and mystical union with God have been relegated to this role.

In *Heichalot* mysticism, the *Aleinu* is said in the first-person singular (*Alai* instead of *Aleinu*). It is the prayer the mystical journeyer utters upon reaching the seventh, final, heavenly hall. In other words, it is the peak experience of prayer as the worshipper stands before God's throne.

Today, we associate *Kaddish* with the prayer for the dead and so conceive of it as a "downer." But how would that help the mourner connect with the deceased? Only when you experience each synonym as a step *up* toward God, and hence toward one's dearly departed, does the *Kaddish* make sense. Laid out on a page, it would appear as it does, in part, below. Begin at the *bottom left* and pray your way *up* the page.

etc.

v'nekhemata

tushb'chata

v'shirata

L'eila min kol birkhata

Sh'emei d'Kudsha, B'rich Hu v'yithalal

v'yitaleh

v'yithadar

v'yitnasei

v'yitromam

v'yitpa'ar

v'yishtabach

Yitbarakh (START HERE, PRAY UP)

and upon all Israel and we say: Amen.
May He who makes peace in His heights,
make peace upon us
Upon us and upon all Israel and we say: Amen
And good life
May there be abundant peace from heaven
And consolations that are uttered in the world and
we say: Amen.
and praise
Beyond any blessing
Be the name of the Holy One, blessed is He
And lauded
upraised
mighty
extolled
exalted
glorified
praised
Blessed
Blessed be His great Name forever and ever.

And soon and we say: Amen.
swiftly
and in the lifetimes of the entire family of Israel
and in your days
in your lifetime
bringing near His Messiah
And cause His salvation to sprout
in the world that He created as He willed.
and sanctified
May His great name grow exalted (START HERE, PRAY UP)

This layout helps remind the worshipper that this is a prayer of mystical ascent. In addition, laying the *Kaddish* out on the page as a prayer of ascension will help condition us to read *up* a page, and it is but a short step from there to being able to read *around* a page. Learning to read *around* a page rather than going linearly through a book is an enormous paradigm shift. If we learn, through prayer, that a Jewish page is different from an English page, then it is just a short step to jump into a page of Talmud itself.

Other *Heichalot* Prayers You Know

There are other prayers in the siddur that come from this school of mysticism. Any time you say the *Kedushah* ("Holy, holy, holy ...") you are praying from this school of mysticism. In addition, any prayer overflowing with synonyms is a *Heichalot* prayer. The parade example of a prayer of synonyms is the prayer after the *Shema*. Haven't you ever wondered why it reads as follows?

> True and enduring,
> correct
> and standing
> and straight
> and faithful
> and beloved
> and dear
> and precious
> and pleasant
> and awesome ... is this word.

Where was the editor? Surely they didn't need all those synonyms. If the task were only to describe God's word, then they would not need such an extensive list. But since this is a *Heichalot* prayer and each word forms a step in a staircase that leads you ever higher and closer to God, then the more words there are, the better!

Clearly, this form of mysticism still had a great deal of significance for the sages who composed the prayer book. And when we understand their origins, these prayers can become more meaningful to us. Then we can see *ourselves* as mystical journeyers, climbing ever closer to God.

The Tree of Life

The Tree of Life and the Garden of Eden were almost immeasurably large for today's human beings. (Adam and Eve were much larger than us, as well.) Their measurements also fit into the *Heichalot* map of the cosmos:

> It was taught: The Tree of Life was as wide as a 500-year jour-ney. Said Rabbi Yehudah bar Rabbi Ilai, "This does not include the width of the branches, but it includes only the width of its trunk.... The Tree of Life is one-sixtieth of the area of the garden. The garden is one-sixtieth of Eden...." And rabbis say, "The number of years it takes to traverse the width of the firma-ment is equal to the sum of the years of the lives of the patri-archs: 173 (Abraham) +180 (Isaac) + 147 (Jacob) = 500."
>
> (Y. BERAKHOT 1:1, 5B3–6A1)

We get both sorts of number systems, base 10 (500) and base 60 (1/60) in this mystical picture. Just saying these numbers aloud allows us to better picture these vast expanses in our mind.

For Us ...

Heichalot mysticism gives us an imaginative Judaism that makes the heavenly realms scalable and exciting. It helps us understand prayers in our prayer books that, all too often, are merely repeti-tive. It lets us imagine our biblical stories in whole new ways.

14

Trailers: Meditation Techniques of the Sages

You don't walk directly from the street into the movie itself. There are trailers. These are not merely advertisements (although they certainly function as such). The trailers help you transition from reality to the world of the film. Transitioning from "the street" to "prayer" is a similar exercise. You don't walk into synagogue ready to pray.

While the Yerushalmi outlines the basic rubrics of prayer (*Shema, Amidah, Birkat Hamazon*, and so on), it also reflects that these bare bones are fleshed out with meditative practices. So, for example, we learn the following:

> Rav Yermiyah said, "Stand to pray only from meditating on a judgment of authoritative tradition [*halakhah*]."
>
> Rav Yermiyah said, "The one who occupies himself with the needs of the public is as if he occupies himself with words of Torah."
>
> (Y. BERAKHOT 5:1, 53A3)

Learning, therefore, is part of praying. In prayer, we speak to God. Through learning, God speaks to us. And taking care of your community is like learning.

The following meditations bespeak the rough-and-tumble reality of Jews in the Land of Israel during this era:

It was said in the name of Rabbi Yochanan, "This verse should always be on your lips: 'The Lord of hosts is with us; the God of Jacob is our refuge. Selah' (Psalm 46:12)." It was also said by the students in the name of Rabbi Yochanan, "'O Lord of hosts, blessed is the one who trusts in You!' (Psalm 84:13)."

Rabbi Chizkiyah in the name of Rabbi Abbahu says, "May it be Your will, Lord our God, and God of our fathers, that You save us from the hard, evil, irreverent times that are going out and storming and coming to the world."

(Y. BERAKHOT 5:1, 53B2)

On the one hand, concentrating on prayer in the hostile environment of Roman-run Israel might have been easy. You would have been praying for survival, hence the deepest wish in your heart. Or concentrating might have been difficult. You would have been under so much stress that you couldn't focus in prayer. Note how the Yerushalmi lists all the things that might make prayer difficult. By listing each trouble (e.g., rebellion, hard times), you systematically set each problem aside and clear your mind for prayer. This passage is a template of prayer during a crisis.

The Yerushalmi stresses that concentration in prayer leads to the fulfillment of the prayers for good:

If you concentrate your heart when you pray, you will learn that your prayer is heard.

(Y. BERAKHOT 5:5, 59B1)

It is as if the greater your concentration, the more force propels your prayers heavenward, and the more likely they are to be fulfilled.

Some of our greatest sages found concentrating during prayer difficult and used their own guided imagery to help them focus:

Said Rabbi Chiyya the Great, "In all my days I never concentrated properly in prayer except for one time when I wanted to concentrate and I meditated, asking myself: Who goes up first before the king? The *arkafta* or the exilarch [two officials at court]?"

　　Shmuel said, "I count young birds."

　　Rabbi Bun bar Chiyya said, "I count rows of bricks."

(Y. Berakhot 2:4, 26a2)

The sages are using things from outside the realm of Judaism and prayer—the hierarchy of people in the court, birds in the sky, bricks—to calm their minds so they can pray. The people at court could be seen as a metaphor for God (the king) and the angels (the courtiers). Shmuel is looking skyward and counting what is there (birds). Rabbi Bun counts what is right in front of him. All three sages know the trick of guided meditation to calm the mind in order to focus in prayer. They have options. We have options.

　　There is consensus that meditation and prayer are aided by being in the synagogue with other worshippers:

"Seek the Lord while He may be found" (Isaiah 55:6). Where may He be found? In the meetinghouses [*batei k'neset*] and study halls [*batei midrashot*]. "Call upon him while He is near" (Isaiah 55:6). Where is He near? In the *batei k'neset* and *batei midrashot*. [Variant: At the time when the public prays.]

(Y. Berakhot 5:1, 54a2)

All these texts (and these are only a small sampling from the Yerushalmi, let alone biblical and post-rabbinic texts) affirm that meditation was an important part of Jewish spiritual practice.

Silent Prayer

Sometimes the best moment in a movie is the one when "nothing" is happening. In *Dear Frankie*, the male and female protagonists spend an almost eternal moment just looking at each other before kissing. It's easily the best moment in the picture. And sometimes the best moments of prayer are when "nothing" is happening.

While the Yerushalmi offers many words for us to say, it also acknowledges that wordless prayer may be the best, for humans lack the words to fully describe the experience of coming into contact with God's essence:

"Praise awaits You [dumiyah tehillah], O God, in Zion" (Psalm 65:2): The highest of all praises is silence. It is like describing a priceless pearl. All who attempt to praise it, no matter how high a price they may set upon it, undervalue it.

(Y. BERAKHOT 9:1)

The Hebrew of Psalm 65:2 lends itself to midrash. *Dumiyah tehillah* is here interpreted to mean "Silence is Your praise, God." Consistent with *Heichalot* mysticism, God is seen as both near and far in the Yerushalmi's system of prayer:

But the Holy One, blessed be He, appears to be distant, yet nothing is closer than He…. See how high the Holy One, blessed be He, is above his world. Yet a person can enter a meetinghouse [beit k'neset], stand behind a pillar, and pray in a whisper and the Holy One, blessed be He, hears his prayer. As it says, "Hannah was speaking in her heart; only her lips moved, and her voice was not heard" (1 Samuel 1:13). Yet the Holy One, blessed be He, heard her prayer.

(Y. BERAKHOT 9:1, 87A1)

In both the Yerushalmi and the Bavli, Hannah is seen as the exemplar of how to pray correctly. Because she prayed in an undertone, so do we. Note that if one wants God to hear the prayers as effectively as God heard Hannah's prayer, the sages urge one to pray in a synagogue. This is significant because much of prayer was done outside the synagogue, when a person ate or encountered boons or hardships during the course of the day. It also presupposes a world in which synagogues exist and are available to the worshipper at relatively short notice.

Yet, the Yerushalmi also acknowledges that a prayer from the heart finds God's ear no matter where it is offered:

> And so too does God listen to all His creatures. As it says, "A prayer of a poor man when he is faint and pours out his complaint before the Lord.... Incline Your ear to me" (Psalm 102:1–2). One who prays to God is like a person who speaks into his fellow's ear and his friend hears him. And is it possible that God could be closer to His creatures than this? For He is so close to His creatures when they pray it is as if they speak directly into God's ear.
>
> (Y. Berakhot 9:1, 87a1)

God is infinitely far away, yet instantly available through prayer. So one can experience immanence and transcendence simultaneously.

Shabbat: Looking for Loopholes

In *Five Easy Pieces*, Jack Nicholson's character just wants an omelet with a side order of toast. The waitress is adamant that there are no substitutions. So he figures out a way to order what he wants within her system of rules. He orders a chicken salad sandwich on toast and asks her to hold the chicken.

As you might expect, the sages and common folk of the Yerushalmi were quite flexible when it came to the observance of Shabbat. If theirs had been the Talmud that won, Shabbat would have been observed in a much more relaxed way. Perhaps nothing says it better than this passage about going to the public baths on Shabbat:

> At first the people of Tiberias would stop up the stoppers to the bath on the eve of the Sabbath, leaving hot water in the bath, and people would come in and wash on the Sabbath. They were suspect of filling the fire below with wood on the eve of the Sabbath. Accordingly, the sages prohibited washing in the water on the Sabbath, since it was heated for that purpose on that day, but they permitted sweating there on the Sabbath.

The sages then suspected the people of going in and bathing and then saying, "We were sweating." Therefore, the sages prohibited both the bathing and sweating.

There were there two baths, one with sweet water and the other with salt water. They were suspect of moving the boards and bathing in the sweet water and saying, "We bathed in the salt water." So the sages prohibited all the baths to them. Once they accepted the sages' authority, the sages, having made their point, gradually permitted them the entire apparatus once again, progressing to the point that they permitted them to use cave water and even the hot springs of Tiberias.

(Y. Shabbat 3:3, PM 23b)

It's an intricate dance. The people would like to bathe, and the sages only grant them license to sweat in the steam room. The sages keep trying to catch them doing something they don't like, but the people find ways to evade the sages' strictures and questions. They even find a way to move from salt water to freshwater. Once the sages establish their authority, however, they are quite permissive.

Women Getting Around the Rules

When women wanted to manipulate the rules regarding Shabbat, they were every bit as adroit at it as the sages. We have this example:

Rabbi Yermiyah and Rabbi Zeira in the name of Rabbi Chiyya bar Ashi: "A clever woman will rinse a cup here, a dish there, and a plate over there, and so turn out to sprinkle water on her house and clean it up on Shabbat."

(Y. Shabbat 2:7, PM 20b)

A clever woman who knows how to manipulate the rules in order to do what she needs to do. And the sages of the Yerushalmi are fine with her doing so.

The *Kiddush* Cup

The Yerushalmi has an elaborate ritual related to the *Kiddush* cup:

> You must hold the cup in the right hand.
> You must hold your hand above the table.
> You must look at it [i.e., you don't set it down to check the oven, for instance].
> Said Rav Acha, "Three things were said about the *Kiddush* cup:
> It should be full.
> It should be decorated (crowned or surrounded with other cups—think: a pyramid of champagne glasses).
> It should be shining."
>
> (Y. BERAKHOT 7:5, 77A1–77A2)

This is a great deal of specificity in a document that isn't rife with it.

Women and Shabbat

Few movies dramatize what's actually going on inside a woman's head. Sadly, this is true of the sages as well. Women were, in general, something of a blind spot for the sages. The sages observed women's dress and other visible behaviors (weaving, dressing, cooking, makeup, jewelry, and how they dressed at weddings), but they displayed almost no understanding of what was going on in women's minds. We have an example of this in the following passage:

> It has been taught: Rabbi Shimon ben Elazar permits wearing an ornament.... Why is it prohibited to wear ornaments on Shabbat? Said Rabbi Ba, "Because women like to display their finery, and she may untie the ornaments to show them to her neighbors and, in forgetfulness, walk about carrying them."
>
> (Y. SHABBAT 6:1, PM 33B)

This characterization of women may evince a wince. Wearing all these ornaments on Shabbat is permitted by one authority and forbidden by another. (No surprise there … it's standard Yerushalmi.) The passage continues:

> Said R. Chizkiyah, "I know the reason for the former ruling and the latter one. There were a lot of little girls in the time of Rabbi Yermiyah. They came and asked him and he asked Rabbi Zeira. Rabbi said to Rabbi Yermiyah, 'Do not forbid and do not permit wearing them.'"
>
> (Y. Shabbat 6:1, PM 34a)

It doesn't get more typical of the Yerushalmi than this, and it also gives us a backstage pass, so to speak, to girls' lives in Israel at this time. Rabbi Zeira, God bless him, takes the brave stance of not permitting and not forbidding. In other words, *he leaves the power to make this decision in women's hands.*

Y. v. B.

The Bavli has less of an emphasis on meditation than does the Yerushalmi and less flexibility when it comes to the standard prayers.

For Us …

The Shabbat of the Yerushalmi looks more flexible than we'd expect. According to the Yerushalmi, there are many valid ways to observe Shabbat. Its observance was far more individualized and fluid than most of us would have guessed. And pretty much everything seems to be up for negotiation among the sages and between the sages and the people. (It sounds an awful lot like Shabbat in America today, doesn't it?)

Part 3

The Holidays

If you had to identify the ten most important Jewish holidays, what would they be? We could probably all agree on Rosh Hashanah, Yom Kippur, and Passover. The sages of the Yerushalmi would list Sukkot and Shavuot, the other two pilgrimage festivals, as well. Next would come the minor holidays, Purim and Hannukkah, as well as two fast days, the seventeenth of Tammuz and the ninth of Av. There are other holidays outlined in both the Yerushalmi and the Bavli, but these are the holidays you're most likely to observe yourself. And now be ready for some surprises. These are the holidays and festivals as you may never have experienced them before. As with everything in the Yerushalmi, there's lots of fun to be had!

15

What Would the High Holy Days Be Like?

The High Holy Days in the world of the movies are the big-budget blockbusters, such as *Titanic* or *The Lord of the Rings*. No expense is spared on these movies, and the response is proportionate. The High Holy Days in Israel were the no-holds-barred production numbers of the Jewish year.

We must begin with what the High Holy Days would have been like while the Temple stood. Perhaps the best way to imagine it would be to combine your ideas of the Superbowl, the State of the Union Address, and the obsessively controlled cleanliness surrounding a person who is about to undergo a bone marrow transplant. (Before a patient has a bone marrow transplant, all his white blood cells are destroyed, making the patient incredibly vulnerable to infection. Such patients stay in rooms that surpass even operating rooms in their cleanliness. The patients are utterly isolated. Only specially garbed medical personnel can come into direct contact with the patient. Family members can only talk with patients through several layers of plate glass.)

The High Holy Days involved a maximum number of priests, levites, sacrificial animals, incense, and more. Imagine a much quieter world, in which you could hear a shofar blown fifteen miles away. Then imagine the barrage of sound that would have emitted from the Temple on the High Holy Days—*shofarot*, trumpets, lyres, animals bellowing—as well as the smell of the burning sacrifices and the incense. Then you'd have some idea of how much "production value" these holidays had for the Jewish people, for the Temple, and for its staff. It was like a blockbuster that was also local news. For the people of the Land of Israel, and of Jerusalem especially, this was something they heard and saw and smelled, even if they never made it to the Temple itself.

God's Three Books

The idea of God's judgment and the sorting of humanity into good, intermediate, and evil categories is fully outlined in the Yerushalmi:

> God has three account books: one for the utterly righteous, one for the utterly wicked, and one for those in between. The utterly righteous receive verdicts of life by Rosh Hashanah.
>
> The utterly wicked receive verdicts of death by Rosh Hashanah.
>
> With regard to those in between, the ten days of repentance between Rosh Hashanah and Yom Kippur were given to them. If they repented, they are inscribed with the righteous; and if not, they are inscribed with the wicked.
>
> What is the proof? "Let them be blotted out of the book of the living, and not be written with the righteous" (Psalm 69:29). "Let them be blotted out of the book" refers to the wicked. "Of the living" refers to the righteous. "And not be written with the righteous" refers to the intermediates. [But they still make it into the book of the living.]
>
> (Y. ROSH HASHANAH 1:3, V 57A)

This midrash uses a common technique for understanding seemingly superfluous words: the sages make them refer to different ideas. They break up the sentence and "fill in the blanks." Here, the sages make the verse apply to God's three books. This imagery survives today in the High Holy Day liturgy.

High Holy Day Services Don't Have to Be So Long

Once the Temple was gone, what could the sages use from such Temple-centered holidays? They were able to keep the shofar on Rosh Hashanah and fasting on Yom Kippur. The best they could do was make prayer and midrash the centerpieces of the day, rather than the sacrifices and the ritual purification of the Temple.

The midrash in the Rosh Hashanah service is most clearly seen in the addition of three sections to the *Amidah*: *Malchuyot* (God's kingship), *Zikhronot* (God's faithful remembering of us), and *Shofarot* (the sound of the shofar). As it is configured today, each one of these sections has ten scriptural verses that relate to that topic. It's more "Scripture surfing" than midrash making, because the verses are just recited one after another. But the Yerushalmi does not configure the service in this way. In fact, the Yerushalmi offers plenty of options on how to pray this part of the service:

> Rabbi Yochanan ben Nuri said, "If one recited three verses, he has fulfilled his obligation. We used to say: three verses from each part of the *Tanakh*, that is, three from Torah, three from Prophets, three from Writings. But it was taught [T. Rosh Hashanah 2:12]: Even if one says three from all of them, that is, one from Torah, one from Prophets, one from Writings, he has fulfilled his obligation."
>
> (Y. Rosh Hashanah 4:7, PM 20b)

Whoever was leading services had the freedom to add or subtract verses to a minimum of three verses for each topic instead of ten each (which we have today). The sages felt your pain at the length of High Holy Day services and allowed congregations to trim them.

Yom Kippur: The Photonegative of a Pilgrimage Festival

While the Temple stood, Yom Kippur was like a Hollywood blockbuster premiere. There were throngs of priests, the handles of the vessels were covered with gold (M. Yoma 3:8), and there was a procession leading the goat to Azazel.

This procession was part of the Yom Kippur ceremony in which one goat was offered as a sin offering and another goat was driven out to the wilderness (Azazel) (Leviticus 16:7–10). The priest placed all the sins of the whole Jewish people onto this goat. It had to be driven out and die in the wilderness, lest it return and bring all our sins back with it. The Yerushalmi records that this was local news:

> The eminent people of Jerusalem used to accompany the priest to the first booth. There were ten booths from Jerusalem to the ravine, a distance of about twelve miles. At each booth they say to him, "Lo, here is food, here is water." They accompany him from one booth to the next except for the man in the last booth, who does not go with him to the ravine. But he stands from a distance and observes what he does.
>
> (M. Yoma 6:4–5)

The requirements regarding the goat of Azazel are in the Torah (Leviticus 16:7–10), but without this mishnah, we wouldn't know that it was accompanied with a sort of parade. This trip to Azazel seems to be the photonegative of the pilgrimage festivals. During those holidays, parades made their way *to* Jerusalem with joy, leading their animals. This "Yom Kippur parade" had an animal being taken *away* from Jerusalem to destroy it. This messy, lonely death is the photonegative of the sacrifice of the other goat in the Temple, which was done before a throng of people and was cleanly sacrificed with a knife. Furthermore, on Yom Kippur the high priest entered the Temple's Holy of Holies alone, while the priest leading the goat to Azazel went, finally, into the ultimate wilderness alone.

Another thing that might surprise you about this mishnah is that the booths along the route bear a striking resemblance to water stations at a marathon. Yom Kippur is, after all, a fast day. Nonetheless, the sages understood reality. A long, midday trek into the wilderness in the fall, before the rains have come in Israel, would dehydrate any man, let alone one who'd been fasting since the night before.

The question the Yerushalmi asks is, "Did anyone ever take the food and water offered at these stations?"

> Why do they offer this food and drink? The evil impulse craves only what is forbidden. This is illustrated in the following. One Yom Kippur, Rav Mana went up to visit Rabbi Chaggai, who was ill. Rabbi Chaggai said to him, "I am thirsty." He said to him, "Go drink something." Rav Mana left him and went away. After a while he came back to him. He said, "What did you do about your thirst?" Rabbi Chaggai said, "When you let me drink, my thirst went away."
>
> Rabbi Chiyya bar Ba told this story: A man was going through the market with his daughter on the Day of Atonement. His daughter said to him, "Father, I am thirsty."
>
> He said to her, "Wait." She said to him, "Father, I am thirsty." He said to her, "Wait." And she died.
>
> On the Day of Atonement, Rav Acha would say before the Additional Prayer, "Brethren, whoever has a child to feed, let him go and take care of the child."
>
> (Y. YOMA 6:4, 44A1–44A2, PM 34A, V 43D)

The Yerushalmi has a grasp on both idealism and realism. Ideally, no one would drink water or eat food on Yom Kippur. But realistically, some people cannot get through Yom Kippur without drinking and/or eating. There is no doubt about the correct course of action regarding children: if they are hungry, skip services, go home, and feed those kids. However, while the Yerushalmi gives us a clear-cut decision on what to do with children, characteristically, it leaves options open for adults. If an adult can cope with it physically or mentally, he or she may continue the fast. This demonstrates a nuanced psychology on the part of the Yerushalmi: if you remove a prohibition, the desire for the prohibited item may abate. But if the person can't cope physiologically, feed and water appropriately!

Yom Kippur Was a Fashion Show

Part of the pageantry of a Hollywood premiere or the Oscars is seeing the spectacular clothes the stars are wearing. And part of the pageantry of Yom Kippur was the spectacle of the priests' robes, not unlike the fashion show that the High Holy Days can be today. Striking the balance between wearing finery appropriate for the day, which helps one pray, and focusing too much on one's clothes was apparently as difficult then as it is now.

> "If the high priest wanted to add finery to the standard outfit, he may add out of his own pocket" (M. Yoma 3:7). It is told that Yishmael ben Piabi's mother made him a tunic worth a hundred *manehs*. And he would stand and make offerings on the altar while wearing it.
>
> Rabbi Elazar ben Harsom's mother made him a tunic worth twenty thousand *manehs*, and he would stand and make offerings on the altar while wearing it. But his brethren, the priests, called him down from the altar, because it was so sheer that he appeared naked while wearing it.
>
> (Y. KIPPURIM 3:6; T. KIPPURIM 1:21–22)

To understand the value of these tunics, we can compare them with the "standard-issue" tunics, which were worth twelve to thirty *manehs*. There seems to be a bit of criticism of Rabbi Elazar ben Harsom's tunic because of its ostentatious price and material. Apparently, it was so finely made that it was transparent (think: the picture of Princess Diana just after her engagement, in a dress through which the light shown to the extent that it was see-through). This is an aspect of the High Holy Days that is not present in the Bavli. This was *local* news.

Y. v. B.

These details, which were so palpably alive for those who wrote the Yerushalmi, were memories the Babylonians heard from distances in space and time. They retold the Mishnah's traditions, but they lack the details that give the recounting the immediacy we find in the Yerushalmi.

For Us ...

Once, my family and I visited Israel and were in Jerusalem the same day that President Bill Clinton paid an unscheduled trip to the city. We couldn't get *anywhere*. It was absolute gridlock. So while the president's visit was international news, we experienced it from a decidedly local point of view. The High Holy Days in Jerusalem while the Temple stood may have been something akin to this.

The Yerushalmi's take on the High Holy Days affirms (1) shorter services are possible and possibly preferable, (2) attention to "production values" must be paid, and (3) not everyone can complete the fast (even the priest who is running a road race without water). In short, this is a more flexible approach to the High Holy Days that still affirms the days' core values.

16

What Would Sukkot Be Like?

The number of movies that have drunken party scenes is too numerous to recount. Pick your favorite from your own memory bank. Or think of the scene in *Titanic* when Rose goes below deck and gets decidedly drunk on beer and loosens up.

When we read about Sukkot in the Yerushalmi, the nostalgia—the genuine wish for Sukkot to be what it once was—is overpowering. There is no effort to rework the holiday. That came from later authors in distant lands. But in the Land of Israel, the site of the greatest party on earth (as Sukkot was), they just wanted the band to play on.

Think of it as Mardis Gras in New Orleans. Even after Hurricane Katrina, they held Mardis Gras. New Orleans without Mardis Gras is not New Orleans. And Israel without Sukkot was an idea so discordant that the sages in Israel could not accept it. So they remembered, treasuring and burnishing the details of what it once had been.

And the people who stayed in Israel were every bit as stubborn as those New Orleanians who returned to the city after Katrina. To some, they seemed crazy. The city had effectively had a nuclear bomb explode in it. Why return to a home flooded up to the second floor, upon whose walls black mold crept like leprosy? But these folks loved their city. So they came back, drained their homes, dusted off what they could, and put down new roots. The Jews of Israel never gave up the dream of returning and remaining in their land and letting the party that was Sukkot return.

And Sukkot really was something like Mardis Gras: an enormous all-night party. It included huge animal sacrifices, prayers for water for the coming rainy season, and an all-night festival, complete with lighting, music, dancing, and rejoicing.

And the Jews of Babylonia? Well, they'd done without the immediacy of the Land for centuries. So their nostalgia may have been for some Sukkot their grandfather attended back in the day. It's as if you'd once attended Mardis Gras in New Orleans and ate a king cake at some point and told your kids about it. But no one in your family drove a float or threw the beads.

Was anything left after the Temple's destruction? A great deal of the religious symbolism remained, as a matter of fact. The animal sacrifices were obviously out, but the special rejoicing at the end of the festival changed into a spiritual wedding ceremony. In the Temple, on the last day of the festival, the priests would circle the altar seven times and then beat the leaves off the willow branches.

Today, this ceremony is adapted in the observance of Hoshanah Rabbah. The Torah scrolls are taken out of the ark and held on the bimah. Then the congregation circles around the Torah scrolls seven times. This is very much an adaptation of what happened in the Temple. It is also an echo of the bride circling the groom in a traditional wedding ceremony. Indeed, the congregation carries their *lulavs* while making these seven circuits, shaking them periodically, and then they, too, beat the willow leaves off the branches. The symbolism could scarcely be more explicit: it is the culmination of a fertility festival, after all. And what is a fertility festival without conception, at least symbolically speaking? Of course, the *lulav* and *etrog* lend themselves to this sort of interpretation. (An egg-shaped item and a long item with shorter items on either side that are waved around together ...)

The Sukkah

The tradition of dwelling in a sukkah for seven days predated the Temple. Once the harvest was in full swing, it was easier to build a lean-to in the field and sleep there rather than trekking home and back again each day. Decorating these booths was part of the merriment of the holiday (think: Martha Stewart–style decorating for an entire country). This goes back to the return from the exile in Babylonia in 516 BCE.

> So they issued the following proclamation and had it passed along to all their cities and in Jerusalem: "Go out to the mountain and bring olive branches, pine branches, myrtle branches, palm branches, and branches of other leafy trees to make booths as it is written."... They made *sukkot* ... and he read from the book of the law of God day by day from the first day until the last day of the celebration.
>
> (Nehemiah 8:15–16, 8:18)

Strangely, an *etrog* doesn't make the list here, and pine boughs are included.

For Us ...

This biblical text leaves the door open for us to include local vegetation in our *lulav* and *etrog*. In the Yerushalmi, the decoration of the sukkah is its harvested produce (Y. Shabbat 3:6). For Sukkot, this means you could make local vegetation part of the *lulav* and *etrog* for the festival. For example, in Vermont, you might take maple leaf branches with local apples for your *lulav*. And you could decorate your *lulav* as nicely as you want. (M. Sukkah 3:8 records that some people bound up their *lulavs* with gold threads.)

Happy Endings

Most movies and movie franchises have happy endings. *Titanic*'s Rose loses Jack but lives a free life. Luke Skywalker is reunited with his father and his sister. Frodo and Sam destroy the ring, and Aragorn becomes king. Sukkot is the Jewish holiday version of such happy endings.

If the High Holy Days are as solemn as a coronation, Sukkot is the street party after it happens. Or, you could say it was like Prince William's wedding to Kate. All was quiet in the cathedral when he put the ring on her finger. But the crowds watching it outside on the big screens let out a lusty cheer that penetrated even those enormous, ancient doors. That crowd and their joy, *that* is Sukkot.

The Yerushalmi emphasizes the role that happiness plays in celebrating Sukkot:

> The Holy Spirit rests only on one whose heart is happy.
>
> (Y. SUKKAH 5:1, 28B1)

The Yerushalmi tells us we can't wait for God to come and make us happy. God is attracted to happiness. And how do we get happy? On Sukkot, we celebrate, we play music, we dance, we do things that delight the heart. The Yerushalmi's Israel isn't an inherently happy place. But its sages urge us, the people, to make the effort.

Sukkot = Spring Break in Florida

In movies, spring break in Florida is shorthand for people singing, dancing, and misbehaving. There was an aspect of this during Sukkot. Perhaps lax morals were associated with the privacy of the impromptu shelters. In addition, the holiday was associated with harvesting grapes and making wine.

> And they went out into the fields, and gathered their vineyards, and trampled the grapes, and made merry, and went into the house of their god, and ate and drank.
>
> (JUDGES 9:27)

The problem for the prophets seems to be that this harvest, including grapes and the making of the wine thereof, was accompanied by a great deal of "merriment."

There was certainly dancing, singing, and juggling. We are even told the lyrics of the songs they sang:

"The pious men and wonder-workers used to dance before them with burning torches in their hands and sang before them songs of praises" (M. Sukkah 5:4).

Some of them would sing, "Happy is my youth that doesn't embarrass my old age." This was what the people of deeds would say.

And some of them would sing, "Happy is my old age that atones for my youth." This was what the repentants would sing.

Both of these groups would sing, "Happy is the one who has never sinned. And one who has sinned, let him return and be forgiven" (T. Sukkah 4:2).

(Y. SUKKAH 5:4; T. SUKKAH 4:2, 29B3)

These are three songs I doubt you've heard in synagogue. They're all the more remarkable because they are the opposite of what we do on the High Holy Days. On those days, we *all* recite the confession so that no one should have to publicly repent his or her sins individually. On Sukkot, everyone publicly owns up to his or her past. It's rather like "What happens in Las Vegas stays in Las Vegas." So when you're in Las Vegas (or in Jerusalem on this festival), everyone gets drunk, dances, and owns up to the stupid things they've done and/or encourages other partyers to do the same.

Mishnah Sukkah 4:5 outlines the dancing and music, ending with the chant/song/refrain *Anu l'Yah ul'Yah eineinu*, "We are for God, and to God our eyes are turned." The English hardly does the Hebrew justice. It doesn't take much imagination to see one person saying the first two words and then the crowd responding with the last two words.

Sukkot = Memorial Day

For Jews in Israel, the culmination of the holiday also had nationalistic tones.

"And on that day they walk around the altar seven times" (M. Sukkah 4:3). Said Rav Acha, "This is a memorial to the victory at Jericho."

(Y. SUKKAH 4:3, 24A4)

Rav Acha associates Sukkot with military victory and conquest of the Land. This nuanced meaning could be intended to bolster the spirits of Israel's Jews, assuring them that the Land is still theirs and that the Romans would one day leave.

Sukkot = Ritual of Rebellion

Rituals of rebellions turn all the rules on their heads. What is normally private is public and, in this case, really public. Priests had to wear certain outfits as mandated in Scripture. But on Sukkot, their underwear, normally never seen, was on display:

> Out of the worn-out undergarments of the high priest they kindled the lamps that were inside the Temple, and out of the worn-out undergarments of the ordinary priests they kindled the lamps that were outside in the courtyard. And there was not a courtyard in Jerusalem that was not lit up from the light of the festivities.... It was taught that a woman could sort her wheat by the light of the fire in the Temple. Would this mean she was violating the rules of sacrilege that state that no one can benefit from something in the Temple while outside the Temple? No, for Rabbi Yehoshua ben Levi said, "Smell, sight, and sound are not subject to the laws of sacrilege." There were six sounds made in the Temple in Jerusalem that they could hear in Jericho: the sound of the great gate opening, the sound of the shovel-flute, the sound of the wooden device Ben Katin made for the laver, the sound of Gavini the crier, the sound of the flute, the sound of the cymbal. There are those who say: Also the voice of the high priest when he said the divine name on the Day of Atonement. From Jericho they could smell the scent of the compounding of the incense. Said Rabbi Elazar ben Diglai, "The goats at my father's house in the mountains of Mikhvar would sneeze from the smell of the compounding of the incense."
>
> (Y. SUKKAH 5:3, 29B1–29B3; M. TAMID 3:8)

First, if you think this is hyperbole, you may be right. On the other hand, I can personally testify, from living in a town with an enormous barbecue competition, that the smell carries for miles. And in the days after Hurricane Ike, when the city was so still, you could hear all sorts of sounds that traveled for miles, when otherwise you wouldn't hear them because your windows would be closed.

Y. v. B.

The feeling we get from the Bavli is something like an article about a society soiree that's published a month after the event. We get the details of where it was held, a list of who attended, a description of the decorations and the menu, and pictures of people all dressed up, but we don't get the feeling of the emotional impact of the day, what it was like to be in that crush of humanity, seeing the lights at night and experiencing the crush of the dancing throng. It's like the difference between being at a fireworks show and seeing them illuminate the whole sky versus seeing a picture, no matter how beautiful, of fireworks in the sky. The picture doesn't come close to the reality. The Yerushalmi is the actual fireworks. The Bavli is the picture.

For Us …

Let me draw your attention to three points. First, the vividness of the memories is almost, quite literally, tangible. (Think of the movie *Avalon*. The difference between actually seeing the circus coming to town and just watching it on television is brought out in the most poignant way.) These are memories of the actual events. Second, the aspect of "local news" is evident again. This is the recollection of Jerusalem not necessarily focused on the Temple itself. This is not a televised, photographed memory of Prince William marrying Kate Middleton. This is the memory of the people who were selling *chachkes* and snacks to the throngs that showed up. These are the people who not only saw those beautiful horses, but also heard them and smelled them. This is the memory of reality. With regard to Sukkot, the sages don't want to make midrash or adapt. They want the party back.

Sukkot v. Passover

One last thing about Sukkot in the Yerushalmi needs to be noted. Biblically, Sukkot is just as big a holiday as Passover. Yet there's far more Mishnah and Gemara on Passover than there is on Sukkot. How can we account for this variation? Was it that Sukkot was so relentlessly anchored in the past? Was Passover celebrated more at home than at the Temple, even in ancient days? Certainly, the Yerushalmi's description of Sukkot is as a Temple-centered holiday. And the sages certainly drew a direct line connecting Sukkot and Passover:

> One must enter both the seder and the sukkah with a ravenous appetite.
>
> (Y. SUKKAH 2:7, 14A5)

17

Passover

So let's take a look at Passover and find out why these two festivals—Passover and Sukkot—ended up with different rabbinic fates.

"The Farmer and the Cowman Should Be Friends"

This section is named for a song in the musical *Oklahoma*. At a barn raising, the farmers and ranchers sing a song in which they trade insults back and forth. Passover is about this eternal fight between ranchers and farmers, specifically, sheepherders and barley growers. Ranchers don't like their ranges blocked by fences. And farmers detest having animals run through and ruin their crops.

Each of these two ways of life had ancient springtime rituals associated with it that predated Judaism by five thousand years. The first spring lamb was slaughtered and its blood was smeared on one's door, where it performed the protective service later conferred by the mezuzah. The lamb was then roasted on a spit and eaten, whole, before midnight, without breaking any of its bones.

At the early barley harvest, as a sign of faith that the barley god would make the coming year a plentiful one, all remaining old barley from the previous year was disposed of, and a heavy, unleavened cake was made and then burnt as a sacrifice to the god. Since all the sourdough starter would have been thrown away, one had to wait until the starter could develop naturally, which would take about seven days.

The Torah never quite manages to blend these two holiday neatly into one holiday. Even in our liturgy today, Passover is known as both Pesach (the lamb holiday) and as Chag Hamatzot (the barley holiday).

The dual nature of the holiday bespeaks Israel's most ancient roots. Seminomadic herders from the south (Jethro's kin at Sinai) gradually moved into the highlands of Judea, where the development of terraced farming allowed them to settle down into a life based on agriculture.

Pesach in Temple Times

When the Temple stood, groups of people who had all bought shares in one lamb traveled to Jerusalem together. The animal was sacrificed and processed, and the groups would use clay ovens to bake the matzah and roast the lamb. Then, as evening fell, the scent of lamb heavy in the air, the groups would drink four cups of wine and retell the whole story of the Exodus from Egypt. They would then eat a true Hillel sandwich of roast lamb, horseradish, *charoset*, and soft matzah (like the Indian bread naan). The last part of the seder would be the eating of the *afikoman*.

After the destruction of the Temple in 70 CE, and especially after the Bar Kokhba Revolt, the sages had to restructure the holiday without the benefit of the pilgrimage or the sacrifice. It's something like asking a movie director who is used to working with 3-D, IMAX, color, and surround sound to make a black-and-white silent picture. But the sages were aided in their reshaping of the holiday by one thing: current events. Yes, the festival would retell the Exodus from Egypt. But the story of a superpower oppressing the Jews and the Jews' eventual, miraculous triumph, resulting in the Jews living freely in their own land, would undoubtedly have been experienced as a contemporary political story that the Jews of Israel wished would come true. They wished that their resistance and defiance of the Romans would end in triumph and that they might soon be free to live in their land, under their own government.

Massaging the Script

Next time you watch a movie, take note of how many writers are credited. Sometimes there's just one or two. But sometimes there are four (and those are only the ones who got credit!). In such cases, the writers had to keep massaging the script until it was filmable. Passover is like that "massaged" script. The sages went over and over it until they had what they wanted. And just as there are many scenes that are written, filmed, edited, and scored that don't make it into the final film, the sages had to leave a lot of Passover seder scenes on the cutting-room floor.

Four Cups

So how did they "massage" Passover's "script"? They added midrash. Lots and lots of midrash ... much more, in fact, than is in the Haggadah we use today. Take, for example, all these alternatives for explaining the four cups of wine:

> Whence did they derive the requirement for four cups?
> 1. Rabbi Yochanan said in the name of Rabbi Benayah, "They correspond to the four redemptions: 'Say, therefore, to the Israelite people: I am the Lord. I will *take* you out from under the burdens of the Egyptians and *deliver* you from their bondage. I will *redeem* you with an outstretched arm and through extraordinary chastisements, and I will *take* you to be My people' (Exodus 6:6–7)."
> 2. Rabbi Yehoshua ben Levi said, "They correspond to the four cups of Pharaoh: 'Pharaoh's *cup* was in my hand, and I pressed them into Pharaoh's *cup* and placed the *cup* in Pharaoh's hand.... And you will place Pharaoh's *cup* in his hand' (Genesis 40:11, 40:13)."
> 3. Rabbi Levi said, "They correspond to the four kingdoms that have oppressed Israel: Babylonia, Media, Greece, and Rome."
> 4. And sages say, "They correspond to the four cups of punishment that the Holy One, blessed be He, will give the nations of the world to drink: 'For thus said the Lord, the God of Israel, to me: Take from my hand this *cup* of wine—of wrath—and make all the nations to whom I send you drink of it' (Jeremiah 25:15); 'Flee from the

midst of Babylon ... for this is a time of vengeance for the Lord. He will deal retribution to her. Babylon was a golden *cup* in the Lord's hand' (Jeremiah 51:6–7); 'For in the Lord's hand there is a *cup* with foaming wine fully mixed; from this He pours all the wicked of the earth drink, draining it to the very dregs' (Psalm 75:9); 'He will rain down upon the wicked blazing coals and sulfur, a scorching wind shall be the portion of their *cup*' (Psalm 11:6). ... And corresponding to these, the Holy One, blessed be He, will give Israel four cups of consolation to drink: 'The Lord is my allotted share and *cup*' (Psalm 16:5); 'You anoint my head with oil, my *cup* runs over' (Psalm 23:5); 'I raise the *cups* of deliverances [i.e., two cups]' (Psalm 116:13)."

(Y. PESACHIM 10:1, 82B1–82B2, PM 68B)

Clearly, there were many alternative explanations for the four cups, only one of which made it into the Passover Haggadah that we have today. Interestingly, it is Rabbi Yochanan's version that becomes the "official" explanation. This is all the more noteworthy because when you have opinions stated by individuals followed by the opinion of the anonymous majority ("sages say"), the anonymous majority always wins. This is classic Yerushalmi: providing many alternatives with no attempt to push any one into supremacy through further discussion.

The last explanation of the four cups, that is, the four cups of retribution, can be found, in a greatly revised form, at the end of the seder. Over the fourth cup, we ask God to pour out anger upon the nations that have oppressed us. (Some Haggadahs have deleted this prayer.)

The fifth cup (Elijah's cup) makes no appearance in the Yerushalmi because it is likely a Babylonian invention. The Bavli tells us of a widely held belief that drinking even numbers of cups leaves you vulnerable to demons, while drinking odd numbers of cups protects you (B. Pesachim 110a; B. Berakhot 51b). So they added a fifth cup to protect those at the seder. When the belief in such demons waned or when

Jews moved away from Babylonia and forgot the origin of this practice, they kept the cup on the table but consigned it to Elijah.

Exile = Slavery

Another midrash compares the oppression of slavery in Egypt to the oppression of exile in Babylonia:

> Just as stone is tougher than brick, so the subjugation to Babylonia was tougher than the subjugation to Egypt.
>
> (Y. SUKKAH 4:3, 24A3)

For the sages of the Yerushalmi, who had tasted life in the Land of Israel, the idea of living away from Israel was worse than slavery. It was a penalty all its own. To live without the Land having once tasted it is worse than living without the Land at all.

The Real Four Questions

I would be willing to wager that you learned to recite the seder's four questions as a child. It is, after all, the premier moment for the kids at a seder. So I hope that it won't come as too much of a shock to you that the four questions you know are not the four questions as they were originally set down. Those four questions are a bit different:

> They filled a second cup for him. At this point, the son questions his father. If the son doesn't know what to ask, his father instructs him to ask, "Why is this night different from all other nights? On all other nights, we eat leavened, and unleavened, bread. Why, on this night, do we eat only unleavened bread? On all other nights we eat all kinds of herbs. Why, on this night, do we eat only bitter herbs? On all other nights, we eat meat roasted, stewed, or boiled. Why, on this night, do we eat it only roasted? On all other nights, we dip once. Why, on this night, do we dip twice?" And according to the child's intelligence, the father instructs him.
>
> (M. PESACHIM 10:4)

The difference between the original four questions and those we ask is the one about roasting meat. This is a natural question for a child to ask. If they are in Jerusalem, they are in the midst of one roasting lamb after another.

Even the minimum second course they eat is roasted. You see, in order for a meal to qualify as festive, there must be two cooked items (besides bread). The sages, always rooting for the folks with no money, make that dish the cheapest cooked dish there is: an egg. And because everything must be roasted, it is placed in the coals and slow-roasted there. The "roasting" question is replaced in our Haggadah with the "leaning" question.

The Miracles of Disabilities

In *Field of Dreams*, an act of faith brings forth a miracle that only some people experience. The Passover story in the Torah involves many miracles, but the sages find even more miracles through midrash:

> When Moses fled from Pharaoh, all Pharaoh's troops were incapacitated: some of them became mute, some of them became deaf, and some of them became blind.
>
> When Pharaoh asked those who were mute where Moses was, they did not speak.
>
> When he asked those who were deaf, they did not hear.
>
> When he asked those who were blind, they did not see.
>
> This demonstrates what the Holy One, blessed be He, said at the burning bush when Moses protested that he had a speech impediment, "Who gave man a mouth or who makes him mute?" (Exodus 4:11).
>
> (Y. Berakhot 9:1, PM 87a2)

The God Moses met at the burning bush miraculously and continuously protects him. This midrash might also hint at the importance of resisting the Romans by not selling out one's fellow Jews.

Catering a Movie: Making the Matzah Look Better

Just as an army moves on its stomach, so a movie set had better have good catering or the extras and featured players aren't going to be able to give their best performances. Pesach is a good bit like this. Even with the limited ingredients available, the cook needs to make every effort to present appetizing food.

The Yerushalmi gives us a tiny peek behind the curtain about Passover cooking in ancient Israel. Women liked to make the meal festive. And entrepreneurs then were just as eager to capitalize on that desire as they are today:

> They fulfill their obligation with Syrian bread (or combed/ colored bread) whether decorated or not, with designs on the bread. Even though they said, "People do not make combed, decorated bread on Passover" (T. Pesachim 2:19). It is taught: Rabbi Yudah said, "Baitos ben Zonin asked Rabban Gamliel and the sages in Yavneh, 'May one make decorated, combed bread on Passover?' They said to him, 'It is forbidden, because a woman tarries over them and they become leavened.' He said to them, 'If so, let them make it in a mold that would enable the unleavened bread to be decorated quickly.' They said to him, 'We cannot permit that, for people would say: All combed breads are prohibited, except for the combed breads of Baitos ben Zonin, which are permitted.'" It is taught: Rabbi Yose says, "They make combed bread thin like wafers, and they do not make thin wafers like white, delicate bread."
>
> (Y. Pesachim 2:4, 20A5–20B1, PM 18A; T. Pesachim 2:19)

The sages don't trust women to heed the time limits on how quickly they must make matzah. However, Baitos ben Zunin saves the day. He was a wealthy resident of Lod who frequently hosted the sages. It was at this man's house that Rabban Gamliel and the other sages had their seder that lasted until dawn, which is mentioned in our Haggadahs (T. Pesachim 10:12). Baitos appears to have been something of a tinkerer and wants to throw the swankiest seder possible.

If this Baitos is related to Marta bat Baitusi, then we are talking about a very wealthy family, indeed. The Baitusians were a group that probably originated with Shimon ben Baitus, who was appointed high priest by Herod the Great in 24 BCE. This was a wealthy clan with strong ties to the Temple in Jerusalem.

I confess, before I read this Yerushalmi, I thought that the all-night seder the sages had in Lod was in a cave, where they were plotting rebellion against the Romans. Once I read this, however, I realized that Rabban Gamliel, a mega-millionaire, would scarcely hold his seder in a cave. It's as if a very rich person today asked to stay in her friend's vacation "cottage" in Aspen, Colorado, for Pesach—the "cottage" with ten bedrooms, a swimming pool, its own ski lift, and a chef to make all the fancy foods for the seder, including the equivalent of matzah made in a waffle iron, or mold.

The take-home for us is that we can make matzah in much prettier shapes and with different technology than we use today. All we have to do is stay within the time limit of eighteen minutes between combining the flour with the water and putting it in the oven.

Lettuce

The Yerushalmi also gives a reason why lettuce is to be included in the seder:

> Just as lettuce is initially sweet but when left in the field becomes bitter, so did the Egyptians do to our ancestors in Egypt. Initially, they were very hospitable, saying to Joseph and his brothers, "The land of Egypt is open before you; settle your father and your brothers in the best part of the land" (Genesis 47:6). Afterward, Pharaoh mistreated them, as it is said, "Ruthlessly, they made life bitter for them with harsh labor at mortar and bricks" (Exodus 1:14).
> (Y. PESACHIM 2:5, 20B2, PM 18A, V 29B; GENESIS RABBAH 95)

The sages assign lettuce a midrashic symbolism. This midrash is left out of most Haggadahs, so we are left with lettuce on the seder plate without really knowing why it was there in the first place. The meaning the Yerushalmi assigns the lettuce would reflect some of Jewish history to that point. It certainly foreshadowed a great deal of Jewish history in the centuries to come. Many times Jews have been welcomed into a country only to be forcefully (and sometimes brutally) made to leave.

Shopping for *Charoset*

Preparations for the seder involved special shopping, just as they do today:

> Vendors of Jerusalem used to say, "Come and take the spices of the commandment!..."
> Rabbi Yehoshua ben Levi said, "It needs to be thick."
> This implies that the *charoset* is a remembrance of the mud.
> There are those who teach, "It needs to stick together."
> This implies that the *charoset* is a remembrance of the blood of the tenth plague and/or the blood on the doorposts that protected the Israelites from that plague.
>
> (Y. Pesachim 10:3, PM 70a, V 37d)

There seems to have been a set of spices and/or ingredients used in the *charoset*. It would be nice to know what the ancient recipe was, but this is all the detail we get. In typical Yerushalmi fashion, we have lots of options for what *charoset* looks like and what it symbolizes.

Fish for the Seder and the Thanksgiving Turkey

Some foods "read" as a certain holiday. All a set decorator has to do is put a turkey with lots of side dishes on a table for the viewer to see "Thanksgiving." For the sages, fish on a table reads as "Shabbat" and/or "Passover."

During Passover, certain food providers took time off:

> The net fishers of Tiberias, the grist makers of Sepphoris, and the grain crushers of Acco took it upon themselves not to work on the intermediate days of Passover. The second and third

make sense, since they work with grain. But the fishermen's ban does not make sense, since they diminish the joy of the festival by decreasing the availability of fish…. Rav Ammi cursed them because they diminished the joy of the holiday….

The people of Mesha took it upon themselves not to sail on the Mediterranean during Passover, because it was dangerous. They came and asked Rabbi Yehudah Hanasi, saying, "Our ancestors were accustomed not to sail on the Great Sea, so what shall we do?" He said to them, "Since your ancestors were accustomed to treat it as a prohibition, do not deviate from the custom of your ancestors, may their souls rest in peace."

(Y. Pesachim 4:1, 29a1–29a2, PM 26a, V 30c–d)

This passage tells us many things. Fish is the symbol of holiday happiness. (In fact, for the Jews of the Judean hills, fresh fish might have been a relative rarity.) Fish continues to be part of the holiday. Gefilte fish, à la the Old Country, is traditionally served on Shabbat and Passover. Old Country–style gefilte fish was fish that was extended by mixing in vegetables and other fillers, since there was not enough actual fish to go around.

Sailing on the Mediterranean was a dangerous business, and ships were regularly lost there during storms, as numerous archeological finds attest. Perhaps the week of Passover tended to be meteorologically volatile, and sailors did not want to go out and get the fish, no matter how much the sages might have cursed them for staying ashore. Rabbi Yehudah Hanasi, displaying the political acumen that allowed him to publish the Mishnah under his imprimatur, allows them to follow the customs of their ancestors. In other words, the sailors can choose what to do. They have options.

The *Afikoman*

We all know that the *afikoman* is a half of a matzah cracker, hidden somewhere so the kids at the seder can find it and collect a handsome ransom for it. Not so fast. The *afikoman* is designed to keep people together, in their groups, lest individuals wander away and not eat the lamb in which they'd bought a stake. Unsurprisingly, the Yerushalmi gives us plenty of options for the *afikoman*.

> Rabbi Shimon said in the name of Rabbi Inani bar Rabbi Sisi, "It is a kind of music."
>
> Rav Ammi [one text says, Rabbi Yochanan] says, "It's a kind of sweet."
>
> Shmuel said, "It's like the mushrooms and pigeons of Chananiah bar Shilat."
>
> (Y. Pesachim 10:6, 85b3, PM 71a, V 37d)

The *afikoman* of the Yerushalmi is certainly *not* a piece of a cracker. But there doesn't seem to be much of a consensus on what it is or even if it's a food. It could be after-dinner entertainment, dessert, or some fancy savory dish. The Yerushalmi feels no need to pick just one or sort through the ideas. It's pretty much anybody's game as to how they're going to end the seder.

How to Be Happy on the Holiday

The Yerushalmi understands that different things make different people happy. And God's spirit rests only on the happy, as we learned above. In fact, a man might want to be particularly nice to his wife after all that cleaning and cooking:

> On a festival, a man is required to make his wife and children happy. With what does he make them happy? With wine. Rabbi Yudah says, "Women, with what is appropriate for them, and children, with what is appropriate for them [T. Pesachim 10:4]. Women, with what is appropriate for them—bright-colored clothes and shoes and belts; and children, with what is appropriate for them—nuts and almonds."
>
> (Y. Pesachim 10:1, 82b1, PM 68b)

The sages understood that the holiday isn't just about pedagogy or worship. It also has to work emotionally, and they were pragmatic enough to know that different things tend to make different groups of people happy.

Fun and Dysfunction at Thanksgiving, and Family Dynamics at the Seder

Family holidays can bring out the best (and worst) in family dynamics. There are numerous movies based on family dysfunction at Thanksgiving and/or Christmas. *Home Alone* and *Avalon* come to mind.

The sages understood that a young bride's first holiday away from her family might bring on a bout of homesickness. Accordingly, the Yerushalmi rules that her feelings should be taken into account when making seder preparations:

> What is a *regel redufin* [a "fleeing festival"]? Said Rabbi Yose bar Rabbi Bun, "This is the first festival after marriage, when her father chases her to her husband's house."
>
> What if she did not go back to her husband's house on the first festival after marriage? May the second festival be considered a *regel redufin*?
>
> In all situations she has a *regel redufin*.
> (Y. Pesachim 8:1, 69A1–69A2, PM 58A–B, V 35c)

Interestingly, only the Yerushalmi mentions this "fleeing festival" (in this passage and in Y. Ketubot 43a). Perhaps this custom only existed in Israel. It's reassuring to know that families have always had trouble with the holidays and that the sages are sensitive to this issue.

Y. v. B.

The Bavli's picture of Passover contains all the main points that the Yerushalmi's does: the banning of *chameitz*, the preparation of the lamb, the four cups of wine, and the seder. But from that point on, the essence of what we find in the Yerushalmi—the fun, the flexibility—is lost. The Bavli wanders off in numerous directions, almost as if the main topic is boring. Perhaps they recognized that the Yerushalmi had basically said it all, so they could feel free to wander into topics such as demonology and parenting.

For Us ...

We would recognize some aspects of the Yerushalmi's Passover: the cleaning, the ban on *chameitz*, the pedagogy, the four cups of wine, the symbols of *maror*, matzah, and *pesach*, the four questions (although they are not our four questions). But family dynamics, the recipe of *charoset*, the very nature of the *afikoman*, the explanation for the four cups of wine, and other details à la the Yerushalmi are limited only by each family's, and each person's, creativity.

18

What Would Shavuot Be Like?

Today, Shavuot is a stunted holiday, bereft of the drama and symbolism that the others festivals have. A group of genetically lactose-intolerant people eats dairy and studies all night? Hardly a compelling holiday.

But if the Yerushalmi had been the Talmud that had won, we would have an entirely different holiday. Think of it as a cross between a marching band contest and a state fair. Everyone would bring his or her very best crops and livestock. There would be a parade into Jerusalem, and the cows would have ornaments put on their horns. Each person would fill a basket with the seven species that the Torah mentions grow in Israel (Deuteronomy 8:8)—wheat, barley, grapes, figs, pomegranates, olives, and dates—and they'd decorate the basket by hanging pigeons off the sides of the basket, as an offering. This isn't just a theoretical construct. A "pane" of a synagogue floor at Sepphorris shows the basket, the species, the pigeons, and the cymbals below them.

But the journey wouldn't stop there. Shavuot really is a holiday all about journeys: from the Red Sea to Sinai, from slavery to freedom, from ancient history to the present.

So you would make your way through the throngs, to the Temple, and there you would recite the narrative of our people's journey and present your first fruits offering to a priest.

This is one of the three times the Torah commands us to *say* something rather than *do* something (the other two are the Priestly Benediction [Numbers 6:22–27] and saying the Blessing after Meals, *Birkat Hamazon* [Deuteronomy 8:10]).

Here is the script and choreography from the Torah:

An Aramean Astray my Ancestor; he went down to Egypt and sojourned there, as menfolk few-in-number, but he became there a nation, great, mighty (in number) and many. Now the Egyptians dealt ill with us and afflicted us, and placed upon us hard servitude. We cried out to YHWH, the God of our fathers, and YHWH hearkened to our voice: He saw our affliction, and our strain, and our oppression, and YHWH took us out from Egypt, with a strong hand and with an outstretched arm, with great awe-inspiring (acts) and with signs and portents, and He brought us to this place and gave us this land, a land flowing with milk and honey. So now—here, I have brought the premier-part of the fruits of the soil that You have given me, O YHWH! Then you are to deposit it before the presence of YHWH your God; and you are to prostrate yourself before the presence of YHWH your God; you are to rejoice in all the good things that YHWH your God has given you and your household, you and the Levite and the sojourner in your midst.

(DEUTERONOMY 26:5–10, THE FIVE BOOKS OF MOSES, TRANS.
EVERETT FOX [NEW YORK: SCHOCKEN BOOKS, 1983])

Of course, these days, the recitation might be a little longer. You would have to include Talmud, Rashi, the Inquisition, and the rebirth of the State of Israel, and so forth, until you could get to the part where you say, basically, "And here I am, still Jewish, still loving Torah, still bound to the Land and to You, God."

This text from Deuteronomy should sound familiar to you. It is the basis for a large part of the Passover seder. But why was it moved to Passover when it was clearly meant for Shavuot? In fact, why did Shavuot, obviously meant to be as wonderful a holiday as Pesach and

Sukkot, turn out to be such an ugly duckling? Well, that would be because, just as there are many kinds of Judaism today, so there were many kinds of Judaism in ancient Israel. And (shocker!) these different groups didn't get along very well.

Why Shavuot Is the Ugly Duckling

In the decades before the Temple fell in 70 CE, there was a group of Jews who lived by the Dead Sea. They disagreed with just about everything that any other Jewish group did. If they had to pick, they'd side with the Sadducees. In addition, Shavuot was their Superbowl of holidays. When this group of Jews died out, the sages, still stung, tried to erase their nemesis's memory, downplaying their favorite holiday so that it ended up the forlorn thing we have today. This is where the movie *Inherit the Wind* comes in. It's a drama about the 1925 Scopes Trial. Two legendary lawyers (William Jennings Bryan and Clarence Darrow) are pitted against each other and, with them, different parts of the town. Darrow really does come off as one of our sages as he demolishes Bryan's biblical literalism.

Reaping the Omer

Nowadays, we *count* the days of the Omer, but in the days of the Temple, they *reaped* the omer. And it wasn't your average "bringing in the sheaves." There was an enormous ceremony that went with it, involving everyone in the area.

How did they make the omer ready for harvest? The messengers of the Court used to go out into the field on the eve of the Festival of Passover and tie the upper part of the grain by handfuls in bunches while it was still connected with the soil, in order to make it easier to reap. And the people of the towns close by assembled there in the evening, at the end of the first day of Passover to reap it with great ceremony.

When it grew dark, the one who was reaping called out to the rest, "Has the sun set?" And they replied, "Yes." He said again, "Has the sun set?" And they answered again, "Yes."

He then asked, "Is this the sickle?" And they responded, "Yes." He repeated the question and they said, "Yes."

He asked, "Is this the basket to hold the grain?" And they said, "Yes." "Is this the basket?" And they said, "Yes."

If it were Shabbat (some say: Saturday night), he asked them, "On Shabbat?" They said, "Yes!" "On this Shabbat?" And they said, "Yes."

"Shall I reap?" And they said, "Reap!" Three times did he call out for each, and to every question, they said, "Yes! Yes! Yes!"

And why was this whole procedure carried out? Because of the Baitusi, who used to maintain that the omer must not be reaped at the end of the first festival day of Passover.

(M. MENACHOT 10:3)

Why such a fuss? Because the Dead Sea Scrolls group and their pals, the Baitusi, didn't think that the sages counted the days of the Omer correctly. The Dead Sea folks lost (as did the Baitusi), and the sages, frankly, stick it to them with this elaborate reaping ritual. If they had known about fireworks, they would have mandated them. They wanted to make sure those Dead Sea guys could hear them counting out the procedure in a way, and on a day, that they thought was in error.

You don't have to use a lot of imagination to see all the revelry (and work) in this ritual. And *no one* would have been able to miss the fact that the reaping was being done on the day the *sages* calculated was the correct one. This almost sounds like a football game, with all the call-and-response shouting going on. It's good to know that the "Horse! Mule!" scene in *Fiddler on the Roof* has ancient antecedents.

Everyone Needs Help with the Hebrew: Ancient Cue Cards

It might seem today as if many people who come to services need help when it comes to reciting the prayers in Hebrew. But guess what? People had the same problem in ancient Israel! We tend to think that Jews in ancient days, and really, up to the last century, were faithfully observant and naturally knowledgeable about Judaism in ways that we are not. Not so, says the Mishnah:

> While the basket was still on his shoulder, he would recite "I profess this day unto the Lord your God" (Deuteronomy 26:3) until the completion of the passage (Deuteronomy 26:10)…. He would then deposit the basket by the side of the altar, bow, and depart.
>
> Originally all who knew how to recite would recite, while those unable to do so would repeat it after the priest. But when people stopped coming and bringing their first fruits, it was decided that both those who could and those who could not recite should repeat the words.
>
> (M. BIKKURIM 3:6–7, 3:4, 24B1–3)

We should take heart! It's always been tough to remember the Hebrew. And this mishnah shows that the proper response when people are having a tough time is to make it easy for them, to give them ways to participate that won't make them feel embarrassed. Indeed, it is incumbent on those who know more to forgo displaying this in order to make it easier for those who know less.

Y. v. B.

Of all the holidays, the difference between the Yerushalmi and the Bavli regarding Shavuot is the greatest because *there is no Bavli on this tractate of Mishnah*. There is silence. Lots and lots of silence.

For Us …

Let's give Shavuot the makeover it deserves. The Bavli never covered tractate Bikkurim (they didn't even want to call the tractate Shavuot), so these observances became lost to us. But studying Yerushalmi helps us know what this holiday once was and what it could be again.

We can transform the Omer counting from the dolorous business it's become to what it probably was before: a countdown that gets more and more raucous the closer we get to the holiday. And we can make Shavuot a parade, a state fair, a farmers' market on steroids. It could be a celebration of our history, from biblical times right up to the present: from Abraham to Moses to Joshua to David, from the destruction of the Temple to the wisdom of the sages, from Babylonia to Spain to Poland to America and back to Israel again. We could present our gifts to the synagogue or to Israel and affirm, as we do so, that we are connected to this long, long line of Jews who have rejoiced in the bounty of the land and the harvest of the spring.

Bottom line? We can do *much* better than staying up all night, eating blintzes and cheesecake.

19

Purim and Hanukkah

There are some movies that the studios are sure will make big bucks: *Pirates of the Caribbean*, *Twilight*, *Harry Potter*, Pixar and Disney animated features. Then there are surprising films that hit it big. People of my generation will remember *Breaking Away*, a film about bike racing in Indiana that was a huge "sleeper" hit. More recently, *My Big Fat Greek Wedding* and *March of the Penguins* were blockbusters that came out of the blue. These sorts of movies are like a character actor compared to a star: they may not be glamorous, but they can tell a great, quirky story. Purim and Hanukkah, when compared with the High Holy Days and the pilgrimage festivals, are like those sleeper films.

Let's take Purim first. Today, Purim is our most flexible holiday. Even the day on which it's observed isn't a given. It could be on a Thursday or a Sunday, on the fourteenth of Adar or the fifteenth, depending on whether you live in a walled city or not. And the religiosity of the day isn't exactly, let's say, deep.

It's possible that the day moves around so much because it's associated with other, earlier holidays. The Yerushalmi even mentions these earlier holidays (Y. Megillah 1:1). The one that's closest to Purim is Nicanor Day (the thirteenth of Adar). On this day, a Greek king who vowed to destroy Jerusalem was himself killed by a small tactical team of Israelis. The king's head and hands were set on pikes outside the city. Purim could also be related to Trajan's Day, the twelfth of Adar. This holiday marks the anniversary of the lifting of Trajan's decrees against Jewish practice.

These both seem like far more legitimate reasons for observing a holiday than a day on which a Jewish girl intermarries and convinces her drunkard husband to dispense mercy to the Jewish people. And we certainly wouldn't be fasting on the twelfth or thirteenth of Adar (as we do today), regardless. These were days of rejoicing. Indeed, there were many days that celebrated various victories in Israel's history before the Second Temple was destroyed.

After the Temple was destroyed, the sages were left with these victory celebrations that simply didn't fit in with their depressed mood and the simple, appalling truth that the Romans weren't going away as other tyrants had done. And victories of any sort against the Romans were thin on the ground, particularly after the defeat Israel suffered following the end of the Bar Kokhba Revolt in 135 CE. So memories of those victories of bygone days were done away with, and a different, more somber feel began to permeate the Jewish calendar. But even so, Purim and Hanukkah remained as days of merriment.

How to Observe Purim: Lots of Options

The text that gives us the four observances of Purim is Esther 9:19:

> Therefore the Jews of the villages, who live in the open towns, celebrate the fourteenth day of the month of Adar, a day for gladness and feasting and holiday making and a day on which they send choice portions to one another.
>
> (ESTHER 9:19)

The sages ask their usual question: why do we have all these separate verbs when one or two might have sufficed? So they give each phrase its own meaning:

> Rav Nachman bar Rav Shmuel bar Nachman said in regard to "gladness," "On this basis we learn that it is forbidden to eulogize the dead.
>
> "Feasting": "On this basis we learn that it is forbidden to fast on that day."

"And holiday making": "On this basis we learn that it is forbidden to do labor on that day."

Said Rav Chelbo, "Many times I sat in session before Rav Shmuel bar Nachman and I never heard this teaching from him."

Rav Nachman bar Rav Shmuel said to him, "Are you saying that you heard everything my father said?"

There is a story about Rabbi that shows he differs. For Rabbi would publicize his deeds on only two days of the year. On the seventeenth of Tammuz he would go to a public bath, and on Purim he would plant a tree.

(Y. MEGILLAH 1:1, PM 3A–B, V 70B)

This passage is surprising for a number of reasons. First of all, today, labor *is* permitted on Purim. In other words, there are no restrictions such as there are on Shabbat or festivals. You may turn on lights, cook food, drive a car, and so on, on Purim. But more surprising is that Rabbi—our Rabbi Yehudah Hanasi, the promulgator of our Mishnah—loses after a public battle. He wins regarding Purim: work is allowed. (Don't you love that his act of work is to plant a tree?) But he loses on the seventeenth of Tammuz: that's still a fast day on which one does not bathe from sunup to sundown. Of course, if Rabbi has to come out so publicly on one side or another, it means that nothing has been decided.

The rest of Yerushalmi Megillah offers a similar picture of a holiday only halfway through formation, if that. It can be read on different days in big cities (i.e., walled cities) versus villages. Whether the *Megillah* (Scroll of Esther) may be read by an individual or by a minyan is still up for grabs. There is even plenty of wiggle room regarding what may be done with the gifts to the poor that are dispensed on Purim:

As to funds collected for the poor for the celebration of Purim, these funds are to be used for Purim....

"They do not enforce the religious requirements given to the poor on Purim in a meticulous way" (T. Megillah 1:5), but whoever puts out his hand to take the money given for the support of the poor is given what he wants.

(Y. MEGILLAH 1:4, PM 5A)

Usually, those who collect and dispense charity do due diligence. You won't be turned away from a soup kitchen for any reason. But if you're looking for some sort of more long-lasting charity, community leaders will want some evidence of your need ... except on Purim. This makes sense if we see Purim as a ritual of rebellion. On this day, all the rules go right out the door. So the normal rules about charity give way to the liberal dispensing of charity, with no means test applied.

A Pedagogical Holiday

So, how did Purim become an established holiday? It wasn't a Temple holiday. There are no sacrifices associated with it. It wasn't even a holiday that originated in the Land of Israel. Why did Purim survive, while Nicanor Day and Trajan Day fell by the wayside?

The fictional nature of the Purim story lends itself to political theater. In addition, it is a pedagogical holiday, that is, it is a holiday based on reading a scriptural text. And this is a template that the sages understood and endorsed.

Which leads us to the next obvious question: Hanukkah? How did *that* happen?

What Would Hanukkah Be Like?

The more you think about it, the less likely it seems that Hanukkah would have a place in the Jewish calendar. A holiday that lasts eight days? That has no foundation in Jewish Scripture? That celebrates the recapture of a Temple that is now so profoundly conquered you'd have to go to Rome to retrieve the guts of the place (the menorah and the ark)? The Yerushalmi recognizes that this holiday exists. But Hanukkah doesn't become the full-blown ritual that we know until it surfaces as such in the Bavli.

Hanukkah really is a victory celebration, something like Armistice Day or VE Day or VJ Day. Tellingly, there is no Mishnah tractate devoted to this holiday. It isn't ever truly discussed systematically in the Yerushalmi (as it is in the Bavli). The midrash collections do discuss it, but there is nothing in our sources from the Land of Israel that approaches the material in B. Shabbat 21a–24a, which is a "mini-tractate" discussing Hanukkah. That's where we find the different ways Beit Hillel and Beit Shammai light the menorah and the story of the oil that miraculously lasted for eight days.

The discussion of Hanukkah in the Yerushalmi is centered on doing away with the holidays in the Fasting Scroll, that is, the list of military holidays celebrated while the Second Temple stood. The scroll gets its name from the fact that fasting on these holidays is prohibited. You could think of it as a list of federal holidays.

> Rabbi Yochanan said, "The Fasting Scroll has been nullified."
>
> Said Rabbi Yochanan, "Last night I was sitting and repeating the following: An incident happened that they decreed a fast in Lod during Hanukkah. Rabbi Eliezer went and told Rabbi Yehoshua about it. Rabbi Yehoshua washed himself [which one mustn't do while fasting] and said to them, 'Go and observe a fast as a penalty for having fasted.' [That is, you shouldn't have fasted on Hanukkah; so now go fast for this sin.]
>
> "Now how can you say, then, that the rules of the Fasting Scroll have been nullified, since the scroll says that one may not fast on Hanukkah and we see that Rabbi Eliezer and Rabbi Yehoshua affirm that, in fact, one may not fast on Hanukkah?"
>
> Said Rabbi Abba, "Even though you maintain that the rules of the Fasting Scroll have been nullified, as to the celebration of Hanukkah and Purim they have not been nullified."
>
> Rabbi Yonatan fasted on the entire eve of the New Year. Rabbi Avin fasted on the entire eve of the festival of Sukkot.
>
> Rabbi Zeira fasted three hundred fasts, and some say, nine hundred fasts, and he paid no attention at all to the days listed in the Fasting Scroll on which one is not supposed to fast.
>
> (Y. NEDARIM 8:1, PM 26B, V 40D)

Once more, the Yerushalmi is all over the board. It's amazing to see those two old foes/friends (Rabbi Eliezer and Rabbi Yehoshua) agreeing with each other for once. Rabbi Eliezer was rich and stubborn and liked a good fight. Rabbi Yehoshua was poor and tractable and tried to avoid fighting. But they both agree here that Hanukkah escapes the fate of the other holidays in the Fasting Scroll. In an unusual display of political maneuvering, Rabbi Yehoshua stands up for Hanukkah. But, typically (for the Yerushalmi), we then find that the picture is far from clear. One sage says not to fast on Hanukkah, while two other very great sages disregard all calendrical considerations in their fasting. In the end, decisions about these observances are left up to the individual.

The *Lulav* and the Hanukkah Lights

Unsurprisingly, the discussion over how to bless the menorah offers an option you haven't heard:

> How do they say a blessing over the Hanukkah light? Rav said, "Blessed … commanded us concerning the commandment to kindle the Hanukkah light [*v'tzivanu al mitzvat ner hanukkah*]."
> (Y. Sukkah 3:4, 18a2–18a3)

This is part of a long comparison of the blessing over the Hanukkah candles and the blessing said before one waves the *lulav*. This is a logical argument. Hanukkah may have originated with a delayed observance of Sukkot. That holiday's observance was of paramount importance, because the water libation ceremony was critical for bringing rain.

After the Maccabees retook the Temple and it was set in order, Sukkot (an eight-day holiday) was observed. A year later, this "second Sukkot" was remembered with the lighting of candles. Thus, a comparison between the waving of the *lulav* and the lighting of the menorah makes sense. It's hard to know when this blessing was dropped and the one we say now was adopted. Regardless, we may feel free to use this blessing from the Yerushalmi, if we like.

A Different Miracle

The Yerushalmi gives us an alternative to the "oil lasting eight days" part of the Hanukkah story:

In the days of the Greek regime, the Jews inside the city would lower two boxes full of gold, and in return, the Greeks would send up two lambs for the daily offering. One time, the Jews lowered the two boxes of gold, but the Greeks sent them up two goats [which are not used for the daily sacrifice]. At that moment, the Holy One, blessed be He, enlightened their eyes, and they discovered two prechecked lambs in the Chamber of the Lambs.

(Y. Berakhot 4:1, 43b2)

This sounds much less like a Hanukkah fairy tale (à la the Bavli) and much more like something that might actually have happened. This passage goes on and tells a very similar story about the Jews of Jerusalem and the Roman siege. The Romans send up two pigs, opening the gates of misfortune and paving the way for the Temple's destruction.

So the Yerushalmi gives us a holiday in the process of "becoming." It's certainly nothing like the holiday described in B. Shabbat 21a–24a.

What's the Point? Resisting the Romans!

So why keep the holiday alive at all? What purpose did it serve? Perhaps it was a form of resistance against the Romans in the land. Such resistance had to take subtle forms. It was a "guerilla" resistance, finding voice where and when it could. The record of that resistance can be found not only in text but also in the stones of Israel. For example, an idol must be utterly destroyed for its toxicity to be broken (Y. Shabbat 9:1). If it wasn't possible to do this, Jews would deface idols and political statuary to show that the stones had no power. You can see such defaced statues in Israel to this very day.

There seems to me to be both a tension and a connection between Purim and Hanukkah. On the one hand, Purim is a text-based holiday. The Scroll of Esther made it into the *Tanakh*, and so it is granted some heft on that account. But it's a story that accepts, even glorifies, diaspora life. On the other hand, Hanukkah is clearly a tale of the Land of Israel and its military prowess. But the books that tell its story (1 and 2 Maccabees) were not included in Jewish Scripture. (They were, however, read in Sephardic synagogues on Hanukkah.) So why did Purim and Hanukkah survive? They should have met the fate of every other such holiday, that is, fallen into disuse. Could they have been a form of protest against foreign occupation? After all, to Greek and Roman eyes, festivals of light during the darkest part of the year would hardly seem odd. (In fact, to Greek eyes, Purim—a drunken festival with some learning thrown in—probably looked like Greek behavior.) Is it possible that the Romans in Israel tolerated Hanukkah because they saw it as a festival of lights, not as a religious or political festival? In that sense, Hanukkah might look a good deal like home Passover celebrations: family gatherings or even just a candle in the window, without any untoward public gathering that might look like rebellion.

Y. v. B.

The biggest contrast here is Hanukkah. For the Bavli, Hanukkah involves a set of elaborate, deliberate procedures in terms of lighting the candles correctly and a recounting of a story about which the Israeli sources know nothing. It is one of the best examples of the Bavli locking down one right way to do something while the Yerushalmi is open to many ways of observance. Purim is also more regimented in the Bavli, but it seems to have been a rather flexible holiday there, as well.

For Us ...

For us, the outcomes of a Yerushalmi-style Purim or Hanukkah are freeing. We can slide the date of Purim around so that its observance does not constitute a burden. We are not locked into one way of lighting and blessing the Hanukkah candles. We are free to make the holidays our own, while remaining true to some of our most ancient texts and tales.

20

Fast Days

The Seventeenth of Tammuz:
Stage the Breaking of the Ten Commandments

Imagine that you are Cecil B. DeMille and you are directing *The Ten Commandments*. How would you stage the breaking of the tablets? Would Moses be angry? Would he throw them? The Yerushalmi offers a scenario that features *Heichalot* mysticism.

One aspect of *Heichalot* mysticism is that it likes to count … anything, right down to the size of the tablets that Moses broke. The fast of the seventeenth of Tammuz commemorates the date on which the tablets were broken (M. Ta'anit 4:5). The Yerushalmi describes the tablets' size, their weight, and their other mystical properties.

Rabbi Yishmael taught, "The Holy One, blessed be He, told him to break the tablets … and afterward said, 'You did well in breaking them.'"

Rabbi Shmuel bar Nachman said in the name of Rabbi Yonatan, "The tablets were six handbreadths long and three broad. Moses held onto two handbreadths and the Holy One, blessed be He, held onto two of them and there was a space of two handbreadths in the middle. When the Israelites worshipped the golden calf, the Holy One, blessed be He, tried to snatch the tablets out of Moses's hand. But Moses's hand was stronger, and he snatched them from God.…"

Rabbi Yochanan said in the name of Rabbi Yose bar Abaye, "The tablets wanted to fly, but Moses was holding on to them...."

It was taught in the name of Rabbi Nehemiah, "The writing itself flew off the tablets."

Rabbi Ezra in the name of Rabbi Yehudah bar Rabbi Shimon: "The tablets weighed forty *seahs*, and the writing was holding them up. When the writing flew off, the tablets became heavy in Moses's hands, and they fell and were broken."

(Y. TA'ANIT 4:5)

According to Rabbi Yochanan, the tablets want to fly. According to Rabbi Nehemiah, it's the writing that flies. And according to Rabbi Ezra, the writing acts like helium in a balloon, keeping the tablets aloft. So the tablets could be seen as living things. We tend to think of them as stones, but they might better be thought of as coral. Coral seems to be a rock, but it's actually a living being. The writing is alive, as well.

All four participants in this story have an independent will: God, Moses, the tablets, and the writing. All four participants witness the Israelites worshipping the golden calf, and all four react in their own way. We could also see the different opinions as describing a step-by-step process rather than alternative scenarios.

At first, the tablets and the writing stay passive, leaving it up to God and Moses. God tries to withdraw the tablets, but Moses overpowers God(!). Then the tablets try to withdraw, but Moses overpowers them, as well. Finally, the writing flies off. The writing is the animating force that makes it possible for Moses to hold up the tablets at all. Once it flies (or flees—the Hebrew words differ by only one letter [*lifvroach/ livroach*]), the tablets become rocks. At that point, Moses simply cannot manage their weight and drops them. This scenario is not to be found in the Bavli or midrash collections. It is recorded only in the Yerushalmi.

The fast on the seventeenth of Tammuz is one that might not have too much meaning for today's Jews. But the Yerushalmi lets us imagine it as an epic moment in which the tablets, themselves, have a say in where they want to go. And this allows us to experience Judaism as a religion in which our holiest things are, in a very real sense, *alive*. This is a life of religious imagination you'll find most vibrantly in the Yerushalmi.

What Would Tisha B'Av Be Like?

Once you have built a set and filmed on it, there's really only one thing left to do: wreck it. In some films, this takes the form of literally blowing up the set, for example, the destruction of Sauron's tower in *The Return of the King* or blowing up Parliament in *V for Vendetta*. Or it could be something a bit less dramatic, such as the shoot-'em-up scene in Spike Lee's *Inside Man*. Tishah B'Av is all about set wrecking.

The first thing to remember is that Tisha B'Av would be local news. And it would not be just religious news. People made pilgrimages to the Temple to bring their sacrifices, fueling a dynamic local economy that included building and maintaining a whole complex of *mikva'ot* to purify those bringing offerings. (No one in a state of ritual impurity could enter the Temple, and one might become ritually impure on the way, perhaps encountering a corpse or a burial ground. So it made sense to put off ritual purification until just before you would enter the Temple.)

In addition to the *mikva'ot*, there was a great market in money changing. People would save money to spend in Jerusalem on their pilgrimage. Indeed, the Temple housed a safe-deposit box system. It was considered the safest place in Jerusalem, since it was guarded twenty-four hours a day.

Instead of bringing an animal, pilgrims might have brought money and bought one in Jerusalem. There was, in fact, a large sheep market outside the Temple for just this purpose. In addition, food vendors, hoteliers, restaurants, tour guides, translators, and the like would have made good use of the opportunity the Temple's attraction would have for Jews of all lands. In your mind, I'd like you to stand in the Temple's outer court and see the bustling world that it was, lifting real estate values, supporting all manner of enterprises.

And now imagine it wrecked. And the Romans didn't just wreck the Temple. They ruined the land itself, both its ecology and its economy. Think of 9/11. Now, of course, we understand that the towers could collapse. But as we watched them burn that day, until the first one went down, their collapse was an inconceivable thought. And the disaster poisoned the atmosphere in lower Manhattan and the first responders who labored to find people in the rubble. Outside of New York City, we experienced the tragedy from a distance. But for those in Manhattan it was an immediate and ongoing peril: they were covered by toxic dust, trapped on the island. (The only way in and out that day was on the water; the bridges and tunnels were closed.) The wrecking and burning of the Temple were something like this, but even worse.

The destruction of the Temple was local news, and it was remembered in the Yerushalmi not only as a day of spiritual calamity, but also as a day of bitterness for a way of life crushed. The Romans ruined a great source of tax revenue in a city that had no great strategic advantage. Jerusalem is up in the hill country, far from the plains that provide easy transport, sea access, and arable land. They destroyed the Temple because it had become a symbol of the Jews' defiance. The Yerushalmi records just how local, and personal, the Temple's destruction was:

"Betar was taken" (M. Ta'anit 4:5). Rabbi would derive by exegesis twenty-four tragic events from the verse: "The Lord has destroyed without mercy all the habitations of Jacob; in His wrath He has broken down the strongholds of the daughter of Judah; He has brought down to the ground in dishonor the kingdom and its rulers" (Lamentations 2:2).

Rabbi Yochanan derived sixty tragic events from the same verse.

Did Rabbi Yochanan then find more than Rabbi did in the same verse? Surely not.

But because Rabbi lived nearer to the time of the Temple's destruction, there were old men in the congregation who remembered what had happened, and when he gave his exegesis, they would weep and fall silent and get up and leave.

(Y. Ta'anit 4:5, PM 24a)

Rabbi's situation is like talking about the Holocaust with actual survivors. The old men who would weep actually remembered the destruction. Rabbi Yochanan is later, beyond living memory of the Temple's destruction.

Still, the Yerushalmi records basic details about the Second Temple's destruction:

> On the seventh of Av they entered the Temple. On the eighth they battered it down. On the ninth they set fire to it, and on the tenth it burned down.
>
> Rabbi Yehoshua ben Levi fasted on the ninth and on the tenth.
>
> Rabbi Levi fasted on the ninth and on the night prior to the tenth.
>
> Rabbi Ba bar Zavda in the name of Rabbi Chanina: Rabbi sought to uproot the ninth of Av that coincided with Shabbat and not celebrate it at all, but they did not concur with him. He said, "Since it has been postponed, let it be canceled this year and not observed at all." They said to him, "Let it be postponed until the next day and observed on Sunday."
>
> (Y. MEGILLAH 1:4, PM 5B)

As ever, we see that there are many different positions, and the details are still in flux, with lots of bargaining going on. And Rabbi, our Rabbi Yehudah Hanasi, loses again.

Messianic Hopes Gone for Good

Have you ever wondered why there is such great nostalgia for the Temple, and why, even today, there are so many people who want to see it rebuilt? It seems an odd wish, in that I doubt many Jews would want to bring animal offerings anymore, though they might want to see a rebuilt Temple and offer grain or wine (or, more practically, gifts of tzedakah). It is likely that had the Temple never been destroyed, it would have gradually evolved and, perhaps, taken a much-reduced place in Jewish thought.

So why is there such yearning for the Temple? It is written into the *Musaf Amidah* for the festivals itself:

> Because of our sins we were exiled from our land and driven far from our country. We cannot go up to appear and bow before You and to perform our duties in Your chosen House, the great and holy Temple that was called by Your name, because of the hand that has stretched out against Your sanctuary. May it be Your will, Lord our God and God of our ancestors, merciful King, that You, in Your abounding compassion, may once more have mercy on us and on Your sanctuary, rebuilding it swiftly and adding to its glory. Our Father, our King, reveal the glory of Your kingdom to us swiftly. Appear and be exalted over us in the sight of all that lives. Bring back our scattered ones from among the nations, and gather our dispersed people from the ends of the earth. Lead us to Zion, Your city, in jubilation, and to Jerusalem, home of Your Temple, with everlasting joy.
>
> (SIDDUR, FESTIVAL *MUSAF*)

Judaism is based on memory, not history. This viewpoint led the sages to assume that history repeats itself in predictable, repeating cycles. So the Jews, seeing that the First Temple was rebuilt in seventy years, assumed that the Second Temple would be rebuilt seventy years after its destruction, as well. It is easy to see the Bar Kokhba Revolt (132–135 CE) as the Jews' attempt to "prime the pump," so to speak, and prepare the way for the rebuilding that would begin in 140 CE.

So when this did not happen, and after the Romans' draconian response to the Bar Kokhba Revolt, the Jews naturally questioned why previous generations merited having the Temple rebuilt for them and they did not. The inevitable answer was that previous generations had some merit that the current generation did not have. The Yerushalmi gives the "diagnosis":

> We have found that the First Temple was destroyed because the Jews of that time worshipped idols, committed adultery, and committed murder.

But regarding the destruction of the Second Temple, we know that the Jews learned Torah, practiced mitzvot, and gave tithes as commanded and that they behaved in all the proper ways. So why was the Second Temple destroyed? It was destroyed because the Jews of that time loved money and hated one another with a baseless hatred [sin'at chinam].

(Y. YOMA 1:1)

The inability of the Jews to work together brought the city down. It's not just a homily. Because they did not fight as a unified force, they gave the Romans the opportunity they needed for victory.

Apparently, Rabbi Akiba believed that the Bar Kochba Revolt would herald redemption … and the rebuilding of the Temple.

Rabbi Shimon bar Yochai taught: Akiba, my master, would interpret the following verse, "A star [kochav] shall come forth out of Jacob" (Numbers 24:17), (Kozva) shall come forth out of Jacob.

When Rabbi Akiba saw Bar Kozva (i.e., Bar Kokhba), he said, "This is the King Messiah." Rabbi Yochanan ben Torta said, "Akiba! Grass will grow in your cheeks and the Messiah will not yet have come!"

(Y. TA'ANIT 4:6, PM 24A)

According to the Yerushalmi, Rabbi Akiba bought into the messianism. (Why wouldn't he? He was still operating on the assumption that history would repeat itself.) He was probably not the only one with these hopes.

What we get from the Yerushalmi is a sense of the immediacy of these events. The revolt happened near where this document was put together. It is one thing to write about things that happened in another country several centuries ago. It's another thing to write a history where there are living people who remember, or whose grandparents remember, the actual reality of the events. The Yerushalmi was written by people who knew where the skeletons were buried, literally.

Purim and Hanukkah and the
Seventeenth of Tammuz and the Ninth of Av

These four holidays balance out the calendar. We have two fast days to commemorate Jerusalem's destruction (the seventeenth of Tammuz and the ninth of Av). Balanced against these, we have Hanukkah, commemorating the victory over the Greeks and the reestablishment of the Temple's service. And we have Purim, commemorating a surprise victory over Haman.

Y. v. B.

The fast days of the seventeenth of Tammuz and the ninth of Av are both observed in the Yerushalmi and the Bavli, but in the Bavli, we miss out on the mystical meanings and the immediate political, economic, and historical grief that is so palpable in the Yerushalmi.

For Us ...

This balancing of the calendar gives us an important message: the Jewish calendar need not be the dolorous thing it has become. Counting the Omer was more likely to have been a countdown to liftoff (i.e., Shavuot). And even the saddest holidays were counterbalanced with happy ones. We are given license, therefore, to keep trimming the mood of the calendar until we have a balance of fasts and festivities.

Part 4

Life Cycle

Although some fifteen hundred years separates our lives from the lives of the sages who composed the Yerushalmi, some things have remained constant over the centuries. We are still born. We still go to school. We still fall in love and get married. We still grow old, and we still die. And the systems and rituals the sages put into place for each of these life-cycle transformations still work for us as well as they did fifteen hundred years ago. But, as with everything else, there are subtle differences between the approaches of the Yerushalmi and the Bavli when it comes to these moments. And the Yerushalmi offers us some surprises, not the least of which is the amount of power women had to control much of their lives.

21

Childbirth
(Women Are in Charge)
and Parenthood

hildbirth in the movies is pretty predictable. The husband flutters about, superfluous. The woman is screaming her head off, and the baby is born looking better than any actual newborn fresh from the womb looks. (In *She's Having a Baby*, this is done to great comedic effect.)

Childbirth in the Yerushalmi is a bit more mysterious ... for the men, that is. Not so very long ago it was standard practice for men to sit in some separate room, anxiously waiting while their wives gave birth to their children in another room. They might have had some indirect input into the proceedings, but basically they were kept out of this process. This image is an apt one when describing the process of childbirth in the sages' day, as well.

For example, even when a question is addressed to a sage on a matter about which he does have authority—what are permissible violations of Sabbath restrictions during childbirth—the sage defers to women's customs. Of course, the sages had come up with a theoretical approach to the problem of childbirth on the Sabbath:

> They may deliver a woman on Shabbat, and they summon a midwife for her from anyplace, and profane the Shabbat on her account, and tie up the navel. Rabbi Yose says, "They even cut it."
>
> (M. SHABBAT 18:3)

Rabbi Yose's opinion is an individual opinion, and therefore, we would think it is not accepted as a general rule. (In general, only the opinions of the anonymous majority are adopted, and individual opinions, though important, do not become normative.) His opinion here is that the umbilical cord may be cut, an additional profanation of Shabbat that the majority apparently feels need not be performed, the tying off of the cord being enough. We find in the following case, however, that Rabbi Yose's opinion is the one used in practice:

> A servant girl of Bar Kappara gave birth to a child on the Sabbath. A woman came and asked Rabbi whether they might tie and cut the umbilical cord. He said to her, "Go and ask the midwife." She said to him, "There is no midwife." He said to her, "Go and follow your usual practice." She said to him, "There is no established practice." He said to her, "Go and cut the umbilical cord, in line with the view of Rabbi Yose" (M. Shabbat 18:3).
>
> (Y. SHABBAT 18:3, PM 85B)

In this case, practice actually followed Rabbi Yose's view. But what is really interesting is that Rabbi would rather not offer an opinion and prefers to leave it up to the midwife. However, when cornered, he offers a lenient ruling based on an individual's opinion.

This whole scenario makes us wonder how many of these decisions were left up to the midwives and the women they aided. Rabbi is willing to let a midwife or even any woman attending the birth decide this issue. Was there a whole set of birth lore and standard rules of practice about birth of which the sages were ignorant? This passage seems to suggest that this could have been the case.

(Il)legitimacy

It may not be surprising that in the unsettled environment of Israel under Roman rule, keeping track of who was a legitimate child and who was illegitimate (i.e., born of an adulterous union) got lost in the shuffle:

God guarded them and an actual case involving illegitimacy
never took place.

> (Y. KIDDUSHIN 1:1, PM 4A; Y. YEVAMOT 1:6, PM 9A;
> SEE B. YEVAMOT 14A FOR THIS SAME DISCUSSION WITHOUT THIS
> CONCLUSION)

In the chaos of Roman-ruled Israel, these sorts of concerns evidently
went by the board. We actually have a parallel to this in modern times.
After the Holocaust, there were untold thousands of widows who
could not prove that their husbands had died. There were no living
witnesses, no bodies, nothing. Yet one rabbi, Moshe Steinberg, made
it his life's mission to find a way to permit every single one of these
women to remarry if they so desired.

Y. v. B.

Here we see a marked difference between the Yerushalmi and the
Bavli. The Yerushalmi doesn't insist that you track down your great-
grandparents to prove you're Jewish. There's so much upheaval
in the land that there's no way to do anything more than give this
business more than a pro-forma going-over. In fact, it bears more
than a little resemblance to Holocaust and post-Holocaust Europe.
It is only when people have lived in peace and stability that these
categories can even begin to become crucial. This phrase, "God
guarded them and no such case of illegitimacy ever happened,"
appears only in the Yerushalmi.

What Parents Must Do for Their Children

What are parents financially obligated to provide for their children?
Parents are obligated to see that their children experience those mitzvot they are too young to observe themselves.

> Any mitzvah that a son is too young to do for himself his father
> is obligated to do for him, that is, circumcise him, redeem him,

teach him Torah, teach him a trade, and marry him off to a woman. Rabbi Akiba says, "He is also obligated to teach him to swim in the water."

(Y. KIDDUSHIN 1:7; T. KIDDUSHIN 1:1, PM 19A)

The sages work out their paradigm of parent-child relationships in terms of the father-son relationship. What must a father do for his son? He must see that he is ritually circumcised and, if the child is the firstborn, redeemed in a ceremony called *pidyon haben*, the redemption of the firstborn son. On the thirty-first day after the boy's birth, the father gives five silver coins to any *kohen*. The *kohen* may keep the coins, return them to the father, or donate them to charity.

Parents are also required to support their children until the age of six. Any care and feeding of the child after that point constitute charity. This was mandated in one of the Decrees of Usha, made after the destruction of the Second Temple (see Y. Ketubot 4:8), meaning times were so desperate that children were not even being fed up to the age of six.

Y. v. B.

Here, for once, the Yerushalmi and Bavli agree with each other. Children do not come gift wrapped on their thirteenth birthdays, ready to be fully functioning Jewish adults. They must be educated in appropriate ways as they grow until they become adults.

For Us ...

We are blessed to live in far more stable times and places than did the sages of the Yerushalmi. They gave us the minimum that we must do, but we are free to do much more for our children. And both the Yerushalmi and the Bavli give us guidelines on how to parent our children until they're independent.

22

School, Coming of Age, and Learning Differences

The number of "coming of age" movies really is too long to catalogue. Pick your favorite: *Breaking Away*, *Hoosiers*, *Say Anything*, *Easy A*, *Temple Grandin*, and *Dead Poets Society* are just the tip of this iceberg. Learning was the heart of the rabbinic endeavor. The sages understood that different people learn in different ways:

> Said Rabbi Yochanan, "It is an established covenant that what one studies in a *beit k'neset*, one does not quickly forget."
>
> Said Rabbi Yochanan of Eintunyata, "It is an established covenant that what one learns alone, one does not quickly forget...."
>
> Said Rabbi Yochanan, "It is an established covenant that when one learns *aggadah* [i.e., stories, midrash] from a book, one does not quickly forget."
>
> Rabbi Tanchum: "One who reasons [*soveir*] when he studies does not quickly forget."
>
> (Y. Berakhot 5:1, 54a3)

The sages understood that people learn in different ways. Some people learn better in public, others in private, some through intense analysis, others through stories. Some learn visually, others aurally.

Also, we see that learning law is certainly *not* the sages' exclusive goal. Not only do the sages want their students to study homiletical materials (*aggadot* = stories), but they also want them to study them *from a book*. So often we're presented with the concept that rabbinic literature was not written down but was passed along orally, from generation to generation. Here we see that this simply wasn't the case. The books already existed in Rabbi Yochanan's day (250–290 CE).

A Learning System or a Legal System?

The Yerushalmi understands that there are different kinds of material to learn:

> Scripture (*Mikra*)
> Mishnah
> Talmud
> *Aggadah*

It also lists the following rabbinic subjects:

> The traditions (*hehalakhot*)
> Stories (*aggadot*)
> *Toseftot*
> Talmud
>   (Y. Peah 2:4, 23a1)

The only kinds of learning that make both lists are *aggadot* and Talmud. *Halakhah* and *aggadah* are also contrasted in Y. Shabbat 1:2. There, we learn that one cannot repeat *halakhot* in a state of ritual impurity, but one *may* learn *aggadot* in such a condition. The question is, is this because *aggadot* are more or less important than the *halakhot*?

The Yerushalmi does *not* reflect a culture that is creating a legal system. Rather, it's a *learning* system. The "halakhic bottom line" mentality with which Talmud is learned today would likely astound and disappoint the Yerushalmi's sages.

Y. v. B.

Learning is the hallmark of the rabbinic enterprise in both the Yerushalmi and the Bavli. But the Yerushalmi sorts different kinds of texts into different types of collections: Mishnah, Tosefta, Gemara, midrash, *aggadah*, and *halakhah*. The Bavli puts all these sorts of documents into one document, that is, the Bavli itself. To step away from our movie analogy, if the Yerushalmi and related documents are fruit salad, in which you can sort out the component ingredients, then the Bavli is a smoothie, in which all the documents are puréed together.

Grandparents Are an Important Part of the Educational Process

The sages were enthusiastic grandparents who played a role in their grandchildren's learning:

> Every Friday afternoon, Rabbi Yehoshua ben Levi listened to his grandson's reading of the Scripture lesson that he studied during the week. Once, he forgot to do so, and when he had already entered the baths of Tiberias, leaning on the shoulder of Rabbi Chiyya bar Ba, he remembered that he had not listened to his grandson's reading of Scripture. So he left the bath right away.... Rabbi Chiyya bar Ba said to him, "Did not Rabbi Yehudah Hanasi teach us that if one has begun taking a bath, one may not interrupt it even for prayer?" (M. Shabbat 1:2). Rabbi Yehoshua said to him, "Chiyya, my son, is it a small matter to you that he who listens to his grandson's reading of Scripture is as though he was hearing it at Mount Sinai? For it is said, 'Make them known unto your children and your children's children, as if it were the day that you stood before the Lord your God in Chorev' (Deuteronomy 4:9–10)."
>
> (Y. Shabbat 1:2, 3a)

This story is set in the baths of Tiberias. The etiquette was that once you started your bath, you normally didn't interrupt it for any reason. But when Rabbi Yehoshua reviews his grandson's learning with him every week, he re-creates the moment of the giving of the Torah at Sinai. And this takes precedence over everything else.

For Us ...

Today, Shavuot celebrates the giving of the Ten Commandments. Perhaps grandparents and grandchildren could participate in a ritual re-creating the revelation on Mount Sinai.

Informal Learning

In the Yerushalmi informal learning is important. For example, one day the teacher doesn't show up. Waiting for their teacher, the children talk about the letters of the Hebrew alphabet that have final forms:

> There is the following story: On a cloudy day, on which sages did not come to the meetinghouse, the children came in and said, "Let us hold a session, so that the study time will not be lost." They said, "Why are there two kinds of *mem, nun, tzadi, pey,* and *kuf*? It means: From one saying of God to another [*mima'amar l'ma'amar*], from the Faithful One to faithful to another [*mine'eman l'ne'eman*], from the Righteous One to the righteous [*mitzadik l'tzadik*], from the Mouth to the mouth [*mipeh l'peh*], from the Palm of the Holy One, blessed be He, to the palm of the hand of Moses [*mikhaf l'khaf*]."
>
> (Y. MEGILLAH 1:9, PM 12B, V 71D)

In these letters, the children see hints regarding the continuous process of passing on the traditions begun at Sinai, one commandment at a time, from one righteous, faithful person to another, throughout the generations. The children were able to learn not only the forms of the alphabet, but the essence of tradition, as well.

Child Development Is an Individual Thing

The pressure kids feel to perform on standardized tests is a common riff in movies, perhaps depicted most successfully in *The Perfect Score.* The sages recognized that different children developed differently.

This allowed a great deal of flexibility in learning instead of a "one size fits all" model of development. (A Houston educator, reading this, wondered why, if they knew this two thousand years ago, we still administer standardized tests ... quite a legitimate question.) A child's development is more important than his/her age:

> If he knows how to wave the *lulav*, he is obligated to wave it.
>
> If he knows how to wrap himself in a tallit, he is obligated to wear tzitzit (fringes).
>
> If he knows how to speak, his father teaches him the *Shema* and Torah and the holy language [Hebrew]....
>
> If he knows how to guard his tefillin, his father procures tefillin for him.
>
> If he knows how to guard his hands against ritual impurity, he may eat *terumah* [food that only priestly families may eat, which must be consumed in ritual purity].
>
> How do they check him? They immerse him in the ritual bath and give him unconsecrated food and tell him it is *terumah*, and they see if he treats it correctly....
>
> Rabbi Yehudah says, "They should not slaughter a paschal offering on his behalf unless he knows how to distinguish food from what is not food. How do we know that he's reached this stage? A child who, when given an egg, takes it and eats it, but when given a stone, throws it away."
>
> (T. HAGIGAH 1:2)

For the sages, intellectual activity (i.e., studying Jewish texts) was also a spiritual pursuit. They did not bifurcate the intellectual and spiritual realms. Theirs was a holistic view of development.

Parental Influence

Parents were involved in their children's education from the beginning of their lives. For example, Rabbi Yehoshua ben Chananyah's greatness is attributed to his mother's diligence in bringing him to the synagogue, starting in infancy:

> Rabbi Dosa ben Harkinas saw Rabbi Yehoshua and recited in
> his regard the following verse: "'Whom will he teach knowl-
> edge, and to whom will he explain the message? Those who are
> weaned from the milk and those taken from the breast' (Isaiah
> 28:9)." I remember that his mother would bring his cradle to
> the synagogue, so that his ears should cleave to the teachings
> of the Torah.
>
> (Y. Yevamot 1:6, PM 8b, V 3a)

Rabbi Dosa ben Harkinas attributes Rabbi Yehoshua's greatness to
his early exposure to Jewish teaching. Rabbi Yehoshua's mother was
obviously motivated to educate her son. (Of course, she might also
have wanted to participate in the learning for herself.)

The verse from Isaiah quoted in this passage is, in itself, a model
for how to teach young children. In it, God despairs of teaching the
adult Israelites who have gone far away from their faith. Therefore,
God decides to teach the youngest children. The verse that follows
the one quoted above (Isaiah 28:9) hints at the way to teach young
children: with repetition, with patience, and with word games, which
must be heard in Hebrew to be appreciated:

> Therefore will God teach these young children *tzav latzav tzav
> latzav* [precept upon precept, precept upon precept], *kav lakav
> kav lakav* [line upon line, line upon line], *z'eir sham z'eir sham*
> [here a little and there a little].
>
> (Isaiah 28:10)

In this verse (Isaiah 28:10) there is obvious wordplay and rhyming
that describe the process of learning. It illustrates how learning is
accomplished: bit by bit, from one's youth, and with a sense of fun, too!

Powerbrokers v. Teachers:
The Teachers Are the Good Guys

In any number of movies, committed teachers have to fight it out
with the powers-that-be for their right to educate their students with

conviction. For example, *Dead Poets Society*'s inspirational teacher is eventually kicked out by the administration, but his teachings live on in the hearts of his students.

The sages faced such problems, as well. Providing children with an education might have slipped to the bottom of some communities' list of priorities, given the desperate conditions in which they found themselves.

> Rabbi Shimon bar Yochai taught: If you see towns that have been uprooted from their location in the Land of Israel, you should know that the inhabitants did not faithfully pay the fee of the scribes and teachers who worked there.... Rabbi Yudan the Patriarch sent Rav Chiyya, Rav Assi, and Rav Ammi to travel among the towns of the Land of Israel to provide them with scribes and teachers. They came to one place and found neither a scribe/Bible teacher [*sofer*] nor a mishnah teacher [*matni'in*]. They said to the people, "Bring us the guardians of the town." The people brought them the town watchmen. They said to them, "Do you think these are the guardians of the town? They are nothing other than the destroyers of the town." They townsfolk asked them, "Who are the guardians of the town?" The sages answered, "The Bible teachers and mishnah teachers are your town's guardians. This accords with what is written, 'Unless the Lord builds the house, those who build it labor in vain. Unless the Lord [not the people] watches over the city, the watchmen stay awake in vain' (Psalm 127:1)."
>
> (Y. HAGIGAH 1:7, PM 6A–B, V 76C)

As the sages traveled about, they urged communities not to put their faith in the political leaders, but rather in those who would provide education for the children. Given the brutality of Roman rule, their advice makes a great deal of sense. Why spend community funds trying to buy Roman favor that is only fitfully given, when they can make an investment in the community's children and in their Jewish identity?

Does Anything Trump Learning?

Almost all coming-of-age movies have, at their core, the teen's negotiation between what's important to the parent and what's important to the teenager. In Judaism, this age-old dilemma is expressed in the tension between emphasizing learning versus doing mitzvot.

> When Rabbi Yehudah would see a corpse being cared for or a bride being praised, he would set his eyes on the disciples and say, "Deeds come before learning, so you should join these processions."
>
> They voted in the upper room of the house of Arim: "Learning comes before deeds."
>
> Rabbi Abbahu was in Caesarea [on the coast]. He sent his son, Rabbi Chanina, to Tiberias to study Torah. The teachers in Tiberias sent word to Rabbi Abbahu, telling him, "He is doing deeds of kindness [i.e., burying the dead] and not learning." He wrote to his son, "Is it because there are no graves in Caesarea that I sent you to Tiberias?"
>
> *And they have already taken a vote in the upper room of the house of Arim in Lod: "Studying Torah is more important than deeds." Rabbis of Caesarea say, "That which you say applies to a case in which there is someone else there who can do the deed required. But when there is no one else available to do the required deeds, then doing religious deed takes precedence over study of Torah."*
>
> Once Rabbi Chiyya, Rabbi Yose, and Rabbi Ammi were late in coming to see Rabbi Elazar. He said to them, "Where were you today?" They said to him, "We had to do a deed of kindness."
>
> He said to them, "And were there no others to do it there?"
>
> They said to him, "He was a foreigner and had no relatives to bury him."
>
> (Y. HAGIGAH 1:7, V 76C)

God bless the sages in the Yerushalmi! They give learners lots of options. Rabbi Elazar seems put out that his three students show up late. However, when he learns that they were engaged in one of the highest mitzvot there is, burying a *meit mitzvah* (a corpse left in the open with no one to bury it), Rabbi Elazar is appeased. We see, above, a dynamic dance between learning versus doing. This is realistic. Sometimes deeds outweigh learning. Sometimes learning outweighs deeds.

The section in italic type in the above passage is the addition of a later editor. You find a great deal of this sort of material in the Bavli and not so much of it in the Yerushalmi. However, it is clearly here. It's that "voice" in Talmud that splits the difference and clarifies a point that is otherwise difficult to understand. The foolproof way to check if something is an interpolation is to take it out and see if the passage reads cogently without it. (This works for all texts, including Scripture.)

23

What Would Your Wedding and Married Life Be Like?

Getting Engaged:
Rabbi Yehudah Hanasi Doesn't Get the Girl

In many a film, the rich guy doesn't get the girl (e.g., *Titanic*). Poor Rabbi Yehudah Hanasi is that luckless rich guy in the Yerushalmi. You would think that the wealthy, wise, and politically well-connected Rabbi would have no trouble attracting women. He was married, that we know. But he never got the girl of his dreams.

> When Rabbi Elazar ben Rabbi Shimon entered the meeting-place, Rabbi's face would darken with sadness. His father said to him, "This is as it should be, for Rabbi Elazar is a lion, son of a lion, while you are a lion, son of a fox [i.e., a distinguished man, of an inconspicuous father]." After Rabbi Elazar died, Rabbi sent and sought his widow in marriage. She said to him, "Will a vessel used for what is holy [i.e., Rabbi Elazar] now be used for what is ordinary [i.e., Rabbi]?"
> (Y. Shabbat 10:5, PM 63b; B. Bava Metzia 84b)

Rabbi glowers every time Rabbi Elazar comes to the meetinghouse not because Rabbi Elazar is smarter. It's because he got the girl. Rabbi Shimon bar Yochai and his son, Rabbi Elazar, spent thirteen years together in a cave evading capture by the Romans. Rabbi Elazar was apparently scarred by the experience and exhibited some rather strange behavior in an attempt to assuage his guilt over actually cooperating with the Romans (see B. Bava Metzia 83b–84a). His widow must have had sterling qualities, because Rabbi apparently carried a torch for her all those years. However, she seems to have had her fill of married life and rebuffed him. In both the Yerushalmi and the Bavli, Rabbi doesn't get his love. Knowing this humanizes Rabbi, whom we might tend to regard as living a charmed life. (Also impressive is Rabbi's father, who seeks to soften the blow by attributing this woman's choice to his own fault, rather than any fault of his son's.)

"Going to the Chapel"? Maybe Not

How many weddings have you seen in movies? *Runaway Bride, 27 Dresses, The Graduate, Seven Brides for Seven Brothers, Wedding Crashers, Father of the Bride, Fiddler on the Roof* ... the list goes on and on. You could easily rattle off the stock components of such scenes in your head: white dress, veil, an officiant, a groom, and perhaps some rice.

A Jewish wedding today is easily described. A wedding contract (*ketubah*) is signed. Under a chuppah, the bride circles the groom seven times. A blessing said over wine precedes the exchange of rings. Then *Sheva Berakhot*, the seven blessings that constitute the actual wedding ceremony, are recited, and a glass is broken. A festive meal is served and the seven blessings are included in the Blessing after Meals. Often, after the meal, dancing, jokes, juggling, and music are performed, in order to make the bride and groom rejoice.

Are these the wedding customs of the Yerushalmi? The Yerushalmi knows about some, but not all, of these customs. Surprisingly, the Yerushalmi does not seem to have heard of *Sheva Berakhot*. Perhaps they were not formulated in Israel at all, or perhaps they were developed after the Yerushalmi closed. For whatever reason, the weddings of the Yerushalmi do not include these blessings. For the sages of the Yerushalmi, the emphasis is on the wedding contract. In those days, it was a real, negotiated contract stipulating what the bride was to bring to the marriage as well as the bride-price the groom had to pay. This wedding contract also stipulated how much money the woman was to receive for food and clothing and how often her husband had to offer to have sex with her.

Sex in the *Ketubah*

Let's face it: cinematic love is pretty routine, from *Gone with the Wind* to *Casablanca* to … (you get the idea). There are conventions about how one arrives at a first kiss and how such a kiss looks. Sex in the Yerushalmi is likewise conventional, with the amount of sex to which a woman is entitled set at the time of the wedding and dependent on the nature of her husband's employment. If he has a job that isn't physically demanding or that does not take him out of town for prolonged periods of time, she is entitled to more sex. The classic place we find out how often people are having sex is in M. Ketubot 5:8 and the commentary to it:

> If someone vows not to have sexual intercourse with his wife, Beit Shammai says this situation can go on for two weeks. Beit Hillel says it can go on for one week. Students can go away to study Torah for thirty days without their wives' permission, thereby depriving their wives of sexual intercourse. Journeymen can go away for one week without permission. People who do not have to do physically demanding work have to offer to have sex with their wives every day. Journeymen have to offer to have sex with their wives twice a week. Camel drivers have to offer to have sex with their wives once every thirty days. Sailors have to offer to have sex with their wives every six months. These are the words of Rabbi Eliezer.
>
> (M. Ketubot 5:8)

This mishnah needs a bit of explaining. In rabbinic literature, women are thought to always want sex, and men are always trying to avoid it. So, in a fit of temper, a man could vow not to have sex with his wife. (Bear in mind that he might have more than one wife.) But this breaks the marriage contract. He must provide his wife with food, sex, and clothing. So after a cooling-off period, he must renounce his vow and divorce his wife, paying her the settlement agreed to in her *ketubah*. (Judaism is remarkable in that it sets the divorce settlement at the time when the man wants the woman the most, i.e., at the wedding, rather than our modern system, when the divorce settlement is set when the man wants her the least, i.e., at the time of divorce.)

Why is there this difference between Beit Hillel and Beit Shammai? Beit Shammai represents those with money, while Beit Hillel represents those who are poor. Beit Shammai's men can afford to pay the *ketubah* price, so we give them two weeks to cool off and reconsider. But Beit Hillel's men will *never* be able to pay off the *ketubah*, so they can be compelled to give up on their fit of temper after one week.

The Yerushalmi then turns to the somewhat puzzling proof text for a wife's right to sex and clothes:

> If a man marries another wife, he cannot diminish her food [*sh'eirah*] [or access to her relatives or her right to progeny or intercourse], her clothing [*k'sutah*], and her conjugal rights [or her oil and cosmetics] [*v'onatah*] [sex or food].
>
> (EXODUS 21:10)

As you might surmise from all the possibilities above, you can see that even the greatest biblical scholars today aren't sure what these words really mean. *The Anchor Bible* on this verse says, "of the three items [in this verse], one is slightly unclear, one is unclear and one is very unclear" (William H. Propp, *Exodus 19–40* [New York: Doubleday, 2006], p. 201). It also states there, "The verse has become an exegetical Rorschach test of what interpreters think a woman should be entitled to, whether as necessities or luxuries." The sages of the Yerushalmi struggled with this verse, as well. (In fact, our passage is originally from the early midrash collection on Exodus, *Mekhilta d'Rabbi Yishma'eil*.)

> Some state: *Sh'eir* is sex, that is, *derekh eretz*. What is *ha'onah* of which the Torah speaks? It was taught: *Onah* is food. Some *tannaim* state: *Onah* is intercourse [*derekh eretz*]. *Sh'eir* is food;

"He let rain on them *sh'eir* [meat] like dust" (Psalm 78:27). *Onah* is intercourse; "If you ill-treat [*t'anneh*] my daughters or take other wives besides my daughters—though no one else be about, remember, God Himself will be witness between you and me" (Genesis 31:50). *Onah* refers to intercourse [*zeh der-ekh eretz*]. Rabbi Eliezer ben Yaakov explains the verse [Exodus 21:10]: "'Her flesh [*sh'eirah*],' means 'her garment,' that is, that her garment should fit her flesh, for he should not give a young woman clothes for an old lady nor give an old woman clothes for a young woman. 'Her garment, her season,' that he should not give her summer clothing for the rainy season, nor clothes for the rainy season in summer."

(Y. Ketubot 5:8; Mekhilta d'Rabbi Yishma'eil, Nezikin 3, Lauterbach p. 374; B. Ketubot 47b–48a, G. p. 281)

This is vintage Yerushalmi. Three legitimate alternatives, complete with proof texts, are offered, but we have no inkling of which the sages prefer. The third alternative is rather novel in that it combines the words *sh'eirah* and *onah* to have them both refer to clothing. Perhaps Rabbi Eliezer ben Yaakov—either Rabbi Eliezer's contemporary (70–90) or a post–Bar Kokhba (130–160 CE) sage—was in the garment trade; he seems attuned to the different sorts of garments a woman needs. On the one hand, he understands that women of different ages wear different sorts of clothes. On the other hand, he understands that women wear different sorts of garments during different seasons. Perhaps garments were used up in a season. (This isn't as far-fetched as you might imagine. Contracts on some cuneiform tablets are "signed" by pressing the hem of one's garment into the clay. The assumption behind this practice is that people had only one garment and could be known by it.)

Then there is the phrase "this is the normal way," *zo derekh eretz*. It might be a delicate way of referring to sex. But this seems strange because later on in this passage, sex is referred to as "eating," and this is called "clean language," *bilshon nekiyyah*. Perhaps the phrase means "This is the way we generally understand this." The passage then continues trying to define what the proof text means:

From where do we derive the obligation to give his wife food? Just as he cannot withhold from her things upon which life depends, so, all the more so, may he not withhold from her things that are not necessities of life [i.e., new clothes twice a year], how much more so may he not withhold from her necessities of life! From where does he get the obligation of periodic intercourse [onah]? Since he many not withhold from her things that do not constitute the main reason for marriage [i.e., clothes], so certainly he may not withhold the things that constitute the main reason for marriage [i.e., sex]!

(Y. KETUBOT 5:8)

The sages continue to expound the proof text to make sure it says what they want it to say—that women are entitled to food, clothes, and sex. Here the argument is logical. Food is an absolute necessity, and sexual intercourse really is one of the reasons for married life in the first place.

The Gemara returns to Rabbi Eliezer's teaching about men's kinds of work determining how often they have to offer to have sex with their wives. Here, we find the proof text he used as a basis for his teaching:

Rabbi Eliezer inferred the periods of intercourse mentioned in our mishnah [above] from the gifts that Jacob, our father, sent as gifts to his brother Esau, for he sent him according to their copulations. "Two hundred she-goats and twenty he-goats," one for ten. "Two hundred ewes and twenty rams," one for ten. "Nursing camels and their offspring thirty" (each) (Genesis 32:15–16). Rabbi Berechiyah said, "Because it is discreet in its sexual behavior, the verse did not publicize the camels' mates, that is, thirty male camels also came with the thirty female camels" (Genesis Rabbah 76:7). "Forty cows and ten bulls," one for four because they are working beasts. "Twenty she-donkeys and ten he-donkeys" (Genesis 32:16), one for two because they are working beasts.

(Y. KETUBOT 5:8)

From this proof text Rabbi Eliezer sees that different animals can provide sexually for different numbers of mates. The more physical labor an animal does, the less energy he has for copulation. Rabbi Eliezer, extrapolating from this, rules that the more physical work a man has to do, the less energy he has for sexual intercourse.

But what about students of the sages? Their work isn't physically strenuous, so they should offer to have sex with their wives every day. It is in the discussion of this problem that we come upon a dictum that almost all Jews know: couples should have sex on Friday nights.

> Rabbi Yermiyah asked, "Should students of the sages be considered as those who do not work?" Rabbi Mana said, "Would it not be more reasonable to compare them to harvesters, since they work even harder?"
>
> Rav said, "She 'eats' with him every Friday night" [as we would say in polite language].
>
> (Y. KETUBOT 5:8)

Again we see that the sages keep trying to get out of sex. Here, they claim a harvester's status and should only have to offer to have sex with their wives once a week. The whole passage ends with Rav's teaching. Even students of the sages, who are busy with Torah study, should offer to have sex with their wives on Friday nights. Eventually, this came to be understood as the norm for everyone.

Y. v. B.

The obligation of a husband to provide his wife with sex is pretty uniform in the Yerushalmi and the Bavli. If anything, people are having more sex in Israel than they are in Babylonia. It is the women of Babylonia who added five more days to the period of impurity, effectively limiting intercourse to roughly two-thirds of the month, while women in Israel were available for sex about three-quarters of the month.

Wedding Crowns

Enough about sex, let's get back to the wedding ceremony. The Yerushalmi tells us that weddings were as big a deal back then as they are today. Some adjustments had to be made to accommodate the sad mood of the country after the Temple was destroyed, but brides still wanted nice weddings. The headdress was an important part of the wedding outfit:

> Rav Yehudah said, "For instance, a Jerusalem of gold."
> Rabbis of Caesarea say, "A golden castle headdress."
> The tale is told that Rabbi Akiba made his wife a golden tiara, and Rabban Gamliel's wife saw it and was jealous of her. She came and told her husband about it.
> He said to her, "If you had done what she did, I would have been glad to make one for you. For she sold her braids of hair and gave him the proceeds so that he might study Torah."
> (Y. Shabbat 6:1, PM 34a; Y. Sotah 9:16)

In one of the versions of the story of how they become betrothed and married, Rabbi Akiba, who was dirt poor when they married, makes Rachel a crown of straw (B. Ketubot 62b-63a; B. Nedarim 50a). From our passage, it appears that once he became wealthy, he gave her an actual Jerusalem of gold. (It is strange that Rabban Gamliel does not buy his wife one. His family was enormously wealthy, and he certainly could have afforded it. And, of course, his wife never needed to sell her hair to support Rabban Gamliel, because he never needed the money.)

As to what the crowns were, in typical Yerushalmi fashion, we're given several different descriptions:

> Rabbi Ba in the name of Rav: "Made of salt and sulfur." Rav Yermiyah in the name of Rav: "Made of salt and olive branches." Rav Nachman bar Yaakov said, "Even of willows." Rav Yermiyah plaited and put on a crown of olive branches [in honor of a bridal couple]. Shmuel heard this and said, "It would have been better for him if he had been beheaded rather than doing this thing."
> (Y. Sotah 9:16, PM 46a, V 24d)

Some say the prohibited crowns were made of rock salt colored with sulfur to appear gold; others say they were made of branches. The only thing we can say for certain about these crowns is that there were many different kinds and that, at some point, they all fell out of favor.

The Chuppah: The Honeymoon Suite

The chuppah did not seem to be an open canopy, as it is today, but rather a tent in which the marriage was consummated.

> The following are grooms' chambers: ornamented sheets with gold-embroidered ribbons hanging on them. It had taut frames for decorative hangings, and he hangs thereon whatever decorations he may desire.
>
> (Y. Sotah 9:16, PM 46a, V 24c)

One is rather forcefully reminded of a sukkah and its decorations. And T. Sotah 15:9 forbids people from decorating their chuppahs with gold. This is the groom's part of the wedding. He'd want to make sure the bride was comfortable and, ahem, willing.

Until now in our discussion, weddings seem to have had a great deal in common with weddings today: the dress, the jewelry, the staging, the chuppah. But when it comes to the ceremony itself, things become less familiar.

Wedding Blessings

There is some blessing of the wedding couple, but the text of that blessing is not given.

> "They bless a wedding couple without ten people present" (M. Megillah 4:4). And do they not give a blessing of a wedding couple in the Blessing after Meals all seven days after the wedding? Rabbi Yermiyah reasoned [savar] that they take the bride out all seven days to the wedding canopy.
>
> (Y. Megillah 4:4, PM 30b, V 75a)

It may come as a shock that the Yerushalmi has never heard of the *Sheva Berakhot*, the seven wedding blessings that are at the core of our weddings today. This part of the ceremony seems pretty much left up in the air. We know what they wear, we know about the contract, we know there's a feast ... we just don't know how they get from point A to point B.

Blessing before Consummation?

The sages were never shy about the purpose of marriage: sexual intimacy and procreation. So, inevitably, logic would lead us to presume that there must have been a blessing before this mitzvah. After all, a blessing is said before performing almost all mitzvot:

> All mitzvot require a blessing before you do them except for blowing the shofar and immersion in a *mikveh* and some say before sexual relations with her husband.
>
> (Y. BERAKHOT 9:3, 91B2)

We can all agree that we say a blessing before we perform a mitzvah. Here, it seems, the logical extension of that idea is that one says a blessing before consummating a marriage. The language in this passage is unclear. The blessing might be "... *vitzivanu al mitzvat kiddushin*" (... who commanded us concerning the commandment of marriage). Even if it were only Alan Shephard's "Astronaut's Prayer" ("Dear Lord, please don't let me screw up"), a prayer of some sort would be appropriate for both bride and groom.

We do find two bits of our contemporary wedding ceremony in the Yerushalmi. The groom says:

> Enter my house and be to me a wife according to the religion of Moses and the Jews [*Lichsheticansi l'veiti t'havyyan l'intu kh'dat Moshe vi'hudaei*].
>
> (Y. KETUBOT 4:8, PM 29A, V 28D)

Today, we say a Hebrew form of this phrase when exchanging rings.

We also have one small part of the *Sheva Berakhot* in a prayer to be said in honor of a cohort of priests who are leaving after a week of serving in the Temple.

> What is this blessing? Said Rabbi Chelbo, "May the One who dwells in the Temple set in your midst fraternity, and love and peace and friendship" [*Hashokhein babayit hazeh yita beineikhem achavah, v'ahavah, shalom v'rei'ut*].
>
> (Y. Berakhot 1:4, 13b1)

This is one line in today's wedding ceremony. To summarize: we know about the contract, the dress, the procession, the meal, and the sex … we just don't know about the ritual that actually joins the bride and groom.

Dancing Before the Bride

The Yerushalmi is certainly clear about one thing: there is dancing at weddings in the Land of Israel. In the Bavli, of course, we have the Beit Hillel/Beit Shammai dispute over how one dances before the bride (B. Ketubot 17a). (That dispute does not show up in the Yerushalmi.) We do learn that the dancing could be somewhat suggestive:

> Rav Shmuel bar Rav Yitzchak would take a branch (or three) and dance before the brides. And when Rabbi Zeira saw him doing this, he would hide away from him. Someone said, "Did you see this elderly man, how he shames us?" When Rav Shmuel bar Rav Yitzchak died, there were three hours of thunder and lightning in the world. A heavenly voice emerged and said, "Rav Shmuel bar Rav Yitzchak, performer of kindnesses [*gamul chasdaya*], has been laid to rest." They went out to perform a kindness for him [*l'migmul lei chesed*; i.e., help with his burial]. A fire descended from heaven and became like a branch of fire between the bier and the people. When they saw this they said, "Look at the life of this elder! His branch stood for him."
>
> (Y. Peah 1:1, 7b1, V 15d; Y. Avodah Zarah 3:1;
> B. Ketubot 17a)

As Rav Shmuel juggled the stick(s) before the bride, God juggles these fiery branches to welcome him into the World to Come. And a voice comes out of heaven and says, "Woe that Rav Shmuel bar Rav Yitzhak has died, the doer of merciful deeds."

The parallel text in Y. Avodah Zarah 3:1 says that Rav Shmuel bar Rav Yitzchak would dance before the bride with a cedar branch. Cedar is part of some biblical rituals (e.g., Leviticus 14:4 and Numbers 19:6).

This may have been a fertility dance. According to Leviticus Rabbah 30:10, the three myrtle branches in the *lulav* represent Jacob and Leah. Just as the myrtle branch is crowded with leaves, so they were crowded with children. So dancing with the myrtle branches might have been a dance blessing the couple with fertility. Myrtle is evergreen and is also associated with Esther's (Hadassah's) good qualities. (Esther's Hebrew name, Hadassah, is very much like myrtle's name, *hadas*.) Myrtle branches are also used to decorate biers as they are carried to the grave. If Rav Shmuel was dancing with a cedar branch, he may have been hearkening back to biblical rituals that use cedar in them (e.g., Leviticus 14:4). Perhaps the cedar branch with which he danced was also covered with leaves. (It is an evergreen.)

The Romans Threaten the Wedding's Joy

The cinematic movie scene that corresponds to this most clearly is the wedding scene in *Fiddler on the Roof*, when the Cossacks violently break up the wedding. Michael Corleone's wedding scene in Sicily, too, has that looming danger as a backdrop. Or it could be pretty much any wedding set during World War II. A looming, dangerous presence overhangs the wedding's joy.

Wedding festivities were literally muted because of the Romans' menacing presence. The Romans claimed the first night with the bride, so the wedding had to be held in secret:

> What was the sign that there was an upcoming wedding? The sound of a cook/baker in the city was understood to mean: A wedding banquet is there! A wedding banquet is there! At the first sight of a light in Bror Hayil [where Rabban Yochanan ben

Zakkai lived] the sign was: "It is the completion of the week for a son, it is the completion of the week for a son so that the circumcision will be taking place now." Even though the persecution came to an end, the custom did not come to an end.

(Y. KETUBOT 1:5, PM 5B, V 25C)

Perhaps the most interesting part of this story is that the custom of not announcing a wedding took root and was observed even after the danger had passed.

As the Roman noose tightened on the Jewish population, more and more wedding customs were abolished:

During Vespasian's [Roman emperor 69–79 CE] war, they banned grooms' crowns and the tambourine. During Titus's [Vespasian's son, who sacked Jerusalem] war, they banned brides' crowns and teaching one's children Greek. During the last war [the Bar Kokhba Revolt, 132–135 CE], they banned brides from being carried in a litter through the city. Our teachers permitted a bride to be carried in a litter through the city.

(M. SOTAH 9:14)

Reading such things, one is reminded of how Jews struggled to live within, or flee from, Nazi Germany after 1939. By this point, Rome was determined to utterly vanquish the Jews, just as the Nazis were bent on exterminating every Jew under their power.

Y. v. B.

The biggest difference between the Yerushalmi and the Bavli is that the *Sheva Berakhot* (seven wedding blessings) aren't in the Yerushalmi or the midrash collections. The Yerushalmi outlines many wedding customs, some observed in the Galilee but not in the south of Israel, some in earlier times and some later traditions. They are presented in the Bavli (B. Ketubot 7b–8a) as a preformed block, with no commentary interspersed among the blessings. Normally, this would suggest that the text has been "cut and pasted" into the text from elsewhere. Strangely, there seems to be no "elsewhere" from which this copying might have occurred. For now, this mystery must remain unsolved.

For Us ...

The Yerushalmi allows us great leeway when it comes to the liturgy for weddings; nothing is set in stone. Brides can dress as they wish, as long as they don't bring harm on the whole community by doing so. As usual, the Yerushalmi grants a lot of flexibility.

24

What Would Old Age Be Like?

In its day, the hit movie *Cocoon* was a daring experiment. The conventional wisdom at the time was that movies about elderly folk just wouldn't go over well with the public. The Yerushalmi wasn't saddled with such biases. However, against the background of a decimated country, an oppressive foreign occupier, and a biblical passage that explicitly says that old people are worth less than young adults (see below), old age might not have been much of a blessing.

Let's begin with the Torah text:

> And God spoke to Moses saying: Speak to the children of Israel and say to them: Whenever a man shall clearly vow the worth of persons to God, then the worth of the male, from twenty to sixty years old, the valuation shall be fifty shekels of silver according to the shekel of the sanctuary. And if it is female, the valuation is thirty shekels.... And when the person is older than sixty, if male then the valuation is fifteen shekels and for a female ten shekels.
>
> (LEVITICUS 27:1–7)

Clearly, anyone over sixty is literally worth less than those younger, and females are worth less than males.

Honoring One's Parents

Given the prominence of the mitzvah of honoring one's parents, you'd imagine that people in the days of the Yerushalmi would have observed it. That would be hopelessly optimistic. The Yerushalmi tells us how it was:

> There is one who feeds his father fattened birds but inherits *Gehinnom*, and there is one who makes his father work at the grind mill and he inherits the Garden of Eden. How could one feed his father fattened birds yet receive *Gehinnom* as his inheritance? A person used to feed his father pheasants. One time, his father said to him, "Son, where did you get these fattened birds?" His son said to him, "Old man, old man! Eat and be quiet about the food, just as dogs eat whatever is before them and don't complain!" Such a person feeds his father fattened birds, yet receives *Gehinnom* as his inheritance.
>
> How could one who yokes his father to the millstones receive the Garden of Eden as his inheritance? A person was grinding at the millstones. A draft came for one member of each household to grind at the royal mill, in service of the king. The son said to his father, "Father, you take up the yoke here in my place, and I shall go take up the harder work of grinding for the king. In this way, should we come to degradation at the royal mill, it will be better for me—me and not you [*tav li ana v'la at*]—to be degraded. Should we receive lashes at the royal mill, it will be better for me—me and not you [*tav li ana v'la at*]—to receive them." Such a person yokes his father to the millstones yet inherits the Garden of Eden.
>
> (Y. Peah 1:1, 6A2-6A3, V 15C)

The father who is being fed the chickens here is clearly worried that his son, to put it politely, "found them after they fell off a truck." And the Romans are always there, in the background, as a menacing presence, forcing parents and children into impossible scenarios.

The Indignities of Aging

The sages understood that as people grow old, they undergo physical changes that may or may not disqualify the elderly from participating in the community as they had been doing all their adult lives. The Mishnah (M. Megillah 4:7) disqualifies a priest with deformed hands from giving the Priestly Benediction in a synagogue. (This is done to keep people from looking at the priest's hands, where God's lethal presence rests during the benediction.) The Yerushalmi builds on the Mishnah and Tosefta and, further, brings reports of cases where this rule was applied selectively:

> A priest who has blemishes on his hands should not raise his hands in the Priestly Benediction (M. Megillah 4:7).
>
> Gemara: It has been taught: If the priest also has blemishes on his face, he should not raise his hands in the Priestly Benediction. It has been taught: "But if he was well-known in his town, he is permitted" (T. Megillah 3:29).
>
> Rabbi Naftali had crooked fingers. He came and asked Rabbi Mana if he might offer the Priestly Benediction. Rabbi Mana said to him, "Since you are well-known in your town, it is permitted."
> (Y. Megillah 4:8, PM 32b, V 75b–c; Y. Ta'anit 4:1, 67b)

Why is the priest with crooked hands shown such leniency? Just imagine a priest who has offered the Priestly Benediction his whole adult life. When he develops arthritis, the Yerushalmi doesn't want this honor taken from him.

Y. v. B.

Regarding honoring parents and the indignities of old age, the Yerushalmi and the Bavli agree that the former is incredibly important and the latter is universally difficult.

For Us …

We have an enormous amount of flexibility when it comes to bending some rules laid down in earlier sources … especially when familiar and beloved members of the community face the ravages of aging. Their feelings are more important than technical rules about proper appearance.

How to Die: Rabbi Eliezer's Deathbed

Deathbed scenes in the movies, from *Gone With the Wind* to *Steel Magnolias* to *Saving Private Ryan*, are a staple of the dramatic arc. One of the most famous stories in all of rabbinic literature is the tale of Rabbi Eliezer's excommunication. Rabbi Eliezer was a strange sort of sage: a magician who was tried for being a Judeo-Christian who was finally kicked out of the Academy, which he so dearly loved (Y. Moed Katan 3:1, V 81c–d; B. Bava Metzia 59b). His deathbed scene is recounted in great detail:

> Rabbi Eliezer was dying at sunset on the eve of the Sabbath. Hyrcanus, his son, came in to remove his tefillin. He said to him, "My son, you have neglected the religious duty of light-ing the Shabbat light, which is integral to Shabbat rest, and the neglect of which leaves one liable to excommunication, and you have come to remove my tefillin, which is only an optional matter."
>
> The son went out crying, saying, "Woe is me, that father's mind is confused."
>
> He said to him, "My mind is not confused. It is your mind that is confused." When his students saw that Rabbi Eliezer had answered his son wisely, they came close to him and asked him questions, and he answered them, saying of what was impure, "Impure," and of what was clean, "Pure," and at the end he said, "Pure," and his soul departed.
>
> They said, "It is obvious that our master is pure." Said Rabbi Mana, "It was obvious before he died."
>
> Rabbi Yehoshua came in and removed his tefillin and bent down and kissed him, weeping. He said, "My master, the

vow against you has been released. 'My master! The chariot of Israel and its horsemen' (2 Kings 2:12)."

(Y. SHABBAT 2:7, PM 20B, V 5B; B. SANHEDRIN 101A; SIFREI
DEUTERONOMY, PISKA 32)

Rabbi Eliezer is consistent to the very end. He knows all the right answers and isn't shy about telling others what they are. Rabbi Yehoshua, his study partner and opponent, makes up with Rabbi Eliezer in this scene, likening Rabbi Eliezer to Elijah and himself to Elisha (Elijah's protégé). When Elisha sees Elijah ascend to heaven, he gives out this cry and puts on Elijah's mantle:

> And Elisha saw it, and he cried, "My father, my father, the chariot of Israel and its horsemen." And he saw him no more; and he took hold of his own clothes and tore them in two pieces. He also took up the mantle of Elijah that fell from him and went back and stood by the bank of the Jordan.

(2 KINGS 2:12–13)

Ever tactful, Rabbi Yehoshua acknowledges that Rabbi Eliezer was his teacher and his better.

What Would Funerals Be Like?

One of the greatest mitzvot in Judaism is burying the dead and comforting the mourners, and the Yerushalmi reflects this. However, in a characteristic Yerushalmi twist, different places are shown to have different customs:

> It was taught: In a place where they were accustomed to greet mourners on Shabbat, they may greet them. And in the south, they would greet them.
>
> Rabbi Hoshia the Great went to a place where he saw mourners on the Sabbath, and he would greet them.
>
> He said to them, "I do not know the custom here, but peace be with you according to the custom where I live."

(Y. BERAKHOT 2:7, 29A2–29A3)

The joy of Shabbat is supposed to supersede the mourning of those sitting shivah. However, the principle of following local custom trumps Shabbat in this case.

Grave Changing

Being laid to rest was a two-step process in Israel in this era. The corpse was buried. Then, after a time, the bones were gathered up and reburied. Something about the following passage may seem oddly familiar to those who know Christian Scripture. (In the Gospels, the stone sealing Jesus's grave is moved after three days.) Here, the sages discuss when the week of mourning begins:

> There is a *tanna* who teaches: Once the rolling stone closes the first grave, the mourning begins.
>
> There is a *tanna* who teaches: Once the rolling stone closes the second grave, the mourning rites begin.
>
> Rabbi Yonah had a case. He asked Rabbi Chananyah, the fellow of the rabbis, who said to him, "Once the stone has rolled over the first grave, the mourning rites start."
>
> Rabbi Yermiyah had a case. He asked Rabbi Zeira and Rabbi Ammi. He said to him, "Once the stone has been rolled over the second grave, the mourning rites start."
>
> He said to him, "You gave a strict ruling." ...
>
> Yehoshua, Drorai's brother, had a case. He came and asked Rabbi Abbahu. He said to him, "Once the second grave has been sealed, mourning starts."
>
> Rabbi Yaakov bar Acha said to him, "I was with you when you asked that question to Rabbi Avodimi of Haifa and he said, 'It is when the first grave has been sealed.'"
>
> He said to him, "I never heard that teaching. But if you heard it, go and teach it."
>
> (Y. MOED KATAN 3:5, PM 14B, V 82C)

The text here is difficult to understand. These customs are related to burial caves that were meant to hold many corpses. Such crypts were designed to be opened more than once. Hence, the large stones at the mouths of the caves closed these crypt caves.

Rabbi's Instruction at Death

Will-reading scenes are another "set piece" we find in films too numerous to note. Perhaps Richard Gere's character in *Shall We Dance* sums it up best. A will may be the document in which a person feels most free to express himself. After all, he will not be around to face the blowback, should there be any. Rabbi Yehudah Hanasi, a moral man to the very last, stipulated three things in his will:

> Rabbi commanded three things on his deathbed: (1) My widow should not move from my house, (2) do not eulogize me in towns along the funeral route, and … (3) do not make voluminous shrouds for me and the bottom of my coffin should be perforated.
> (Y. KILAYIM 9:3, 79A4)

First, Rabbi's wife is to stay in their house and live just as well as she did while Rabbi was alive, that is, very well indeed. She is to live as if her husband is overseas and she is still under his protection.

Second, he doesn't want to burden small communities with the cost of a memorial (think: the difference between having London host the wedding of Prince William and Kate Middleton versus some small hamlet having to foot that bill). Also, it would delay his actual burial if the corpse were to make a stop at every community along the route from Sepphoris to Beit She'arim.

Third, and perhaps most interesting, is Rabbi's request to be buried in simple shrouds with holes in the bottom of his coffin. Rabbi, a millionaire, could have afforded to be buried in silk and mahogany. But he wanted to fulfill the verse "dust to dust" (Genesis 3:19) as quickly and as unostentatiously as possible.

Other Sages' Shrouds

What one wore in the grave was an important spiritual/fashion decision. Some sages specified how they wanted to be buried. And in typical

Yerushalmi fashion, there's no one right answer—just lots of different right ones.

> Rabbi Yochanan stipulated, "Dress me in beige [or gray], neither white nor black. If I rise among the righteous, I shall not be ashamed. If I rise among the wicked, I shall not be ashamed."
>
>   Rabbi Yoshiyah stipulated, "Dress me in clean white." They said to him, "In what way are you better than your teacher Rabbi Yochanan?" He said to them, "Why should I be ashamed of my deeds?"
>
>   Rabbi Yermiyah stipulated, "Dress me in clean white, dress me in my socks, put my shoes on my feet and a walking stick in my hand, and lay me on my side. When the Messiah comes, I will be ready."
>
> (Y. Kilayim 9:4, 79b2)

This is just one part of a huge aggadic section here. Rabbi Yochanan is unsure of how he'll end up in the World to Come. He could, perhaps, be suffering from a guilty conscience at the way he mistreated his study partner, Reish Lakish. (The Bavli suggests that Rabbi Yochanan was responsible for Reish Lakish's death. See B. Bava Metzia 84a.) Rabbi Yoshiyah seems pretty sure of himself. But it's Rabbi Yermiyah who hopes to be like Ezekiel's dry bones, which rise again, fully fleshed, and head to Jerusalem. In other words, he does not see death as the final station but as just a part of the journey that leads to the messianic era.

Buried with a Bit of the Land of Israel

One thing hasn't changed in all these centuries: people still want to be buried with a bit of earth from the Land of Israel.

> Rabbi Bar Kirya and Rabbi Elazar were walking in the road, and they saw coffins being brought into the Land of Israel from abroad. Rabbi Bar Kirya said to Rabbi Elazar, "What good is that going to do them? I apply this verse to them, 'And I brought you into a plentiful country, to eat its fruit and its goodness;

but when you entered, you defiled my land, and My inheritance you considered an abomination' (Jeremiah 2:7) during
your lifetime. 'You came and defiled my land' in your death."
Rabbi Elazar said to him, "When they reach the Land of Israel,
they take a bit of earth and put it on the coffin, as it is written,
'His earth atones for His people' (Deuteronomy 32:43)."

(Y. KILAYIM 9:3, 82A1, V 32D)

Israel's earth has magical powers, making atonement for whatever sins
the person has committed. No matter how hopeless Israel's situation
seemed, no matter how permanently the Romans seemed to be staying,
no matter how dim the prospect of a genuine, successful return to the
Land may have grown, the pull of Israel never waned, over all those
centuries.

And it remains with us to this very day. The pull of Israel's Talmud
calls us to learn and practice in new ways.

Y. v. B.

Burying the dead with appropriate dignity is important in both the
Yerushalmi and the Bavli, although customs varied over time and
space, just as they do today. (Just go to an older graveyard and you
can see how "fashions" in tombstones developed, grew, and gave
way to newer "fashions.")

Conclusion:
What We Can Recapture

I once had the distinct pleasure of teaching at a hilltop retreat in Harpers Ferry, West Virginia. This town changed hands eight times during the Civil War and, I swear, you could still hear the horses charging through the trees and the rifle fire. And not in some imaginative way. I mean the echoes were still there. That's what I think of when I learn Yerushalmi. It's alive and you can hear the echoes of our ancestors.

So, what would have happened if we'd learned more Yerushalmi than Bavli? What kind of Jews would we be? We'd be more relaxed in our observance in the sense that we'd allow people to explore their options. And we'd be more tolerant of others who did things differently than we did. Gossip would be the thing we would avoid like the plague, and we would have incredibly joyful, rich holidays. Shavuot, especially, would be changed almost beyond recognition into a sort of state fair/Mardi Gras. In other words, we'd have more fun and less fighting, more flexibility and less rigidity. It's here for the taking. Let's go get it!

Abbreviations

B.   Bavli

G.   Guggenheimer edition of Yerushalmi

M.   Mishnah

PM   P'nei Moshe edition of Yerushalmi

T.   Tosefta

V   Venice edition of Yerushalmi

Y.   Yerushalmi

When, Who, and Where

Year (CE)	Israel	Babylonia
220	Rabbi Chanina	Mar Ukba
	Rabbi Yehoshua ben Levi	Shmuel
		Rav
250	Rabbi Yochanan ben Nappaha	Rav Huna
	Rabbi Shimon ben Lakish	Rabbi Tanchum bar Hanilai
	Rav Adda bar Ahavah	
	Rabbi Yose bar Chanina	
290	Shmuel bar Nachmani	Rav Chisda
	Rabbi Abbahu	
	Rav Ammi	Rabbah bar Chana
	Rav Assi	
	Rabbi Chiyya bar Abba	Rabbah bar Nachmani
	Rabbi Zeira	Rav Yosef
320	Rabbi Yermiyah	Abaye
	R. Chelbo	Raba
	Rav Huna	Rav Nachman bar Yitzchak
	Rav Dimi	
350	Avin	
	Rabbi Yonah	Rav Pappa
	Rabbi Berechiyah	Rav Chama
	R. Yose bar Avin	
375		Rav Ashi
		Mar Zutra
		Rafram
		Ravina

Orders and Tractates of the Mishnah

Orders of the Mishnah

Seder Zeraim (Seeds): Traditions relating to agriculture, particularly in the Land of Israel. Contains tractate Berakhot (Blessings), which deals with the recital of the *Shema, Amidah,* and other prayers.

Seder Moed (Appointed Time, Festival): Traditions pertaining to Shabbat, festivals, and fasts.

Seder Nashim (Women): Traditions regarding marriage, divorce, contracts, and vows.

Seder Nezikin (Damages): Traditions about civil and criminal damages, e.g., corporal and capital punishments, the administration of Jewish courts, and rules regarding testimony. This order contains tractate Avot, the Sayings of the Fathers.

Seder Kodashim (Holy Things): Traditions pertaining to the sacrifices offered in the Temple and the rules of keeping kosher.

Seder Toharot (Purity): Traditions of ritual purity and impurity.

Tractates of the Mishnah/Gemara

Within the six orders, we find the following tractates. (The tractate name is followed by the common abbreviation of that name.)

Seder Zeraim

Berakhot (Ber.): "Blessings." Traditions regarding the *Shema, Amidah,* blessing for food, etc.

Peah: "Corner" of the field. Traditions concerning leaving the corners of one's fields unharvested so that the poor might glean food there.

Demai (Dem.): "Doubtful(ly Tithed)." What to do with produce when you don't know whether it has been tithed.

Kilayim (Kil.): "Mixtures." Outlines agricultural traditions regarding the mixing of species.

Shevi'it (Sheb.): "Seventh." How to observe the Sabbatical year, which occurs every seven years.

Terumot (Ter.): "The Priests' Portion of the Harvest." The traditions of *terumah*, the gift of produce given to the priests.

Ma'asrot (Ma'as.): "Tithes." The traditions of tithes, i.e., giving away 10 percent of one's produce.

Ma'aser Sheni (MS or Ma'as Sh.): "The Second Tithe." The traditions of the second tithe.

Hallah (Hal. or Ha.): "Dough." The traditions of separating some bread dough and giving it to the priests or burning it.

Orlah (Or. or Orl.): "Uncircumcised Fruit." Outlines the prohibitions against using the fruits of trees during the first three years after their having been planted.

Bikkurim (Bik.): "First Fruits." Description of the first fruit offerings at the Temple, i.e., the holiday Shavuot.

Seder Moed

Shabbat (Shab.): "Sabbath." The traditions governing Shabbat.

Eruvin (Er.): "Mergings." A continuation of tractate Shabbat.

Pesachim (Pes.): "Passover Offerings." The traditions of Passover.

Shekalim (Shek.): "Shekels." The annual shekel contribution to the ancient Temple and how it was used.

Yoma (Yom.): "The Day." Traditions regarding the Day of Atonement.

Sukkah (Suk.): "Booth." Traditions of Sukkot.

Beitzah (Bez.): "Egg." Traditions that apply to all festivals.

Rosh Hashanah (R.H.): "New Year." The traditions of Rosh Hashanah.

Ta'anit (Ta'. or Ta'an.): "Fast." When and how public fast days were observed.

Megillah (Meg.): "Scroll." The traditions regarding reading the Scroll of Esther and some rules regarding Torah reading.

Moed Katan (M.K.): "Minor Festival." Rules regarding Chol Hamoed, the intermediate days of a festival.

Hagigah (Hag.): "Festival Offering." Special festival offerings. (Also some material on mysticism.)

Seder Nashim

Yevamot (Yeb.): "Sisters-in-Law." The traditions regarding levirate marriage, i.e., when a man leaves his widow childless and she marries his brother (based on Deuteronomy 25:5–10).

Ketubot (Ket.): "Wedding Contracts." The traditions regarding weddings and marriage.

Nedarim (Ned.): "Vows." The traditions concerning vows.

Nazir (Naz.): "Nazirite." How to become a nazirite (e.g., like Samson). A nazir dedicates his/her life, or a part thereof, to God and vows not to cut his/her hair or drink alcohol, among other behaviors.

Sotah (Sot.): "A Woman Suspected of Adultery." Traditions regarding the suspected adulteress (based on Numbers 5:11–31).

Gittin (Git.): "Bills of Divorce." Traditions governing divorce.

Kiddushin (Kid.): "Betrothals." Traditions regarding how a woman is betrothed.

Seder Nezikin

Bava Kamma (B.K.): "The First Gate." Traditions regarding civil and criminal law.

Bava Metzia (B.M.): "The Middle Gate." Traditions regarding business law.

Bava Batra (B.B.): "The Last Gate." Traditions regarding partnership, inheritance, sales, etc.

Sanhedrin (San.): "Sanhedrin." The traditions regarding capital punishment.

Makkot (Mak.): "Lashes." Corporal punishment.

Shevuot (Shevu. or Shebu.): "Oaths." Traditions regarding public and private oaths.

Eduyot (Ed. or Eduy.): "Testimonies." A collection of *mishnayot* on several different subjects, organized according to who said them.

Avodah Zarah (A.Z.): "Idolatry." Rules governing relations between Jews and non-Jews.

Avot (Ab.): "Fathers." A collection of sages' sayings, organized according to who taught them.

Horayot (Hor.): "Decisions, Rulings." Traditions regarding rabbinical courts.

Seder Kodashim

Zevachim (Zev.): "Animal Sacrifices." Traditions regarding the offering of various animal sacrifices.

Menachot (Men.): "Meal Offerings." The traditions regarding grain offerings, tzitzit, and tefillin.

Hullin (Hul.): "Ordinary, Unhallowed." Traditions regarding kosher slaughtering (*shechitah*).

Bekhorot (Bek.): "Firstlings." The traditions concerning firstborn male animals.

Arakhin (Ar.): "Valuations." The traditions regarding dedicating items to the Temple.

Temurah (Tem.): "Substitution." The traditions regarding substituting one sacrifice for another.

Keritot (Ker.): "Excisions." Those sins for which the punishment is *kareit*, i.e., being cut off from the community.

Me'ilah (Me'il.): "Sacrilege." The traditions regarding the unlawful use of things dedicated to the Temple.

Tamid (Tam.): "Daily Sacrifices." The traditions of the daily service in the Temple.

Middot (Mid.): "Measurements." Traditions regarding the architectural plan of the Temple and its measurements.

Kinnim (Kin.): "Birds' nests." Traditions regarding the sacrifices of birds.

Seder Toharot

Keilim (Kel.): "Vessels." Traditions regarding the various forms of ritual impurity that apply to vessels.

Ohalot (Oh. or Ohal.): "Tents." Traditions regarding ritual impurity of tents that contain dead bodies.

Negaim (Neg.): "Leprosy." Traditions regarding leprosy and its purification.

Parah (Par.): "Heifer." The traditions regarding the red heifer (based on Numbers 19:1–22).

Toharot (Tohor.): "Purifications." Various traditions regarding ritual impurity.

Mikva'ot (Mik.): "Ritual Baths." Traditions regarding the construction and use of the ritual bath.

Niddah (Nid.): "Menstruating Woman." Traditions regarding a menstruating woman.

Makhshirin (Maks. or Maksh.): "Preparations." Traditions regarding how foods may become ritually impure.

Zavim (Zav.): "Those suffering from secretions." Traditions regarding the ritual impurity of persons with venereal diseases.

Tevul Yom (T.Y.): "Immersed during the Day." Traditions regarding one who takes a ritual bath during the day but is not considered ritually pure until evening.

Yadayim (Yad.): "Hands." Traditions regarding the ritual washing of hands.

Uktzin (Uk. or Ukz.): "Stems." Traditions about ritual impurity regarding stems and the fruits attached to them.

Commentaries on the Mishnah

The Mishnah provides the skeletal structure of the Talmudic literature. Below are the tractates of the Mishnah with indications of which documents comment upon them. Note that Tosefta is the most complete commentary on Mishnah but that not even Tosefta covers every tractate of Mishnah.

Seder Zeraim

Berakhot	Mishnah	Tosefta	Yerushalmi	Bavli
Peah	Mishnah	Tosefta	Yerushalmi	
Demai	Mishnah	Tosefta	Yerushalmi	
Kilayim	Mishnah	Tosefta	Yerushalmi	
Shevi'it	Mishnah	Tosefta	Yerushalmi	
Terumot	Mishnah	Tosefta	Yerushalmi	
Ma'asrot	Mishnah	Tosefta	Yerushalmi	
Ma'aser Sheni	Mishnah	Tosefta	Yerushalmi	
Hallah	Mishnah	Tosefta	Yerushalmi	
Orlah	Mishnah	Tosefta	Yerushalmi	
Bikkurim	Mishnah	Tosefta	Yerushalmi	

Seder Moed

Shabbat	Mishnah	Tosefta	Yerushalmi	Bavli
Eruvin	Mishnah	Tosefta	Yerushalmi	Bavli
Pesachim	Mishnah	Tosefta	Yerushalmi	Bavli
Shekalim	Mishnah	Tosefta	Yerushalmi	
Yoma	Mishnah	Tosefta	Yerushalmi	Bavli
Sukkah	Mishnah	Tosefta	Yerushalmi	Bavli
Beitzah	Mishnah	Tosefta	Yerushalmi	Bavli
Rosh Hashanah	Mishnah	Tosefta	Yerushalmi	Bavli
Ta'anit	Mishnah	Tosefta	Yerushalmi	Bavli
Megillah	Mishnah	Tosefta	Yerushalmi	Bavli
Moed Katan	Mishnah	Tosefta	Yerushalmi	Bavli
Hagigah	Mishnah	Tosefta	Yerushalmi	Bavli

Seder Nashim

Yevamot	Mishnah	Tosefta	Yerushalmi	Bavli
Ketubot	Mishnah	Tosefta	Yerushalmi	Bavli
Nedarim	Mishnah	Tosefta	Yerushalmi	Bavli
Nazir	Mishnah	Tosefta	Yerushalmi	Bavli
Sotah	Mishnah	Tosefta	Yerushalmi	Bavli
Gittin	Mishnah	Tosefta	Yerushalmi	Bavli
Kiddushin	Mishnah	Tosefta	Yerushalmi	Bavli

Seder Nezikin

Bava Kamma	Mishnah	Tosefta	Yerushalmi	Bavli
Bava Metzia	Mishnah	Tosefta	Yerushalmi	Bavli
Bava Batra	Mishnah	Tosefta	Yerushalmi	Bavli
Sanhedrin	Mishnah	Tosefta	Yerushalmi	Bavli
Makkot	Mishnah	Tosefta	Yerushalmi	Bavli
Shevuot	Mishnah	Tosefta	Yerushalmi	Bavli
Eduyot	Mishnah	Tosefta		
Avodah Zarah	Mishnah	Tosefta	Yerushalmi	Bavli
Avot	Mishnah			
Horayot	Mishnah	Tosefta	Yerushalmi	Bavli

Seder Kodashim

Zevachim	Mishnah	Tosefta		Bavli
Menachot	Mishnah	Tosefta		Bavli
Hullin	Mishnah	Tosefta		Bavli
Bekhorot	Mishnah	Tosefta		Bavli
Arakhin	Mishnah	Tosefta		Bavli
Temurah	Mishnah	Tosefta		Bavli
Keritot	Mishnah	Tosefta		Bavli
Me'ilah	Mishnah	Tosefta		Bavli
Tamid	Mishnah			Bavli
Middot	Mishnah			
Kinnim	Mishnah			

Seder Toharot

Keilim	Mishnah	Tosefta		
Ohalot	Mishnah	Tosefta		
Negaim	Mishnah	Tosefta		
Parah	Mishnah	Tosefta		
Toharot	Mishnah	Tosefta		
Mikva'ot	Mishnah	Tosefta		
Niddah	Mishnah	Tosefta	Yerushalmi	Bavli
Makhshirin	Mishnah	Tosefta		
Zavim	Mishnah	Tosefta		
Tevul Yom	Mishnah	Tosefta		
Yadayim	Mishnah	Tosefta		
Uktzin	Mishnah	Tosefta		

Glossary

Additional Prayer: See *Musaf*.

aggadah (**pl.** *aggadot*): Stories in the Talmud text. Differs from midrash in that these stories are not necessarily related to a Torah text.

aggadic: Of or concerning *aggadah*.

aliyah/aliyot: Literally, "going up." Refers to blessing/reading the Torah in services.

altar: Sacrifices were offered on the main altar in the Temple courtyard. Incense was offered inside the Temple on a smaller altar.

am ha-aretz (**pl.** *amei ha-aretz*): Literally, "a people of the land." A person who isn't careful about taking "Jewish taxes" from his/her food. The opposite of an *am ha-aretz* is a *chaveir*.

Amidah: Literally, "Standing." The prayer par excellence in Judaism. It contains nineteen benedictions and is said standing three times each day.

Azazeil: Entire removal of sin and guilt from sacred places into the desert on the back of a goat, symbolizing entire forgiveness (Leviticus 16:7–10).

Bavli: The Talmud of the land of Babylonia.

BCE: Before the Common Era, i.e., BC.

Beit Hillel: Literally, "House of Hillel." The school that developed to expound the ideas of Hillel, one of the last of the *zugot*. Its opinions are almost always adopted over those of Beit Shammai.

beit k'neset (**pl.** *batei k'neset*): Literally, "house of meeting." A synagogue.

beit midrash (**pl.** *batei midrashot*): Literally, "house of expounding." An academy of rabbinic learning.

Beit Shammai: Literally, "House of Shammai." The school that developed to expound the ideas of Shammai, one of the last of the *zugot*.

berakhah (**pl.** *berakhot*): A blessing. Today, it usually contains the formula "Blessed is the Lord our God, Ruler of the universe ..."

bimah: The raised portion in a synagogue.

Birkat Hamazon: The blessing over food said after a meal. It is derived from Deuteronomy 8:10, "When you have eaten and are satisfied, you will bless the Lord your God for the good land He has given you."

CE: The Common Era, i.e., AD.

challah: Loaf; dough. A portion of dough is to be given to the priests (Numbers 15:20). A private person was to give 1/24th and a commercial baker was to give 1/48th. Today, a person gives only a small part, which is separated from the dough and burned.

chameitz: Leavened grain. A person is forbidden to eat or own *chameitz* during Passover.

chaveir (**pl.** *chaveirim*): Literally, "an associate" or "colleague." The opposite of an *am ha-aretz*. Someone who was dedicated to the strict observance of the mitzvot, particularly regarding tithes.

chayyot: Living being. A type of angel mentioned Ezekiel's vision of the celestial chariot (Ezekiel 1).

chazzan: An officiant at worship services.

chuppah: A wedding canopy.

darshan: One who makes midrash and/or who gives the sermon during services.

demai: Literally, "suspicion." Food that was purchased from a person who may not have taken out the tithes.

derekh eretz: Literally, "the way of the land." Good manners. May also refer to making a living or marital intercourse.

dinar: A silver coin.

duchen: To offer the Priestly Benediction during services.

first tithe: *Ma'aser rishon* in Hebrew. When a crop is harvested, first *terumah* is set aside (1/40th to 1/60th of the total harvest). Then this first tithe, i.e., 1/10th of the remaining crop, is set aside for the Levites. (The second tithe is an additional part of the crop set aside after *terumah* and the first tithe have been taken out. This produce was to be consumed in Jerusalem or traded for money that was then expended on food in Jerusalem. This tithe was collected during the first, second, fourth, and fifth years of the Sabbatical cycle.)

gabbai: An officiant who helps run services.

Gemara: The commentary on the Mishnah, composed 200–425 CE in the Yerushalmi and 200–650 CE in the Bavli.

Haggadah: Literally, "a story." The book used as a service at the Pesach seder.

halakhah: Literally, "the way." A reliable tradition. Today, it colloquially means "Jewish law." In the Yerushalmi, it can refer to a mishnah or to the Gemara.

Havdalah: Literally, "difference." The ceremony that concludes the Sabbath on Saturday evening. Prayers are said over wine, spices, and a braided candle.

Heichalot **mysticism**: A form of mystical ascent through seven heavenly halls.

Holy of Holies: The part of the Temple that housed the ark. Access to this area was permitted only to the High Priest on the Day of Atonement.

Kaddish: "Holy" in Aramaic. A prayer of praise to God recited at funerals, during mourning, after communal study, between major sections of a worship service, and at other times.

Kedushah: A part of the liturgy and an important feature of *Heichalot* mysticism. "Holy, holy, holy is the Lord of hosts; the whole earth is full of His glory" (Isaiah 6:3).

ketubah: A wedding contract.

Kiddush: Literally, "Sanctification." The prayer said over wine to sanctify Shabbat and festivals.

kohen (**pl.** *kohanim*): A priest. One who blesses the congregation and may eat *terumah*. This is a hereditary position.

maror: Bitter herbs. A necessary component of the Passover meal.

Megillah: Scroll. Five scrolls are included in the Hebrew Bible: Esther, Song of Songs, Ruth, Lamentations, and Ecclesiastes.

Mekhilta d'Rabbi Yishma'eil: The Portion of Rabbi Ishmael. The early midrash collection on the book of Exodus.

menschlichkeit: Acting with goodness and decency.

mezuzah: Literally, "doorpost." A parchment on which are written the words of Deuteronomy 6:4–9 and 11:13–21. The parchment is then affixed to the doorpost of a dwelling.

mikva'ot: Ritual baths. Immersion in these waters purifies the ritually impure.

mishnah (pl. *mishnayot*): Literally, "teaching." The Mishnah is the collection of tannaitic learning compiled by Rabbi Judah Hanasi in 200 CE. A mishnah is an individual segment within that compilation.

mitzvah: "Commandment." A deed that one must perform or an action one must refrain from doing.

Musaf: Literally, "addition." The additional public sacrifices brought on Shabbat, the New Moon, and festivals when the Temple stood. Also the name of the extra service recited on days when this sacrifice would have been brought.

nasi: Exalted. It denotes a leader. The term *nasi* may refer to many different time periods and to people who do many different sorts of things. Its precise meaning has not been determined.

Nishmat: The soul [of all living things]. A prayer of praise in the introductory portion of the service on Sabbaths and holidays.

Olam Haba: "The World to Come." The pleasant realm in the afterlife where the righteous are rewarded.

payytan: One who composes and performs *piyyut*, a special song for each Shabbat.

Pentateuch: The first five books of the Bible: Genesis, Exodus, Leviticus, Numbers, Deuteronomy.

Pesach: Literally, "to pass over." The festival in the spring that celebrates the Exodus from Egypt. This holiday marks the end of winter.

pesach: The Passover sacrificial offering of a lamb.

piyyut: A poem that was composed for each Shabbat and performed during services.

Priestly Benediction: The threefold blessing found in Numbers (6:24–26).

proof text: A verse from Scripture that supports a sage's teaching.

Rosh Hashanah: Literally, "The Head of the Year." The Jewish New Year, which occurs in the fall. It is a time of judgment and repentance.

Scriptures: The Torah, Prophets, and Writings. Torah is considered to be divinely revealed in traditional Judaism. Prophets and Writings have a lower level of holiness and authority.

Shabbat: The seventh day of the week. A day of rest that lasts from Friday sundown to Saturday sundown.

Shekhinah: God's indwelling presence.

Shema: Literally, "hear." The central creed of Judaism, which consists of Deuteronomy 6:4–9, Deuteronomy 11:13–21, and Numbers 15:37–41. The first line must be said with intention.

Sifrei Deuteronomy: The early midrash collection on the book of Deuteronomy.

stamma: Literally, "explainer." The later editors of the Talmuds.

Sukkot: The harvest festival of the fall. With this festival commence prayers for rain and the winter season.

Tallit: The garment that has the tzitzit tied to its four corners. A Jewish garment worn during prayer. (When the tzitzit are worn all day long, under one's clothes, they are attached to a garment called the *arbah kanfot*, "the four corners.")

Tanakh: The Hebrew acronym for the Scriptures: Torah, *Nevi'im* (Prophets), and *Ketuvim* (Writings).

tanna: A repeater. One who repeated the teachings of a certain school, which the sages (*chachamim*) would then discuss.

tefillah/tefillin: Phylacteries, cube-shaped leather boxes that are tied to the hand and head. They contain the following passages written on parchment: Deuteronomy 6:4–9, Deuteronomy 11:13–21, Exodus 13:1–10, and Exodus 13:11–16.

terumah: The offering whose basis is Deuteronomy 18:4 and Numbers 18:12. This is an offering given to the priests from one's produce. It could be anywhere from 1/40th to 1/60th of the total amount. (See Numbers 18:12 and Deuteronomy 18:4.)

Torah: The first five books of the Bible: Genesis, Exodus, Leviticus, Numbers, and Deuteronomy. Also used to refer to Jewish learning in general.

Tosefta: Literally, "addition" or "supplement." Tannaitic material collected into a compendium at the same time as the Mishnah, i.e., 200 CE.

tractate: A volume of Talmud.

triennial cycle: The practice of reading the Torah over three years in the Land of Israel, as opposed to the Babylonian practice of reading all of it in one year.

tzedakah: Literally, "justice" or "righteousness." Charity.

tzitzit: The fringes attached to our garments to remind us to do the mitzvot. They are mentioned in the third paragraph of the *Shema*, Numbers 15:37–41.

Yerushalmi: Literally, "the Jerusalem One." The Talmud of the Land of Israel.

zug **(pl. *zugot*)**: Literally, "pair." The pairs of leaders who presided over the Sanhedrin. The pair consisted of the *nasi* (president) and the *av beit din* (vice president). The era of the *zugot* lasted from approximately 175 BCE to 10 CE.

zuz: A coin.

The Sages

There are many sages in Yerushalmi about whom we have almost no information. Only one or two statements are attributed to them and that is all we know. In addition, spelling of sages' names in the Yerushalmi is not uniform. So the same sage could be referred to as Rabbi Elazar and Rabbi Lazar, or Chiyya bar Ba is called elsewhere Chiyya bar Abba. Because the Yerushalmi did not receive the centuries of "grooming" that the Bavli did, these variations occur much more frequently here.

Rabbi Abbahu (280–320) was a sage from Caesarea. He was a disciple of Rabbi Yochanan. He had a thorough knowledge of Greek and favored Greek culture. He was held in high esteem by the Roman authorities and had great political influence.

Rabbi Acha (fourth century) was a sage of Israel who is extensively quoted in the Yerushalmi, but seldom in the Bavli. His younger colleagues called him "the Light of Israel." He was merciful and gentle by nature. On the day of his death, it is reported that stars were visible at noontime.

Rabbi Acha bar Yaakov (290–320 CE) was a Babylonian sage.

Rabbi Akiba ben Joseph (110–130) grew up illiterate but became one of the most influential rabbis. He helped arrange the Mishnah into its present form. He died a martyr at the hand of the Romans for publicly teaching the Jewish tradition.

Rav Ammi (290–320) was an Israeli sage and a student of Rabbi Yochanan and Rabbi Hoshayah. He was a respected teacher in Tiberias and is often mentioned with Rav Assi and Rav Hiyya II.

Rav Avin (290–320) came from Babylonia to Israel. This could also be his son of the same name, who frequently appears in orders Nashim and Nezikin in the Yerushalmi as well as the midrash collection *Tanchuma*.

Avtalyon was the other half of a pair of leaders, with Shammai. His place was taken by Hillel.

Bar Kappara (Rabbi Elazar ha-Kappar, early third century) had an academy in Caesarea. He held original views, greatly valued the study of the natural sciences, and used the Greek language. He disliked metaphysical speculation and opposed Gnosticism and asceticism. He was a talented poet and authored many fables, epigrams, and prayers.

Rabbi Benaya b. Sisi was a sage in Israel, 200–220 CE. His teachings are quoted by Rabbi Yochanan bar Napacha.

Ben Zoma (Shimon ben Zoma, c. 90–130) was one of the four sages who entered "paradise."

Rabbi Berechiyah (290–320) was a student of R. Chelbo.

Rabbi Chaggai (fourth generation) was a student of Rabbi Zeira and was a respected member of the academy in Tiberias.

Rabbi Chama bar Bisa was the father of R. Hoshaya.

Rabbi Chanina bar Pappa (end of third to beginning of fourth century) migrated to the Land of Israel in his youth and studied under Rabbi Yochanan and others. He was considered a paradigm of holiness, and it is said that even the night spirits feared him.

Rabbi Chiyya (ben Gamda) (200–220) lived in both Israel and Babylonia. He transmitted traditions in the names of Simai and Yose ben Shaul.

Rabbi Chiyya bar Abba (279–320) emigrated from Babylonia with his brother Shimon bar Abba and became a disciple of Rabbi Yochanan. He was a distinguished teacher, but very poor.

Rabbi Chiyya bar Ba (Abba) may have been a student and friend of Rabbi Yehudah Hanasi. He was of Davidic descent, born in Babylonia but lived in Tiberias. He was active in the silk trade. This could also be a later sage who immigrated to Israel from Babylonia in his youth and became Rabbi Yochanan's student.

Rabbi Chiyya the Great (200–220) (not the later sage of the same name) was a Babylonian who came to Israel when he had already reached an advanced age. He became Yehudah Hanasi's disciple and friend.

Rabbi Chizkiyah (350–375) was a student of Rabbi Yermiyah and led the academy in Caesarea.

Rabbi Dosa b. Harkinos (90–130 CE). See Avot 3:10.

Rabbi Elazar could be Rabbi Elazar ben Pedat (d. 279). He was a member of a priestly family and was born in Babylonia. There, he studied under Samuel and Rav. After the latter's death, he moved to the Land of Israel. He was extremely poor. This could also be Rabbi Elazar ben Shammua, a sage from approximately 150. He was one of the last pupils of Rabbi Akiba and was one of the rabbis ordained by Yehudah ben Baba. Later midrashim include this Elazar among the ten martyrs of the Hadrianic persecutions.

Rabbi Elazar b. R. Shimon (bar Yochai) was the son of Rabbi Shimon bar Yochai, who lived in Israel around 170–200. He worked with the Roman government.

Rabbi Eliezer ben Hyrcanus (80–120) was a faithful conservator of decisions handed down from earlier generations and opposed any modification in them. He was an adherent of Beit Shammai and thus frequently differed with his colleagues. Being persistent in his opinion and conforming to it even in practice, he was excommunicated by his own brother-in-law, Rabban Gamliel II.

Rabbi Eliezer b. Yaakov (130–170) took part in creating the rulings of Usha (B. Ketubot 49a–50b) after the Bar Kokhba Revolt.

Elisha ben Abuyah was a sage in the first half of the second century. He was born before the year 70 CE in Jerusalem, where his father was a prominent citizen. He rejected Judaism. He is also known as Acher, "the Other."

Rabban Gamliel (70–90 CE) was a leader in Yavneh after the Second Temple was destroyed in 70 CE and a disciple of Rabban Yochanan ben Zakkai. He wanted to secure Yavneh's status as the spiritual center of Judaism. To that end, he exercised his authority as *nasi*, the president of the Academy, so harshly that he was eventually expelled from office. He was, however, reinstated shortly thereafter.

Hillel was Shammai's partner in the last of the *zugot*. He tended to favor those with less money and interpreted the Torah more liberally than Shammai.

Rabbi Hoshia the Great (Oshaya) (200–220) collected *mishnayot* and was Rabbi Yochanan's teacher.

Imma Shalom was Rabban Gamliel's sister and Rabbi Eliezer's wife.

Rabbi Levi (290–320) was a student of Rabbi Yochanan's known for his *aggadah*.

Rabbi Liyya [Ilai?] (110–135) was a younger student of R. Eliezer ben Hyrcanus, father of Yehudah bar Ilai, who often passed on the tradition of Rabbi Eliezer.

Rav Mana (250–290) was a sage of Israel (either 250–290 or 350–375). If the former, he was Rabbi Yochanan's contemporary.

Rabbi Meir (139–165) was ordained by Rabbi Akiba quite early in his career and was the most prominent of Rabbi Akiba's students. He continued Rabbi Akiba's work in arranging the material of what would become the Mishnah of Rabbi Yehudah Hanasi. Rabbi Meir's opinions are mentioned in almost every book of the Mishnah.

Rabbi. See **Rabbi Yehudah Hanasi**.

Rav (175–247) was an important sage in Babylonia. His real name was Abba Areca.

Reish Lakish. See **Rabbi Shimon ben Lakish**.

Rabbi Shimon bar Yochai (139–165) was a sage from the Galilee. He was one of Rabbi Akiba's most distinguished disciples. Persecuted by the Romans, he hid himself in a cave for several years with his son, Elazar, eating only carob to sustain himself. He opened an academy in Tekoa in the Galilee. He followed Rabbi Yishmael's methods of textual interpretation. He is regarded as the author of *Sifrei*, the midrash collection on Deuteronomy.

Rabbi Shimon ben Elazar (ben Shammua) (110–135) was Rabbi Meir's student and often disputed with Rabbi Yehudah Hanasi.

Rabbi Shimon ben Lakish (known as **Reish Lakish**, 219–279 CE) was a gladiator before he became a sage. He had extraordinary intellectual and analytical gifts. He was not only good friends with Rabbi Yochanan, but his brother-in-law as well.

Rabbi Shimon ben Pazzi (second half of third century) was Rabbi Yehoshua ben Levi's student. He lived in the south of Israel.

Mar Shmuel (180–254) was from Nehardea, Babylonia. Like his colleague Rav, he went to Israel, and there he became a disciple of Yehudah Hanasi. Shmuel was interested in medicine and astronomy. Although he and Rav often differed, their relationship was friendly. After Rav's death in 247, Shmuel became the highest religious authority in Babylonia.

Rabbi Shmuel b. Nachmani (290–320) was born in Israel and went to Babylonia twice and settled in Tiberias. He was a student of R. Yonatan ben Elazar and is quoted by Rav Chelbo.

Summachos bar Yosef (165–200) was a prominent disciple of Rabbi Meir's who was known for his great dialectical powers. However, after Rabbi Meir's death, he was excluded from Rabbi Yehudah Hanasi's school, charged with indulging in disputes designed to show off his intellect.

Rabbi Tarfon (80–110) came from a priestly family from Lod and was the teacher of R. Yehudah bar Ilai. Most of his discussions are with Rabbi Akiba. He strongly favored the priests.

Rabbi Yaakov bar Idi was a student of Rabbi Yochanan, whose teachings he transmitted to later generations.

Rabbi Yehoshua (ben Chananyah) (80–120) was Rabbi Eliezer ben Hyrcanus's study partner. He was gentle and nonconfrontational whenever possible. He was an impoverished man who sold charcoal for a living.

Rabbi Yehoshua ben Levi (220–250) was from Lod. He was a prominent teacher in Israel and a student of Bar Kappara and R. Pinchas ben Yair. He was the teacher of R. Shimon ben Pazzi and R. Tanchum bar Hanilai.

Rav Yehudah (bar Yechezkel) (257–299) was a Babylonian sage who was a disciple of both Rav's and Samuel's. He founded the academy in

Pumbedita and also headed the academy at Sura for the two years before his death in 299.

Yehudah ben Tabbai was one half of a *zug* with Shimon ben Shetach.

Rabbi Yehudah Hanasi (165–200) was simply called Rabbi. He was well versed in Jewish traditions as well as in secular subjects, such as the Greek language. He became the chief authority of his generation. Although personally wealthy, he lived simply and sustained many students by his charity. He completed and promulgated the Mishnah begun by Rabbi Akiba.

Rabbi Yermiyah (320–359), a native of Babylonia, came to Israel and became a disciple of Rabbi Zeira. In his younger days, he indulged in posing puzzling questions of little import, probably intending to ridicule the dialectical methods used in the academies. For this reason, he was expelled from the Babylonian academy. He then moved to Israel and was better appreciated there, being acknowledged as a great authority.

Rabbi Yishmael (ben Elisha) (90–130) was the student of Rabbi Nechunya ben Hakanah. His methods opposed those of Rabbi Akiba. *Mekhilta*, the early midrash on Exodus, is attributed to him.

Rabbi Yochanan bar Napacha (c. 199–279) is usually called simply Rabbi Yochanan. He was the central author of the Yerushalmi. He founded his own academy, which became the principal seat of learning in the Land of Israel.

Rabbi Yohanan ben Nuri (110–135) was a sage in Rabban Gamliel's circle. Rabbi Akiba was his adversary.

Rabbi Yoshiyah (c. third century) was a pupil of Rabbi Yochanan and Rabbi Kahana and was held in high esteem by his contemporaries.

Rabbi Zeira (279–320) was a Babylonian but did not like the hair-splitting techniques of study used in the academies there, so he immigrated to Palestine, where he was ordained. He was known for his extreme piety.

Index

AVAILABLE FROM BETTER BOOKSTORES.
TRY YOUR BOOKSTORE FIRST.

Spirituality

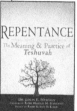

Repentance: The Meaning and Practice of *Teshuvah*
By Dr. Louis E. Newman; Foreword by Rabbi Harold M. Schulweis; Preface by Rabbi Karyn D. Kedar
Examines both the practical and philosophical dimensions of *teshuvah*, Judaism's core religious-moral teaching on repentance, and its value for us—Jews and non-Jews alike—today. 6 x 9, 256 pp, HC, 978-1-58023-426-9 **$24.99**

Tanya, the Masterpiece of Hasidic Wisdom
Selections Annotated & Explained
Translation & Annotation by Rabbi Rami Shapiro; Foreword by Rabbi Zalman M. Schachter-Shalomi
Brings the genius of *Tanya*, one of the most powerful books of Jewish wisdom, to anyone seeking to deepen their understanding of the soul.
5½ x 8½, 240 pp, Quality PB, 978-1-59473-275-1 **$16.99**
(A book from SkyLight Paths, Jewish Lights' sister imprint)

A Book of Life: Embracing Judaism as a Spiritual Practice
By Rabbi Michael Strassfeld 6 x 9, 544 pp, Quality PB, 978-1-58023-247-0 **$19.99**

Bringing the Psalms to Life: How to Understand and Use the Book of Psalms
By Rabbi Daniel F. Polish, PhD 6 x 9, 208 pp, Quality PB, 978-1-58023-157-2 **$16.95**

Does the Soul Survive? A Jewish Journey to Belief in Afterlife, Past Lives & Living with Purpose By Rabbi Elie Kaplan Spitz; Foreword by Brian L. Weiss, MD
6 x 9, 288 pp, Quality PB, 978-1-58023-165-7 **$16.99**

First Steps to a New Jewish Spirit: Reb Zalman's Guide to Recapturing the Intimacy & Ecstasy in Your Relationship with God By Rabbi Zalman M. Schachter-Shalomi with Donald Gropman 6 x 9, 144 pp, Quality PB, 978-1-58023-182-4 **$16.95**

Foundations of Sephardic Spirituality: The Inner Life of Jews of the Ottoman Empire
By Rabbi Marc D. Angel, PhD 6 x 9, 224 pp, Quality PB, 978-1-58023-341-5 **$18.99**

God & the Big Bang: Discovering Harmony between Science & Spirituality
By Dr. Daniel C. Matt 6 x 9, 216 pp, Quality PB, 978-1-879045-89-7 **$16.99**

God in Our Relationships: Spirituality between People from the Teachings of Martin Buber By Rabbi Dennis S. Ross 5½ x 8½, 160 pp, Quality PB, 978-1-58023-147-3 **$16.95**

The Jewish Lights Spirituality Handbook: A Guide to Understanding, Exploring & Living a Spiritual Life Edited by Stuart M. Matlins
What exactly is "Jewish" about spirituality? How do I make it a part of my life? Fifty of today's foremost spiritual leaders share their ideas and experience with us.
6 x 9, 456 pp, Quality PB, 978-1-58023-093-3 **$19.99**

Judaism, Physics and God: Searching for Sacred Metaphors in a Post-Einstein World
By Rabbi David W. Nelson 6 x 9, 352 pp, Quality PB, inc. reader's discussion guide,
978-1-58023-306-4 **$18.99**; HC, 352 pp, 978-1-58023-252-4 **$24.99**

Meaning & Mitzvah: Daily Practices for Reclaiming Judaism through Prayer, God, Torah, Hebrew, Mitzvot and Peoplehood By Rabbi Goldie Milgram
7 x 9, 336 pp, Quality PB, 978-1-58023-256-2 **$19.99**

There Is No Messiah ... and You're It: The Stunning Transformation of Judaism's Most Provocative Idea By Rabbi Robert N. Levine, DD
6 x 9, 192 pp, Quality PB, 978-1-58023-255-5 **$16.99**

These Are the Words, 2nd Edition: A Vocabulary of Jewish Spiritual Life
By Rabbi Arthur Green, PhD 6 x 9, 320 pp, Quality PB, 978-1-58023-494-8 **$19.99**

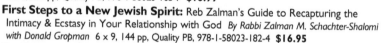

Or phone, mail or e-mail to: **JEWISH LIGHTS Publishing**
An imprint of Turner Publishing Company
4507 Charlotte Avenue • Suite 100 • Nashville, Tennessee 37209
Tel: (615) 255-2665 • www.jewishlights.com
Prices subject to change.

Spirituality/Prayer

Making Prayer Real: Leading Jewish Spiritual Voices on Why Prayer Is Difficult and What to Do about It *By Rabbi Mike Comins*
A new and different response to the challenges of Jewish prayer, with "best prayer practices" from Jewish spiritual leaders of all denominations.
6 x 9, 320 pp, Quality PB, 978-1-58023-417-7 **$18.99**

Witnesses to the One: The Spiritual History of the *Sh'ma*
By Rabbi Joseph B. Meszler; Foreword by Rabbi Elyse Goldstein
6 x 9, 176 pp, Quality PB, 978-1-58023-400-9 **$16.99**; HC, 978-1-58023-309-5 **$19.99**

My People's Prayer Book Series: Traditional Prayers, Modern Commentaries *Edited by Rabbi Lawrence A. Hoffman, PhD*
Provides diverse and exciting commentary to the traditional liturgy. Will help you find new wisdom in Jewish prayer, and bring liturgy into your life. Each book includes Hebrew text, modern translations and commentaries from all perspectives of the Jewish world.

Vol. 1—The *Sh'ma* and Its Blessings
   7 x 10, 168 pp, HC, 978-1-879045-79-8 **$29.99**
Vol. 2—The *Amidah* 7 x 10, 240 pp, HC, 978-1-879045-80-4 **$24.95**
Vol. 3—*P'sukei D'zimrah* (Morning Psalms)
   7 x 10, 240 pp, HC, 978-1-879045-81-1 **$29.99**
Vol. 4—*Seder K'riat Hatorah* (The Torah Service)
   7 x 10, 264 pp, HC, 978-1-879045-82-8 **$29.99**
Vol. 5—*Birkhot Hashachar* (Morning Blessings)
   7 x 10, 240 pp, HC, 978-1-879045-83-5 **$24.95**
Vol. 6—*Tachanun* and Concluding Prayers
   7 x 10, 240 pp, HC, 978-1-879045-84-2 **$24.95**
Vol. 7—Shabbat at Home 7 x 10, 240 pp, HC, 978-1-879045-85-9 **$24.95**
Vol. 8—*Kabbalat Shabbat* (Welcoming Shabbat in the Synagogue)
   7 x 10, 240 pp, HC, 978-1-58023-121-3 **$24.99**
Vol. 9—Welcoming the Night: *Minchah* and *Ma'ariv* (Afternoon and Evening Prayer) 7 x 10, 272 pp, HC, 978-1-58023-262-3 **$24.99**
Vol. 10—Shabbat Morning: *Shacharit* and *Musaf* (Morning and Additional Services) 7 x 10, 240 pp, HC, 978-1-58023-240-1 **$29.99**

Spirituality/Lawrence Kushner

I'm God; You're Not: Observations on Organized Religion & Other Disguises of the Ego
6 x 9, 256 pp, HC, 978-1-58023-441-2 **$21.99**

The Book of Letters: A Mystical Hebrew Alphabet
Popular HC Edition, 6 x 9, 80 pp, 2-color text, 978-1-879045-00-2 **$24.95**
Collector's Limited Edition, 9 x 12, 80 pp, gold-foil-embossed pages, w/ limited-edition silkscreened print, 978-1-879045-04-0 **$349.00**

The Book of Miracles: A Young Person's Guide to Jewish Spiritual Awareness
6 x 9, 96 pp, 2-color illus., HC, 978-1-879045-78-1 **$16.95** *For ages 9–13*

The Book of Words: Talking Spiritual Life, Living Spiritual Talk
6 x 9, 160 pp, Quality PB, 978-1-58023-020-9 **$18.99**

Eyes Remade for Wonder: A Lawrence Kushner Reader *Introduction by Thomas Moore*
6 x 9, 240 pp, Quality PB, 978-1-58023-042-1 **$18.95**

God Was in This Place & I, i Did Not Know: Finding Self, Spirituality and Ultimate Meaning 6 x 9, 192 pp, Quality PB, 978-1-879045-33-0 **$16.95**

Honey from the Rock: An Introduction to Jewish Mysticism
6 x 9, 176 pp, Quality PB, 978-1-58023-073-5 **$16.95**

Invisible Lines of Connection: Sacred Stories of the Ordinary
5½ x 8½, 160 pp, Quality PB, 978-1-879045-98-9 **$15.95**

Jewish Spirituality: A Brief Introduction for Christians
5½ x 8½, 112 pp, Quality PB, 978-1-58023-150-3 **$12.95**

The River of Light: Jewish Mystical Awareness
6 x 9, 192 pp, Quality PB, 978-1-58023-096-4 **$16.95**

The Way Into Jewish Mystical Tradition
6 x 9, 224 pp, Quality PB, 978-1-58023-200-5 **$18.99**; HC, 978-1-58023-029-2 **$21.95**

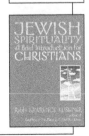

Theology/Philosophy/The Way Into... Series

The Way Into... series offers an accessible and highly usable "guided tour" of the Jewish faith, people, history and beliefs—in total, an introduction to Judaism that will enable you to understand and interact with the sacred texts of the Jewish tradition. Each volume is written by a leading contemporary scholar and teacher, and explores one key aspect of Judaism. The Way Into... series enables all readers to achieve a real sense of Jewish cultural literacy through guided study.

The Way Into Encountering God in Judaism
By Rabbi Neil Gillman, PhD
For everyone who wants to understand how Jews have encountered God throughout history and today.
6 x 9, 240 pp, Quality PB, 978-1-58023-199-2 **$18.99**; HC, 978-1-58023-025-4 **$21.95**
Also Available: **The Jewish Approach to God:** A Brief Introduction for Christians
By Rabbi Neil Gillman, PhD
5½ x 8½, 192 pp, Quality PB, 978-1-58023-190-9 **$16.95**

The Way Into Jewish Mystical Tradition
By Rabbi Lawrence Kushner
Allows readers to interact directly with the sacred mystical texts of the Jewish tradition. An accessible introduction to the concepts of Jewish mysticism, their religious and spiritual significance, and how they relate to life today.
6 x 9, 224 pp, Quality PB, 978-1-58023-200-5 **$18.99**; HC, 978-1-58023-029-2 **$21.95**

The Way Into Jewish Prayer
By Rabbi Lawrence A. Hoffman, PhD
Opens the door to 3,000 years of Jewish prayer, making anyone feel at home in the Jewish way of communicating with God.
6 x 9, 208 pp, Quality PB, 978-1-58023-201-2 **$18.99**

The Way Into Jewish Prayer Teacher's Guide
By Rabbi Jennifer Ossakow Goldsmith
8½ x 11, 42 pp, PB, 978-1-58023-345-3 **$8.99**
Download a free copy at www.jewishlights.com.

The Way Into Judaism and the Environment
By Jeremy Benstein, PhD
Explores the ways in which Judaism contributes to contemporary social-environmental issues, the extent to which Judaism is part of the problem and how it can be part of the solution.
6 x 9, 288 pp, Quality PB, 978-1-58023-368-2 **$18.99**

The Way Into Tikkun Olam (Repairing the World)
By Rabbi Elliot N. Dorff, PhD
An accessible introduction to the Jewish concept of the individual's responsibility to care for others and repair the world.
6 x 9, 304 pp, Quality PB, 978-1-58023-328-6 **$18.99**

The Way Into Torah
By Rabbi Norman J. Cohen, PhD
Helps guide you in the exploration of the origins and development of Torah, explains why it should be studied and how to do it.
6 x 9, 176 pp, Quality PB, 978-1-58023-198-5 **$16.99**

The Way Into the Varieties of Jewishness
By Sylvia Barack Fishman, PhD
Explores the religious and historical understanding of what it has meant to be Jewish from ancient times to the present controversy over "Who is a Jew?"
6 x 9, 288 pp, Quality PB, 978-1-58023-367-5 **$18.99**; HC, 978-1-58023-030-8 **$24.99**

Theology/Philosophy

The God Who Hates Lies: Confronting & Rethinking Jewish Tradition
By Dr. David Hartman with Charlie Buckholtz
The world's leading Modern Orthodox Jewish theologian probes the deepest questions at the heart of what it means to be a human being and a Jew.
6 x 9, 208 pp, HC, 978-1-58023-455-9 **$24.99**

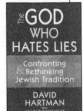

Jewish Theology in Our Time: A New Generation Explores the Foundations and Future of Jewish Belief *Edited by Rabbi Elliot J. Cosgrove, PhD; Foreword by Rabbi David J. Wolpe; Preface by Rabbi Carole B. Balin, PhD*
A powerful and challenging examination of what Jews can believe—by a new generation's most dynamic and innovative thinkers.
6 x 9, 240 pp, HC, 978-1-58023-413-9 **$24.99**

Maimonides—Essential Teachings on Jewish Faith & Ethics: The Book of Knowledge & the Thirteen Principles of Faith—Annotated & Explained
Translation and Annotation by Rabbi Marc D. Angel, PhD
Opens up for us Maimonides's views on the nature of God, providence, prophecy, free will, human nature, repentance and more.
5½ x 8½, 224 pp, Quality PB Original, 978-1-59473-311-6 **$18.99***

The Death of Death: Resurrection and Immortality in Jewish Thought
By Rabbi Neil Gillman, PhD 6 x 9, 336 pp, Quality PB, 978-1-58023-081-0 **$18.95**

Doing Jewish Theology: God, Torah & Israel in Modern Judaism *By Rabbi Neil Gillman, PhD*
6 x 9, 304 pp, Quality PB, 978-1-58023-439-9 **$18.99**

Hasidic Tales: Annotated & Explained *Translation & Annotation by Rabbi Rami Shapiro*
5½ x 8½, 240 pp, Quality PB, 978-1-893361-86-7 **$16.95***

A Heart of Many Rooms: Celebrating the Many Voices within Judaism
By Dr. David Hartman 6 x 9, 352 pp, Quality PB, 978-1-58023-156-5 **$19.95**

The Hebrew Prophets: Selections Annotated & Explained
Translation & Annotation by Rabbi Rami Shapiro; Foreword by Rabbi Zalman M. Schachter-Shalomi
5½ x 8½, 224 pp, Quality PB, 978-1-59473-037-5 **$16.99***

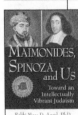

Maimonides, Spinoza and Us: Toward an Intellectually Vibrant Judaism
By Rabbi Marc D. Angel, PhD A challenging look at two great Jewish philosophers and what their thinking means to our understanding of God, truth, revelation and reason. 6 x 9, 224 pp, HC, 978-1-58023-411-5 **$24.99**

A Living Covenant: The Innovative Spirit in Traditional Judaism
By Dr. David Hartman 6 x 9, 368 pp, Quality PB, 978-1-58023-011-7 **$25.00**

Love and Terror in the God Encounter: The Theological Legacy of Rabbi Joseph B. Soloveitchik *By Dr. David Hartman* 6 x 9, 240 pp, Quality PB, 978-1-58023-176-3 **$19.95**

A Touch of the Sacred: A Theologian's Informal Guide to Jewish Belief
By Dr. Eugene B. Borowitz and Frances W. Schwartz
6 x 9, 256 pp, Quality PB, 978-1-58023-416-0 **$16.99**; HC, 978-1-58023-337-8 **$21.99**

Traces of God: Seeing God in Torah, History and Everyday Life *By Rabbi Neil Gillman, PhD*
6 x 9, 240 pp, Quality PB, 978-1-58023-369-9 **$16.99**

Your Word Is Fire: The Hasidic Masters on Contemplative Prayer
Edited and translated by Rabbi Arthur Green, PhD, and Barry W. Holtz
6 x 9, 160 pp, Quality PB, 978-1-879045-25-5 **$15.95**

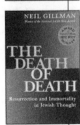

I Am Jewish
Personal Reflections Inspired by the Last Words of Daniel Pearl
Almost 150 Jews—both famous and not—from all walks of life, from all around the world, write about many aspects of their Judaism.
Edited by Judea and Ruth Pearl 6 x 9, 304 pp, Deluxe PB w/ flaps, 978-1-58023-259-3 **$18.99**
Download a free copy of the *I Am Jewish Teacher's Guide* at www.jewishlights.com.

Hannah Senesh: Her Life and Diary, The First Complete Edition
By Hannah Senesh; Foreword by Marge Piercy; Preface by Eitan Senesh; Afterword by Roberta Grossman
6 x 9, 368 pp, b/w photos, Quality PB, 978-1-58023-342-2 **$19.99**

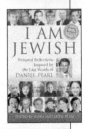

**A book from SkyLight Paths, Jewish Lights' sister imprint*

JEWISH LIGHTS BOOKS ARE AVAILABLE FROM BETTER BOOKSTORES. TRY YOUR BOOKSTORE FIRST.

About Jewish Lights

People of all faiths and backgrounds yearn for books that attract, engage, educate, and spiritually inspire.

Our principal goal is to stimulate thought and help all people learn about who the Jewish People are, where they come from, and what the future can be made to hold. While people of our diverse Jewish heritage are the primary audience, our books speak to people in the Christian world as well and will broaden their understanding of Judaism and the roots of their own faith.

We bring to you authors who are at the forefront of spiritual thought and experience. While each has something different to say, they all say it in a voice that you can hear.

Our books are designed to welcome you and then to engage, stimulate, and inspire. We judge our success not only by whether or not our books are beautiful and commercially successful, but by whether or not they make a difference in your life.

For your information and convenience, at the back of this book we have provided a list of other Jewish Lights books you might find interesting and useful. They cover all the categories of your life:

Bar/Bat Mitzvah	Life Cycle
Bible Study / Midrash	Meditation
Children's Books	Men's Interest
Congregation Resources	Parenting
Current Events / History	Prayer / Ritual / Sacred Practice
Ecology / Environment	Social Justice
Fiction: Mystery, Science Fiction	Spirituality
Grief / Healing	Theology / Philosophy
Holidays / Holy Days	Travel
Inspiration	Twelve Steps
Kabbalah / Mysticism / Enneagram	Women's Interest

Stuart M. Matlins, Publisher

Or phone, mail or e-mail to: **JEWISH LIGHTS Publishing**
An imprint of Turner Publishing Company
4507 Charlotte Avenue • Suite 100 • Nashville, Tennessee 37209
Tel: (615) 255-2665 • www.jewishlights.com
Prices subject to change.

For more information about each book, visit our website at www.jewishlights.com

Printed in the USA
CPSIA information can be obtained
at www.ICGtesting.com
JSHW022221140824
68134JS00018B/1184

9 781683 364092